The Sensitive Self

OTHER WESLEYAN BOOKS BY MICHAEL EIGEN

Ecstasy (2001)

Rage (2002)

The Sensitive Self

MICHAEL EIGEN

Wesleyan University Press MIDDLETOWN, CONNECTICUT

Published by Wesleyan University Press, Middletown, CT 06459
Copyright © 2004 by Michael Eigen
All rights reserved
Set in Carter Cone Galliard by B. Williams & Associates
Manufactured in the United States of America

ISBN 0-8195-6684-5 (cloth)
ISBN 0-8195-6685-3 (pbk.)

Cataloging information for this book is available from the Library of Congress.

Portions of this book were previously published, in somewhat different form, and
are reprinted here with permission, as follows:

Chapter 2, "A Basic Rhythm," is based on "A Basic Rhythm," *The Psychoanalytic Review* 89 (2002): 721–40. © National Psychological Association for Psychoanalysis.

Chapter 3, "Mysticism and Psychoanalysis," comes from "Mysticism and Psychoanalysis," *The Psychoanalytic Review* 88 (2002): 455–81. © National Psychological Association for Psychoanalysis.

Chapter 4, "Half and Half," was published as "Half and Half" in *fort da* 8 (2002): 7–17. Reprinted with permission of the Northern California Society for Psychoanalytic Psychology.

Chapter 5, "A Little Psyche-Music," was published as "A Little Psyche-Music," *Psychoanalytic Dialogues* 12, no. 1 (2004). Reprinted with permission of *The Analytic Press*.

Chapter 11, "Sensitivity and Vulgarity," is based on an interview with the author conducted by Robert Marchesani for *The Psychotherapy Patient* 12 (2003): 99–110. Its original title was "Up, Down, All Around: Interview with Michael Eigen." This issue of the journal was also published as a book edited by E. Mark Stern and Robert B. Marchesani (2003), *Inhabitants of the Unconscious: The Grotesque and the Vulgar in Everyday Life* (Binghamton, N.Y.: Haworth Press). The interview is used with the permission of Haworth Press.

5 4 3 2 1

To the National Psychological Association for Psychoanalysis

and the New York University Postdoctoral Program in Psychotherapy

and Psychoanalysis for years of support, challenge, and collegial

participation—and loose threads galore

CONTENTS

ACKNOWLEDGMENTS

Some of these chapters began as talks, and I would like to thank the institutes and organizations that asked me to share my ideas with them. They include the International Association for Relational Psychoanalysis and Psychotherapy, the Northwest Alliance for Psychoanalytic Study, the Northern California Society for Psychoanalytic Psychology, the Psychoanalytic Institute of Northern California, the Christian Theological Seminary, the Westchester Institute for Training in Psychotherapy and Psychoanalysis, the European Association of Psychotherapy together with the Irish Council of Psychotherapy, the Blanton Peale Graduate Institute, and the Sheppard Pratt Health System. I'm grateful to members of these groups who sought me out and made talks possible. They include Adrienne Harris, Jessica Benjamin, Felicity Kelcourse, Ross Skelton, Scott Lines, Marvin Lifschitz, Maureen Sawyer, and Kathryn Madden.

For publication of some of these chapters, I want to thank Martin Schulman and *The Psychoanalytic Review,* Alan Kubler and *fort da,* and E. Mark Stern and *The Psychotherapy Patient*. I am grateful to the staff of Other Books, a jewel of a store, for two lovely book parties, and, like many of my colleagues in New York City, I am sad that it closed. Thanks to Judith Newman, Edith Laufer, and Judy Ann Kaplan and the National Psychological Association for Psychoanalysis for consistently providing outlets for me to talk about my work. Many thanks to Robert Marchesani and Jeff Eaton for their thoughtful and fun interviews of me, which have been converted into the last two chapters of this book. They gave me a chance to explore informally a range of human sensitivity from vulgarity to the aesthetics of psychosocial life and to comment on the therapy field.

Thanks to internet sites where mixtures of communication and anticommunication rage. I've made many good friends through sites run by John Stone, Silvio Merciao, Robert Young, and Cheryl Martin. I discover networks of amazing workers who are contributing to the expansion of what it is possible to experience and express. These are dangerous times of heightened anxiety and grief, but they are, too, times of heightened awareness, with world communities becoming more closely knit, as well as split. It becomes harder not to recognize vast differences between people and harder not to open up to the growth processes differences require. Human sensitivity takes many forms and must evolve to find responses that enhance life.

Special thanks to Anthony Molino, an energetic editor, translator, and author, for letting Wesleyan University Press know about me. This is my third book with Wesleyan, and I'm grateful to all who have helped me there, including Tom Radko, Susanna Tamminen, Leonora Gibson, Leslie Starr, Ron Maner (who copyedited all three books), and Richard Hendel (who designed them).

My family and patients inspire me and keep me close to the possible. One learns constantly how to be with others and oneself. My Bion, Winnicott, and Lacan seminar, ongoing for nearly three decades, provides a seriously playful space to let imagination roam. All this involves being sensitive to sensitivity and grueling, joyful staying with it and staying with it some more.

Precautions have been taken to disguise the identity of patients, using composites, changing details, while trying to remain faithful to affective realities at work. Most chapters have been shown to individuals who contribute to portrayals and are included in this book with their approval. In a work like this, the psychic realities expressed are the important thing. What is taken from individuals for public use lights up difficulties many face.

The Sensitive Self

Man has no body distinct from his Soul for that called Body is a portion of Soul discerned by the five Senses, the chief inlets of Soul in this age.

—William Blake *The Marriage of Heaven and Hell*

I will put a new spirit within you; and I will take away the stony heart out of your flesh, and I will give you a heart of flesh.

—Ezekiel 36:26

CHAPTER 1 *Introduction*

Without sensitivity what would life be like? Sensitivity nurtures us, gives life color, expressiveness, charm—provides a basis for terror. Sensitivity, feeling, and thinking feed each other, are part of each other. Thinking and feeling are ways sensitivity unfolds or grows. We speak of emotional sensitivity, reflective sensitivity, not just the raw life of sensations. But without the sensory sea we take for granted, feeling and thought would dry up and die.

We have the capacity to focus on different aspects of our experiential matrix, to select a bit of experience and zoom in on it, detach it from other aspects of experience for a time and try to see what it is made up of. Attempts have been made to abstract sensation from the flow of experience and study its qualities. Freud wrote of chaotic sensory fields streaming through the body, involving inside and outside of skin, mucus membranes, glands, aliveness of tissues. This readily expands to include proprioceptive and kinesthetic sensation, nerves, muscles, even a vision of cellular aliveness. Not all or most sensations throb and pulse, but one well knows what the latter mean. For Freud, such sensitivity is mediated by what he calls a pleasure or body ego, an idea that resonates with older writings on "the flesh," "concupiscence," mischievous, destructive, enlivening Eros.

In addition to the vague, sometimes sharp and insistent tumult, spread, and fluctuation of body sensation, one can focus on what philosophers called primary (e.g., size, shape, mass) and secondary (e.g., color, sound, odor, taste) qualities. One can tease out sensory elements from the perceptual flow and imagine them to be building blocks of experience, as if what we see is made of sensation bits compounded into unities. It is, indeed, possible to decompose the world into bits and pieces, focusing on intensity of hue, textures, line fragments. Stare at a surface long enough and it loses form, dissolves, changes contour, challenges categories. But the fact that we can tune into and break up our experiential field in lots of ways does not make any one way primary.

We can focus on the rise and fall of sensations or on the wholeness of objects. Or we can try to relax focus and let the perceptual flow splash through us. The fact that such an attentional capacity exists at all is amazing. That it provides us with the ability to create worlds of experiencing by subtly blending sensation, perception, feeling, and thought is even more amazing.

M. Klein and W. R. Bion apply the bits-and-pieces vs. wholeness categories, which characterize earlier writings on sensation and perception, to emotional life. Klein believes unconscious fantasy mediates affective movement from part to whole object experience, for example, seeing mother as breast or nipple vs. seeing her as an actual person, a subject in her own right. In the first, the other exists in terms of a partial function or service. If the function runs well, the other is felt as good, and good feelings result (or, vice versa, good feelings produce a sense of a good object). If things do not go well, affect is negative, allied with negative object perception. It is as if, Klein suggests, there are two worlds of feelings and objects, good and bad, depending on the emotional sensation dominant at the moment. If things go very badly, affect may not only split into positive and negative valences, but fragment and disperse (proliferation of splitting), dovetailing with a sense of self and object fragmentation. If affect dispersal goes far enough, feeling diminishes and, finally, is lost.

In the simplest case, the psychic universe divides into good and bad affect, self, object. For Klein, the defense mechanisms that mediate this division include splitting and projection. One tries to preserve the good self-object-affect by splitting off and projecting the bad. This basic attempt to preserve a good affect nucleus at the heart of the psyche is bolstered by denial, idealization, and the manic defense. One has to deny what is happening in the psyche as a whole in order to split off bad feelings (one hand not knowing what the other is doing), and this denial is intensified by idealizing the good core one tries to maintain. A chronic manic position develops, in which some portion of the psyche tries to keep good feeling above the bad, sweeping the latter elsewhere, into other parts of the world or self. This solution is only apparently stable. Defenses reshuffle, and what is good at one time may be bad at another, and the personality may end up reorganizing and hardening around a bad affect-self-object core (a rigidity ultimately linked with instability). Klein calls the psyche's reliance on splitting, projection, denial, idealization, and the manic defense the paranoid-schizoid position.

Development proceeds toward bringing split-off affects and fantasies together in an attempt to see self and other more fully. The infant begins to realize that the hated witch mother (bad affect core) and the loved, divine one (good affect core) is the same person in different aspects, and the loving, hating being is oneself in different moods. Good and bad experiences are part of what happens between people, part of the necessary brew, as one enters more deeply into the life of injury and repair. The pain one receives and inflicts (in fantasy, in reality) and the pleasure as well are part of what whole people do together. Klein notes a depressive tone to the realization that injury is part of intersubjectivity, that we cannot escape pain by splitting it off, that caring and reparation must evolve, partly, to make up for and heal some of the consequences of splitting. She calls this growth in making room for opposite affects and differing viewpoints the depressive position. A certain mourning attends awareness that injury and disturbance are inevitable and that faith in a good core must undergo much development in order to meet the challenges within and without.

Bion has enlarged on Klein's part-whole affective dialectics. He sees the movement from splitting to reparation as a particular case of more general psychic operations, which involve incessant breaking into parts and building into wholes. He thus placed a biconditional sign between paranoid-schizoid and depressive positions (PS ↔ D), indicating two-way movement at once simultaneous, oscillating, and periodic. For example, he depicts an analyst patiently waiting in a semifragmented, bits-and-pieces state until a take on the emotional reality of the session clicks into place. He describes this as a movement from patience to security that never ends. There is something

Joblike about Bion's description. Waiting in unknowing can become intense indeed, characterized by a heightened sense of decomposition and persecution rewarded by a moment of enlightenment.

Sense of decomposition ↔ sense of enlightenment. The double-headed arrow insists on movement between form and formlessness, but more. A mix of determinacy-indeterminacy is implied. Parts are wholes and wholes are parts, depending on one's focus. For example, Bion stresses that causal notions. useful as they may be, often are misused as substitutes for other ways of experiencing. Causality can close off experiential flow, putting brakes on, slanting it this way or that. A common but frequently lethal mode of causal thinking is "moralistic," assigning blame: "It's my fault" or "It's your fault." Reactive blaming is a commonplace use of causality to escape opening to more complex dimensions of living. In this case, precocious causality = precocious moralistic closure of growth. Bion finds causal thinking suffocating. He does not want it to close off sensitivity to the larger flow.

Proper use of causality views it as a selective configuration that organizes larger processes in certain ways for certain purposes. Any part of reality tapped by a causal apprehension precedes, succeeds, and exceeds the latter's use. Causal thinking organizes transformational processes of which it is part and needs to be seen as one tool the mind uses. It is not always the only or best filter for expressing and amplifying the full range of possibilities human sensitivity opens. Organizing life via causal thought (whether scientific, theological, moralistic, psychological, or commonsensical) contributes to the community of voices, the checks and balances of tendencies, our mixed and varied makeup of capacities—none of which has the last word. In such a mix of ingredients in process, the meaning of part-whole keeps changing.

To further complicate matters and bring out a challenge sensitivity opens, the idea, whole, intuitive sense or gestalt formed in the movement from PS to D may itself be explosive, threatening, destabilizing. The analyst waits in patience in chaos to be thrown for a loop by the emergence of a thought that is hard to handle. Bion calls this thought (or feeling) messiah or genius because of its challenge to personality. A messiah or genius aspect of self threatens the status quo, which Bion calls establishment. He likens the potentially creative idea or feeling or intuition to a big-bang birth of the psychic universe. It takes time to catch up with, assimilate, make use of intuitive leaps.

Thus we arrive at a position in which the movement toward security, the formation of an idea, intuition, feeling, sense, or transforming slant concerning our attitudes and makeup is a funny kind of security indeed. What the analyst waits for in the decomposing unknown is a transformative sense of emotional reality that initiates and is part of a prolonged birth process (gestation ↔ big bang). One moves from one sort of annihilation to another (waiting in chaos for the formation of a transformative pattern: both chaos and formation threaten to blow self away).

What sort of security is this? It is the security one gets from trying with all one's being to make contact with oneself, with another, with emotional reality. There is hunger for reality, for truth about life, oneself, others. A certain security comes from following that hunger, coming through the upset, living with the turbulence. Truth is highly charged, explosive, and if used wrongly, can wreck life. But without it, the soul is dead. For Bion, there is an emotional nourishment that comes with seeking the truth about ourselves, albeit use of truth in a compassionate or hateful way makes all the difference. Bion was fond of Samuel Johnson's remark: "Let us endeavor to see things as they are, and then enquire whether we ought to complain. Whether to see life as it is will give us much consolation, I know not; but the consolation that is drawn from truth, if any there be, is solid and durable; that which may be derived from error must be, like its original, fallacious and fugitive."

A remark like this opens many cans of worms: what is truth, how does one contact it, how does one use it, how does one relate to fanatic use of "truth," hallucinated truth, the omnipresence of error and truth, and so on? The Greek categories Johnson assumes are filled with holes now. Yet the sense of what he means comes through. Whatever difficulties and impossibilities plague this kind of discourse, one feels the reality of what Johnson appeals to. It is this kind of security—maddening, perplexing, challenging—that comes from struggling with oneself, trying to open to the real. Bion describes this, too, as becoming at-one (at-onement) with oneself and transforming in O, his sign for unknowable ultimate reality.

Bion associates O with catastrophic impact. Even if it is a good O, a fruitful, potentially creative O-impact, there is a degree of shattering. The big-bang moment is ubiquitous, ongoing, unpredictable, potentially exploding into new universes of experience—insofar as one is receptive or can take it or make use of it. The impact of reality is far greater than our ability to process it. We can't take too much reality. Our equipment simply is not up to it. If we are lucky, persistent, patient, hungry enough for the real, our equipment grows into the job, building more capacity to work with what is. Nevertheless, we are always behind the impact of moment, at best able to process crumbs broken off from the whole. But those crumbs can be rich indeed!

Reality is processed through incessant transformations of impacts. Bion's work can be viewed as descriptions of transformations that his sensibility and ability could manage. His particular bent makes him sensitive to impact as disaster or potential disaster. He has a special gift for delineating psychotic deformations in response to disaster (big-bang explosions, meteoric black winters). Any increase in reality or consciousness may stimulate disaster dread. Bion redefines resistance as resistance to the real. Emotional and mental life may turn off to variable degrees, becoming numb, vacuous, deadening, in response to dread of heightening (and vice versa, heightening may ward off deadness). Therapy provides support for the psyche's attempts to process what bits of reality it can. It aids the psyche's attempts to sustain and digest the fact that we are alive and trying to learn something about living.

Psychoanalysis is a response to a sense of disaster that pervades psychic life. Its catalogue of anxieties—those associated with birth, separation, intrusion, abandonment, castration, and even life and death—expresses a sensitivity to injury with many forms, a wound with many faces. Psychoanalysis works with damage done and signifiers of disaster. It is a creative response to disaster, as so much of culture is.

We keep trying to regularize disaster, wish it away, tone it down. Science puts pressure on reality to fit formulas. It squeezes reality into patterns that enlarge our ability to control unwanted events. We are dazzled by ideas about reality generated by thinking that will not give up. Science makes things better. But disaster does not go away. Heart attacks, cancer, terrorist attacks, emotional and physical and economic abuse—feed disaster anxiety. Our psyche partly forms around an internal sense of disaster that links with rich arrays of disaster fantasies. Not infrequently, unconscious hallucinated disaster molds external reality, as well as vice versa.

D. W. Winnicott describes this internal sense of disaster as a kind of madness or deformation the personality undergoes as it begins to form. The self keeps growing, and personality makes a go of it, following threads of good experiences to offset the bad, insofar as it can. One tries to absorb deforming traumas and go on. But a nuclear sense of disaster anxiety persists in the background, sometimes erupting as part of hysterical, obsessive, or phobic dreads that persecute daily life. Winnicott describes a double tendency, a need to go toward yet escape basic madness. The paradoxical result of reaching toward one's basic madness and the traumatized self is feeling more alive and real. The model is not control so much as opening one's experiential field.

Bion calls this opening faith. One opens oneself to reality (O) not because the latter is good or bad—it may be both and neither—but because it is. It is the only O we have and are, and we'd best learn to become partners with ourselves, with it. Faith is an open attitude that lets things register. It is not the closed faith of a particular religious dogma, ready to do violence to what is outside it. The faith Bion has in mind is part of the need sensitivity has to taste life, to feel impacts and digest them in ways that lead to more life.

This kind of faith is an attempt not to do violence to experience, an attempt that must fail, perhaps. But the attitude it embodies is significant—a caring, devotion, sincerity, respect, an imaginative loving objectivity, a drive to do life justice, a need to do right by experience. If taken seriously, one possible result of this kind of faith is increased ability to wait on each other, wait for each other—a sensitivity to emotional smell, spirit, affective attitude, a desire to taste each other and our mutual impacts. Waiting, patience, a certain passivity are important in order to let impacts build and unfold: sensitivity grows around them and they stimulate growth of sensitivity. It is a faith that comes back for more, that keeps opening and opening in the face of trauma waves, that registers impacts and learns to work with them.

One may need to pull back from sensitivity for a time, keep things down. But sooner or later sensitivity drives past the manageable, seeks heightened impacts, raw aliveness, fresh air. It needs to taste and shatter and stretch.

We will see throughout this book dramas sensitivity goes through, involving too much, too little, and more subtle nuances of quality. Sensitivity may be too much or too little for itself, moving between flooding and starvation, whether in sensory, emotional, social, aesthetic, ethical, intellectual, or spiritual domains. Therapy provides moment-to-moment possibilities of hiding, deforming, dying out, rerouting, regrouping, coming back to open up once more, to try another way around or through, to find ways to work with one's sensitive self, to let sensitivity speak.

GLIMPSES OF THE CHAPTERS THAT FOLLOW

"A Basic Rhythm" (Chapter 2) describes variations of a drama sensitivity undergoes, relating to injury and recovery. Work by Elkin, Winnicott, and Bion amplify this theme in complementary ways, adding to our sense of what happens when we are wounded. Freud tended to emphasize a kind of ego sensitivity, narcissistic humiliation. In the standard English translation, a word often used is "mortification," instinctively associating wound with death. There is much in Freud's writings to show he was sensitive to impacts that resound through the entire personality. As early as *Studies on Hysteria*, Freud spoke the language of injury, spontaneously connecting wound and image. He pointed to links between neurotic and poetic sensitivity with everyday language, noting how wounded sensitivity spontaneously translates into a "blow to the face," a "stab in the heart." Psychoanalysis can be viewed as a semipoetic elaboration of what happens when sensitivity is wounded—a particular kind of expressive language for wounded sensitivity.

In later work Freud suggested that something can go wrong with drives too. Not only ego, but also id can be damaged. As I've suggested elsewhere, a monstrous ego is underwritten by a deformed id. Trauma blasts through all agencies of personality, even if psyche works hard to isolate and circumscribe the damage. Bion adds that primary process and dreamwork, elementary attempts to process affects, can be damaged. Damage reaches unconscious processing ability and the therapist becomes an auxiliary dreamworker (including an auxiliary dreamer), not just an auxiliary ego worker. The scope and depth of injury to sensitivity demands increased scope and depth of therapeutic sensitivity.

For Winnicott trauma that hits personality as it begins to form leaves a sense of damage associated with beginnings, including the start of emotional processing. To connect this with Bion, fear of feelings is deep because ability to process feelings is damaged. Damage permeates links between self and other, between different functions and capacities of personality, and extends to the ability of dreams to work with disturbances they express.

H. Elkin describes an underlying rhythm involving dying out and reawakening of self that can go awry and take skewed turns. Winnicott and Bion converge on this theme, adding layerings and possibilities to what we go through in order to establish workable rhythms of injury and recovery, renewal of our sensitive self.

Chapter 3 traces intersections between mysticism and psychoanalysis. O's impact on sensitivity opens varying worlds of experience and ways of organizing experience. We can experience the world "naturalistically" and "mystically," often together, an eye on each. We may be better off giving various sides of our nature their due than fighting truth wars. We have a lot to learn from the capacities that make us up, each making contributions to our sense of life. There is no sense in taking sides with one and throwing rocks at others, which is what we often seem inclined to do. Better to put our energy into learning how to use what is given to us, the ins and outs of our makeup.

Mystical apprehension of reality, like any other approach to the real, opens creative and/or destructive doors of perception. Some people are more sensitive to mystical experience than others, and there is no one type of mystical sensitivity, no more than there is one type of aesthetic sensitivity. This is so for psychoanalysts, as for any other group. The analysts discussed in this chapter—among them, Freud, Federn, Milner, Bion, Matte-Blanco, and Elkin—tend to be mystic-friendly, variously emphasizing paradox, mystery, shatter, communion, separation, oneness, and nameless nuances difficult to pin down. They combine critical and poetic sensibility, analysis and intuition.

After connecting psychoanalysis and mysticism, the chapter moves toward positive and negative work of destruction. Destructive experience plays an important role in personal and spiritual development. There are times positive and negative aspects of destruction are indistinguishable or mirror images of each other. We detour through Lacan, Kerouac, Spielberg, a homeless man, Jewish mysticism, a depressed musician, and an enraged psychologist and gain a view of how furious many are at destruction dressed as helpfulness today. In these portrayals, wounded sensitivity speaks, simultaneously undergoing deformation and trying to right itself. There is inconsolable rage and grief in these portrayals, although faith does not disappear in a final way. It regroups, persists, obscurely awaiting openings.

Wounded sensitivity is a basic structure in cases Bion describes. His writings emphasize a sudden shock to sensitivity that tends to freeze the self. Chapter 4 ("Half and Half") elaborates this nucleus, drawing on a case in which Bion's client could not bear a waitress (hallucinated? actual?) bringing him a half-empty cup of coffee. I take off on the proverbial half-empty/half-full conundrum and show how Bion's client cuts off, becomes enraged and contemptuous, turns imaginary or perceived lack into something absolute, total, irreversible. This individual lives in a wound world where everything associated with wounding is subject to hyper–hallucinatory magnification, so that a sense of shock and disaster that informs personality never has a chance to thaw out. The tendencies discussed are important for a wide range of issues bearing on relations between narcissism and social feeling.

Chapter 5 ("A Little Psyche-Music") amplifies themes in earlier chapters and stresses the importance of unconscious processes working well enough to support personality. When trauma hits as personality begins to form, unconscious processing of affects can be damaged. Dreamwork, involved in processing emotional impacts, can be damaged. To try to begin processing affects with a damaged affect processor places one in a perilous position. Beginnings remain associated with catastrophe, so that unconscious background dread gathers force and persecutes personality when growth occurs. As stressed in Chapter 2, sessions become a vehicle for experiencing (partial) breakdown and (partial) spontaneous recovery, enabling a basic rhythm of injury and repair to be established and unconscious processing of wounding impacts to evolve.

Chapter 5 suggests that wounded sensitivity exploits a hallucinatory halo that limes human experiencing and, to some extent, uses mystical experiencing as a kind of salve. An invisible mutilated trauma space became visible, for some, in the violent demise of the World Trade Center, which now plays a role in children's dreams. A working unconscious that can support us in living must endure and work with much mutilation. It must try to process events that damage processing, so that Sisyphus takes on new meaning. A generative unconscious supports the play of naturalistic and mystical tendencies, enabling the subject to use both as a lens on reality, collapsing neither in an absolute or final way.

Chapters 6–10 take up individual cases in detail, each varying the focus on nuances of wounded sensitivity and sensitive appreciation of experiencing. It is wondrous how individuals traverse immense ranges of agonies and joys and many less dramatic states in everyday life that are impossible to pin down, adding to the taste of life. The worst are endured for the latent promise of evolution they hold or simply because they cannot be avoided, and one tries to outlast them until something better happens. For the most part, we will meet individuals trying to stick close to themselves, touching meaningful cores of experience, evolving with them. In those instances when things grow worse rather than better, at least one gains more of a sense of what one is up against and appreciates the resistance of the materials with which one works.

In "Alone with God" (Chapter 6), a highly traumatized individual with deep mystical sensitivity wrestles with a fatal illness. She discovers inlines and outlines of trauma in her God, as exquisite psychomystical tendrils take her to new places, many of which she'd rather not be in. She drinks the only cup she has to drink, and, I believe, we benefit from where she takes us. It is a tribute to the power of her quest that not only is she alive today (three years after this chapter was written, six years after the onset of an illness that was supposed to claim her before the chapter was begun), but she has not let down an inch in her drive and ability to explore what life offers her. She is more radiant, open, and shrewd than ever.

"I Could Do It" (Chapter 7) explores the use of hate to dampen sensitivity. In this person's milieu, sensitivity was maimed, crushed, and mutated by parents experienced as emotive high-velocity particle accelerators. Sensitivity was in a position where it could do nothing but tolerate the destruction that destroyed it, as it spun off into various states, including terror fragments, pain nuclei, hate waves and coating, and sensitivity splitting into hypersensitivity and insensitivity. The sense of basic reality was altered and scarred. As my patient grew up, the realization that sensitivity subjects you to such horror was unendurable, and he tried to mute it, even blank it out with hate, which compounded the difficulties. Now a shield of hate stood between him and himself and this cleavage at the heart of sensitivity became unbearable: "I bury sensitivity with hate, yet nothing hurts me more than the hate I'm buried in."

This person began to hate his sensitivity and, therefore, himself because of what sensitivity subjects him to. He wished there could be sensitivity without injury. At the same time, he was moved by the fact that sensitivity gives him access to the suffering of others, to awareness of the pain in life all over our globe. Sensitivity registers the inhuman in human affairs, recoils, and forms the urge to help.

"Totalities" (Chapter 8) takes recoil against one's sensitivity further. It discusses a case in which the results of trauma impacted in such a way that raw sensitivity itself felt like an attack. Raw sensitivity rendered this person so vulnerable that vulnerability itself became amplified. Vulnerability mutated. It became a spiraling mixture of vulnerable sensitivity and defenses against the latter, a whirling blend and blur of vulnerability-invulnerability, supersensitive and dead at the same time. This man became addicted to his sensitivity. He could not take an eye off vulnerability for a moment, which so pressured him that he, also, incessantly sought oblivion. He was addicted to what caused him most pain, his sensitivity attacks. Part of the inner logic seemed to be that if sensitivity attacked itself enough, it would become less sensitive. A life of attacking the unbearable. Through it all he was aware that sensitivity was basically a vibrating sensitivity, opening doors to the universe, a pulse gone wrong but not silent. He is riveted by the terror that life cannot stand itself, cannot take its own aliveness, that aliveness attacks aliveness.

"Dancing" (Chapter 9) portrays ways in which individuals struggle to make a place for sensitivity, let sensitivity in, and also attempt to evacuate it. In the first case considered, my patient, a therapist, dreamt of his patient dancing. His patient used drink and drugs to regulate feelings, dampening and heightening them, increasing-decreasing sensitivity. My patient's patient expressed levels of heartbreak that mirrored something in my patient's soul, while also mirroring a longing for potential healing and growth. My patient struggled with the need to let his patient in, to make use of him in dreaming. According to Bion, anxiety in the analyst signals the latter's resistance to the patient's reality, fear of letting the patient in, dread of dreaming the patient. Dreaming the patient is making the patient real. The patient wins a place inside the therapist and becomes part of the latter's own transformation process. The dance of sensitivities evolves together. Writing this is a kind of waking dreaming of my patient dreaming his patient, a chain of psychic digestion, a chain we hope can spread, to the point of all human beings finding ways to dream each other, making use of what each offers, the realness of people, self everywhere.

At the same time, the tendency to push away, get rid of, evacuate is an important part of feeling real too. Either side, taking in or pushing out, can metastasize, harden, go haywire. The second case examined in this chapter studies the intricacies of a man who becomes a dancer and uses dancing in a quasi-psychopathic way. The failures in his life, the crashes, unconsciously portray heartbreak he cannot feel, a trauma history gone blank, the latter mimicking heartlessness. Dancing enlivened him but turned into a business — not only a business, but a way of manipulating others, a way of keeping life at bay. A kind of control that once fed ego but ended by starving emotional reality. The two cases taken together provide a glimpse of the tension between sincerity and psychopathy, a kind of dialectic sensitivity undergoes.

"Not Enough" (Chapter 10) studies aspects of erotic sensitivity. It begins with the sliding of erotic feeling from one person to another, the "not enough" that is a latent part of erotic hunger. Unconscious fury at one's partner (whom one also appreciates) condenses sliding "not enoughs," concentrating them into spikes of discontent aimed at whoever one is stuck with. The sliding of erotic feeling that aims at increasing erotic sensitivity turns into a kind of erotic bleeding. Sensitivity bleeds, thins out, even as it spikes. Insofar as my patient in this chapter is sensitive, there is someone somewhere who can make him glow, but a net result is that his feelings bleed and thin and something about him slackens.

"Enough! or Too much," writes William Blake, meaning only too much is enough. My patient seeks excess to make up for not enough, but too much is a reality in its own right. Excess is real, inviting, tantalizing. Other experiences pale by comparison, nothing good enough. But excess undoes itself and leads to psychospiritual hangovers. In the long run, it is important to wriggle psychically in such a way that not enough and too much become friends.

Chapters 11 and 12 ("Sensitivity and Vulgarity" and "Is There Room for Heaven in Psychoanalysis?") are interviews with me conducted, respectively, by Robert Marchesani and Jeffrey Eaton. The relationship between sensitivity and vulgarity is complex and highly significant for who we are, how we operate and experience the world. Sensitivity spans many dimensions and symbolic worlds, making use of sexual sensitivity and symbolism, on the one hand, and mystical sensitivity and symbolism, on the other. The extremes can seem vast indeed but also connect and fuse in many ways, as in sexualizing God or deifying sex. Psychoanalysis teaches that sex connects with everything. Religions teach that God connects with everything. It is no surprise that psychoanalysis and mysticism have deep inner connections, if both connect with everything. Instinct and spirit are not only at war, but also deeply feed each other.

In the past I have written that "the asshole holds the body together." I said this because of the wealth of associations that link other body parts with anal imagery. In psychoanalytic trains of asso-ciation (e.g., mouth-anus-vagina; nipple-feces-penis/clitoris) top-bottom, front-back, and inner-outer meanings pass through and re-volve around anal links. Phallic and cavity associative "equations" include the anal area, which combines both. Vulgarity has, partly, a unifying effect and flavor. When one swears, one feels stronger, more together, more united for a moment. "Fuck" is a kind of elemental self-assertive expression, at once hostile-sexual (at times a hostile re-sponse to and use of sexuality, as well as a sexualization of hostility).

Some of the most powerful vulgar expressions link fuck with anality—for example, "up your ass!" And although we do call some-one cunt or prick, calling someone an asshole cuts into a deeper level of negative self-image. To be a shit or piece of shit or asshole distills a sense of worthlessness, self-hate, abasement, lowliness. The imagery of weaponry and destruction ("spoil," "wipe out," "bomb") is more anal than phallic, as life is fecalized, laid waste. When we act big and try to phallicize our sense of power, we should beware the hidden swamp and quicksand of hidden anality, sucking life from behind into the black hole. Sensitivity to links between body and symbol (including body as symbol and symbol as body) opens rich tapestries of experiencing, which, too often, are short-circuited and play themselves out in insensitive mixtures of calculated and blindly destructive acts.

Chapter 12 brings out an aesthetic core in life and psychoanalysis and allies this core with a kind of ethics. Aesthetic and ethical sensi-tivity do not always intersect, but there is a kind of experiential beauty and ethics to psychoanalytic work that expresses areas of con-vergence. This chapter discusses alternative therapy models, shifting winds in the therapy field, and brings out what I've taken from voices who influenced me. My own work places less emphasis on control than on discovery, the opening of experiential fields, some-times just in subtle shifts and nuances. One particular focus is sensi-tivity to beatific experience, for good and ill, since the heaven within fuses with destructive or generative currents.

–18. For

CHAPTER 2 *A Basic Rhythm*

Rebirth images have a long history. Ancient mysteries focused on moving from "lower" to "higher" consciousness. Biblical rebirth images involved healing damage or cleansing corruption: the blind will see, the lame walk, the burden of sin will be lifted. Rebirth images are associated with the wish to live forever but are not limited to the latter. They are connected with changing states of being, moods, feelings, growth processes—referring, for example, to shifts between feeling dead and awakening to life.

Symbolic life is partly concerned with describing what its own activity feels like and discovering what it can do. Art, for example, disrupts itself in order to explore its processes and discover further possibilities. I've heard artists speak of killing their work (babies), repeatedly destroying what they do until what emerges feels closer to a birth they can say yes to. In such a process successive destructions and births fuse yet support and lend strength to what results.

The psyche generates rebirth images to help organize sensitivity. To speak of a new spirit, new person, new soul implies something wrong with the old one, perhaps a perennial insufficiency built into experience. We refer to someone "getting better," not just as a movement from illness to health but as part of a drive to surpass or transcend oneself, a never-ending birth. Disruption supersedes disruption as one keeps stretching. We *want* to be better, to go beyond or correct ourselves.

Rebirth images also track trauma. Sensitivity suffers wounds. We are very sensitive beings, more easily injured than we like to think. As Bion writes, "When two personalities meet, an emotional storm is created." At the same time, we are extremely resilient. This mixture of sensitivity and resilience is part of our strength. But one way or another, sensitivity makes us casualties of our development. We keep trying to find better ways to survive ourselves, to be better partners with processes that constitute us, although these processes are largely unknown.

The very notion of rebirth refers to a rhythm involving disruption and continuity. Winnicott believes disruption is part of continuity or adds deeper continuity to living if things go well enough. Sometimes I get the feeling that continuity makes Bion claustrophobic and that shatter almost has the last word. But, in his work, going through a shattering process can lead to something larger. Sensitivity is ripped apart by life. There are wounds that never heal—perhaps shouldn't heal. But even these wounds can feed a drive for the better: to create a better world, to be a better person.

Processes by which wounds feed evolution are registered in rebirth imagery. A particular psychoanalytic turn to this age-old effort has to do with the ins and outs of going through trauma. Ancient myths and stories portray effects of trauma: turning to stone, becoming a monster, turning into a flower or a closed shell. It is not crippled limbs that are at stake but wounded selves, blocked, frozen, deformed, rigid. Socrates addressed sickness of soul, and a riveting concern with infected mind or spirit informed Shakespeare's language. It would be a crazy idealization of life to think we can do away with what deforms us. What psychoanalysis does is incorporate block, shock, and disability into a larger rhythm of decimation and flow. In one way or another, agonies sensitivity suffers are tasted or gone through, over and over, and something else happens, an opening, a recovery, a movement toward another place. Neither blockage nor flow falls away. Both evolve and contribute to nuances of tensions that are part of the texture of experiencing.

It is unclear to what extent the psyche can regenerate itself or what its regeneration might mean. Psychoanalysts, like prophets, refer to another chance at new beginnings. For our purposes in the present chapter, this does not mean leaving trauma behind. Trauma is one part of a larger rhythm. Psychoanalytic writers have made important contributions to the sense of this rhythm, the movement between blockage and flow, trauma and new beginnings. Ideas from three contributors—Elkin, Winnicott, and Bion—will be developed here, complementary profiles of a basic rhythm that takes many forms.

Elkin delineates an emotive-spiritual drama that arises with self-other awareness, prior to awareness of materiality as such. He believes the infant's smiling in response to a face or face representation expresses awareness of self and other, but not in the usual framework of spatial limits. Since primordial self and other are experienced before a coherent body image develops, they have an immaterial, ineffable quality (in another context, Bion speaks of the basic psychic reality as "infinity"). It takes time to learn that mind, spirit, feeling, intentions are bounded by material forms and we must be where our body is. Meanwhile, the human face becomes the center of a fluid world, undergoing immense changes as affective dramas ensue.

Initial primordial consciousness moves from ineffable bliss through disruptive crises to restoration of well-being, undergoing momentous shifts of relational significance. The dawn of self-awareness is supported by a background Other (akin to Buddha encompassed by the void). Surges of self-other feeling spike as the encompassing, nonmaterial Other smiles and hearts blend through expressive faces. Smile triggers smile, feeling reverberates. There are echoes of this resonant state in movies portraying the meeting of true lovers, face-heart connection radiantly blooming. One can envision an expressive face as the radiant center of the cosmic mandala.

Trouble comes and disrupts this bliss. Need, pain, distress, agony —something wrong, perhaps hunger, illness, thermal imbalance, respiratory mishap, a bad spirit. The baby lacks a material frame of reference for its distress, and the latter spirals toward infinity when the Other fails to respond and bring relief. The radiant face-heart connection shatters in the face of mounting anxiety, panic, rage (aspects of Bion's "nameless dread," Winnicott's "primitive agonies"). Loss of goodness mushrooms. The infant's helpless inability to change its state for the better swings from anxiety to impotent despair, possibly dropping into stupor or nervous sleep. The Other, concomitantly, is experienced as "omnipotent, inscrutable, terrifying, indifferent, or cruelly mocking," a face burning hell in one's soul (myths of turning to stone, dying upon glimpsing the unbearable). From pristine radiant awakening to mental-spiritual agony and death, loss of primordial consciousness, a breaking of heart-to-heart, eye-to-eye, face-to-face contact. Simple radiant identification of primordial self with primordial Other tastes destruction.

In time the Other's ministrations take hold and primordial consciousness is reborn. Or perhaps the infant experiences a spontaneous change of state, with correlative shifts of self-other feeling. The overall movement is a kind of death-resurrection sequence. However, with rebirth of consciousness, the Other acquires new significance. The self experiences regeneration in consequence of the Other's raising it from death. Spirit has been fanned back to life with awareness of "the Other as the eternal, numinous, Source of Being; that is, of light, or consciousness itself."

No primordial experience is lost, so that initial radiant self-other identification, intermediate dread, rage and stupor vis-à-vis a menacing Other, and culminating faith in the divine Other's merciful love embrace each other, fuse, ebb and flow, interpenetrate, threaten, support and feed emotional life. "For the Self has realized," as Elkin concludes, "that its very existence depends on the merciful love of the often inscrutable, seemingly cruel or indifferent, yet eternal, omniscient, and omnipotent Other. Only when the child learns to rely trustfully, when beset by instinctive fears, on the divine *Loving-Cognition*, does his mind-spirit remain fixed in the light of primordial consciousness."

Elkin tends to see the initial moment as more Hindu ("I and God are one," "Atman Brahman"), the culminating moment as more Judeo-Christian (rebirth through the Other: "Yea, though you slay me, yet will I trust you."). Various threads of mystical and psychotic experience draw on oscillating combinations of these and intermediate phases.

WINNICOTT'S "SPONTANEOUS RECOVERY"

"In every calm and reasonable person," Phillip Roth writes, "there is a hidden second person scared witless about death, but for someone thirty-two the time between Now and Then is ordinarily so vast, so boundless, that it's no more than a couple of times a year, and then only for a moment or two and late at night, that one comes anywhere near encountering that second person and in the state of madness that is the second person's everyday life." Roth links madness with fear of death, in a second, hidden person, beneath a calm and reasonable one. It is somewhat a literary ploy to create a calm and reasonable person for whom madness is a second soul. Here sanity and madness are treated as dramatic foils, when much of the time we are probably neither too sane, nor too mad.

Yet Roth picks a thread that Winnicott elaborates into a kind of therapeutic principle. Winnicott finds it important for many people to use therapy as a place to break down and recover, dip into that "second person" a little at a time. One's madness becomes a second home, or, at least, one grows a little less afraid of it, or has a better sense of what there is to be afraid of.

In the last case, one may see that there is reason for fear, more than one dared to realize. For the madness Winnicott speaks of has as its nucleus not only fear of physical death, but also psychological agonies over loss of mind and self and functioning, inchoate dreads involving unbearable impacts as self comes into being. Madness is tied to sensitivity, a consequence of the latter and part of the latter. We would not be mad if we were not sensitive. For Winnicott, "Some experience of madness, whatever that may mean, is universal, and this means that it is impossible to think of a child who was so well cared for in earliest infancy that there was no occasion for overstrain of the personality as it is integrated at a given moment."

Overstrain. In popular talk we speak of getting bent out of shape. Personality undergoes distortions, deformations. In certain instances, breakdown is deformation past a certain point. Many individuals get used to deformations and adapt to them. We may feel safe in a state of chronic collapse, less than ourselves, and play down awareness of our loss. One makes do with the personality one inhabits and works with what is available. The madness we are unconscious of spreads through skin, muscles, organs, cells, the air that we breathe. It may be so ubiquitous we cannot locate it.

Winnicott goes farther: "Psychosis has to do with distortions during the phase of the formation of the personality pattern." He means by this "environmental distortion at the phase of the individual's absolute dependence." There is an environmental factor in the psychosis Winnicott is thinking about. The holding environment needed to support psychic life is seriously flawed, and warp marks "the formation of the personality pattern." Something goes wrong as personality begins to form, at the onset of self-organization, so that birth of self goes awry. One suffers distortion or is blown away. One tightens oneself to get through, but self-tightening creates distorted casings around distorted insides, hardening and poisoning self. One holds vast areas of self at a distance, but poison spreads and there is no safe haven.

Winnicott speaks of two kinds of persons, "one who does not carry around with them a significant experience of mental breakdown in earliest infancy and those who do." Those who do try to escape breakdown with one foot and move toward it with the other. Therapy provides a place to embrace this double movement and develop a better rhythm so that the breakdown-recovery movement can be fruitful.

Thus fear of madness may be fear of a return of madness, reexperiencing the dreaded breaking of personality as the latter began to form. Fear of madness draws upon a sense of damage at the start of self. We will see, when discussing Bion, more ways beginnings trigger dread. Winnicott provides a developmental background for association of beginnings with madness if, at the onset of self-formation, breakdown regularly intruded.

Interpreting breakdown is not enough. Individuals must go through it repeatedly in circumscribed form. Intellectual awareness may help or hinder, but what is most important is tasting and living it. The idea that one is partially experiencing a breakdown present at one's beginnings and that one is trying to establish the rhythm of breakdown and recovery now—this idea can provide a kind of cognitive frame that enables opening long enough to experience bits of what is needed. It is an idea allied with trust that coming through breakdown is possible (overlapping with Elkin's primordial consciousness coming through agonizing despair and psychospiritual death). However, this idea is not enough. One must feel the Other's fidelity in order to risk finding the place of breaking and coming together, in order to establish this psychic pulse-beat. As Winnicott says, "Madness that has to be remembered can only be remembered in the reliving of it."

There are impediments to reliving originary madness. One is the impossibility of going through an experience as totally as an infant might. It is not possible to recapture original breakdown because one is alive only now. One can work only with what is available in one's developed state. Winnicott makes an important clinical contribution, suggesting that sometimes individuals create or organize lesser pains as entrée to primordial agonies. For example, he describes a girl who complains of too much homework and overstress at school. With this as a jumping-off point, her sense of strain escalates into severe headaches and hours of screaming. She moves from teacher as stressor to therapist, from whom even a word becomes unbearable. She reaches a point of raw sensitivity, where impact of otherness is too much. She uses an everyday frustration to reach a more total sense of impingement and breakdown, from which she now can recover. In therapy one practices letting go into breakdown, followed by reversal into renewal. This girl admitted to Winnicott that school was not as bad as she made it out to be, but she needed its badness to get into something worse. She is practicing recovery by stimulating the sense of trauma. She may not get to the original madness, but Winnicott suggests she gets to an extreme of agony next door to it.

Another impediment to reaching the original madness (or reaching toward it) is the difficulty of finding an analyst who grasps what the person is trying to do. For example, a therapist's sanity, logic, or fear might put a damper on the agony escalation the girl in the preceding example needed to experience. Too sensible a therapist might short-circuit the spiraling toward madness this girl worked so hard at achieving. Winnicott felt his patient worked at creating the state she needed to recover from, and she needed a therapist to help create an atmosphere in which this was possible.

The drive to get better urges the person toward the madness that needs experiencing. The drive toward health partly overcomes the desire to flee, so that one tastes letting go into breakdown. In this context, movement toward madness is part of health. Flight from madness reinforces an overly defensive or even sick sanity. The individual is caught between "fear of madness and the need to be mad." Too often psychiatric aid does not see the positive aspect of breakdown, which Winnicott suggests can be a first step toward health. Winnicott is not speaking about breakdowns that ruin a person's chance at living and have ghastly, chronic consequences for self and family, with no way out. He refers to growing the capacity to use breakdown states so that individuals, over time, can touch the madness that threatens and freezes personality in a way that adds to living. By going through momentary breakdown more openly, one becomes friendlier with oneself. "Cure only comes if the patient reaches to the original state of breakdown," says Winnicott. Reaches to, not reaches. In reaching toward, a directional movement, one is less focused on stopping oneself than on letting a little more happen.

Ordinary psychoanalytic remembering is not the issue, because one cannot remember what one did not experience. That is, originary breakdown involves not being able to experience what one is undergoing. One lacks resources to hold what is happening and memory breaks as it forms or defensiveness substitutes for it. "In the simplest possible case there is therefore a split second in which the threat of madness was experienced," according to Winnicott, "but anxiety at this level is unthinkable. Its intensity is beyond description and new defenses are organized immediately so that in fact madness was not experienced. Yet on the other hand madness was potentially a fact."

I am reminded of screams of psychotic patients changing levels of consciousness during insulin shock treatment. One person described it thus: "I would come in and out of awareness, more like coming in and out of life. Comas are uneven, but I didn't know that. I would start becoming conscious, and the coma would start coming back, and I screamed and screamed, afraid I was dying. There was nothing but screaming death. More horrible than death—you're stuck in something agonizing, and you scream and scream and that's all there is until you're out."

To some extent, the coma replicates what Elkin describes as terror, rage, stupor, and death of primordial consciousness, the "split second" Winnicott makes us feel as self gives way to traumatic impact.

A Basic Rhythm : 25

Human beings live with this sequence in the back of their beings: intimations of potential madness, in which momentary breakdowns draw on the originary breakdown, which cannot be experienced, which is always about to happen, a terrifying something worse than death.

For Winnicott, the pain of originary madness, if it could be experienced, would be indescribable. He accesses it through lesser psychotic anxieties, such as disintegration, unreality feelings, lack of relatedness, depersonalization, lack of psychosomatic cohesion, split-off intellectual functioning, falling forever, ECT panic. Even actual psychosis is not total, but a part of what psychosis might be. A problem for psychotic individuals is that they are stuck in states they are unable to suffer through. They can neither get out of nor go through what takes them over. The terror that cannot be experienced takes the form of an experience that cannot be processed. A psychotic is too afraid of his madness to work with it—nothing is more terrifying to a mad individual than his own madness. The "technically" mad individual is in the same position as the rest of us, insofar as his madness is a barrier against greater madness, defensively organizing what threatens organization.

Winnicott calls the Ur-madness, the madness that can't be reached, X, and goes on to say, "What is absolutely personal to the individual is X." Winnicott touches a place where madness makes us feel real. If we fail to reach for the most frightening point of all, we may miss what is most personal in our beings. If we fail to include the point of breakdown in our search as persons, we will be leaving a crucial fact of self out. Winnicott points to a terror too terrifying to experience as a truth needing digestion, a moment searching for someone to endure it, if only a little, or a little at a time. Terror at the heart of life has been pointed to by myth, religion, literature, war, and the lust for power. Therapy seems a feeble response in light of the immensity of what we face, but it provides a place where people sit together and dip into processes that all too readily spin out of control in the world at large.

Winnicott is not simply speaking of psychotic or neurotic individuals. He is speaking to us. In analysis "the patient continually reaches to new experiences in the direction towards X," living through "localized madnesses." The analyst does not reach for sanity so much as enable "the madness to become a manageable experience from which the patient can make a spontaneous recovery." Madness gets dosed out. The key here is *spontaneous recovery*, as crucial for actually psychotic individuals as for those who dip into madness symbolically. I think Winnicott is urging the human race to take in the fact of madness in daily life, so that humanity will not have to go (or stay) mad. Here he adds his particular twist, so important in self-feeling, that the capacity to live through an experience has broken down and needs support to begin its work.

BION'S FREEING MURDER

In *Cogitations*, Bion writes of being murdered, then being all right. He likens a psychotic seeing blood mounting up on his sleeve to being murdered in reverse. The patient dreads annihilation as his blood is restored. It is an annihilation he must risk if he is to come alive, if the blood of meaning and feeling is to flow in his psychic veins: "At the point when his blood will be fully restored to his circulatory system he will experience being murdered. And then he will be all right." The closer to life, the closer to murder as a rite of passage.

Murder as gateway on the way toward aliveness, as psychic circulation increases, contrasts with images of bleeding to death. Bion writes about loss of blood as an image of loss of feeling or splattering of common sense. Hemorrhage expresses injury to thinking and feeling processes.

Here are two deaths, one associated with loss of psyche, the other with filling out of psyche, a double dread connected with loss and gain of aliveness. Bion's shorthand notation for the murder one passes through in order to gain life is the "murderous superego," annihilating object par excellence. As one comes alive, the object that murders life is intensely activated. As one puts oneself together, one also puts together the annihilating object. To have blood may be more frightening than not having blood. In the former, one risks trauma all over again. In the latter one is protected by hopelessness; one already is dead.

The murderous object one passes through on the path to life sounds like Winnicott's depiction of trauma hitting at the beginning of personality formation. Beginnings are henceforth associated with annihilation or, at least, serious damage. To begin to come alive risks retraumatization. In Winnicott's account, one goes through dread of traumatization repeatedly, in somewhat handleable doses (e.g., momentarily breaking down and recovering in sessions). Bion fuses breakdown with murder, which adds an extra grain of intensity. It is not just breakdown one fears, but annihilation, a multiplicative state of affairs in which breakdown and murder infinitely heighten each other.

Winnicott speaks of breakdown that cannot be experienced because one cannot be there to experience it. Therapy works with the sense of personality being decimated as it begins to form and builds capacity to experience breakdown and formation. Bion raises the possibility of being there to undergo the murder that made it impossible to be there. Even attempting to go through this impossibility can help build capacity to process elements of the murderous object that stops processing. To be murdered or broken is one thing, to face being murdered and broken another. In the latter instance, one experiences devastation to the extent one can, in a more fully, open way, or begins to notice this is something one cannot do. To start to process and relate more fully to one's inability to process is a kind of beginning. One can, at least, begin to speak of and undergo dread of beginnings.

Elkin's dying out and return of primordial consciousness seems a general, underlying, background pulse, which can happen in more deforming or sustaining ways, an archetypal structure of a basic rhythm. The self goes through infinities of agonies before dying out, prior to joyous infinities of return, an essential death-resurrection sequence. Here is a rhythmic basis for the sense of infinite return, self dying out in horror, awakening through love. It is a good resurrection, rebirth through a caring, merciful Other. The intermediate phases, including visions/perceptions of indifferent, inimical otherness one cannot bear, are encompassed by a sense of the overarching goodness of life. It is akin to the rhythm of the Psalms: the soul repeatedly returns from devastation, as life blooms again through God's love.

The rebirth sequence is not always gone through fully and openly. Often subjects go through it in a pinched, defensive way. Sometimes one is reborn as a monster. There are destructive, even evil, rebirths if the face at the center of personality is demonic, terrifying, ever traumatizing. Life freezes around the ugly core. One may not be able to pass through the kindness needed in order to incorporate the dreadful or malignant Other into a larger sense of life. Most rebirths are semiaborted, semisuccessful combinations of rigidity and openness. One keeps trying to go through it better.

In Elkin's case, death precedes restoration. In Bion's, restoration precedes death, then further righting of self, which faces more death, in a continuing cycle The two are not antithetical, since the death-rebirth-death-rebirth rhythm is a constant. Bion singles out a particular moment of this ongoing sequence, a particular aspect of annihilation anxiety. It is vintage Bion to depict being murdered as the restorative moment climaxes. If one can't undergo murder properly, one can't feel all right. To go through murder is part of the psyche's journey. One comes together, partly, in order to face death (à la Winnicott's building capacity to better go through breakdown and recovery).

Bion's account incorporates bits of body into the psychic journey —murder is not only soul murder. Annihilation resonates through physical, psychical, spiritual dimensions: psychosomatic murder (somewhere) *and* murder of psyche (nowhere, everywhere). One murder vibrates through others, a murder chorus ricocheting through personality. An example of a murder chorus in literature is the reverberations of infanticide-matricide-patricide in Greek tragedy. Another example involves the Freudian primal scene. "Primal scene" is a term referring to variations of fantasy and observation revolving around parental intercourse: who is doing what to whom? A child rightly or wrongly may feel that father and mother are injuring or destroying each other, or playing with each other. Mixtures of destruction and creation are variably weighted. Babies born from creative-destructive unions may be imagined as deformed or divine, worse or better than oneself. The world and self may be populated by armies of corpses or superalive beings. Many shifting forms of aliveness-deadness have roots in experiences/fantasies of parental attitudes that pervade bodies.

There is something finite about murder. One cannot murder everything. One murders this or that person or group, trying to get rid of particular obstacles, traits, qualities, powers. Murder often is encoded in the desire to win, whether a game or a war (one says in games, "you're killing me"). In suicide the individual may try to get rid of a part of personality that is wounding him, a particular wounding presence within.

When murder reaches past a certain point, it dissolves into a more formless sense of destruction, a diffuse disaster anxiety, an over-whelming catastrophic dread threatening to sweep self away. Particular murderous fantasies or acts try to put the brakes on illimitable dread, act as filters, give particularity to nameless annihilation. In a way, murder attempts to master annihilation. The victim (individual or group) comes to stand for annihilation. For an instant, the mur-derer has the intoxicating illusion that annihilation itself is putty in his/her hands. One manufactures annihilation, has power over it, imagines annihilation helpless. The grandiosity of murder is destined to boomerang, since part of its psychology couples victory with im-potence (fused extremes undergo reversal).

There are many kinds of murder and responses to it, diverse min-glings of guilt, anxiety, excitement, gain, and loss. Murder can make one feel more alive. I don't simply mean thrill murder or boundless excitement of rage. I mean experience of one's power and energy rip-ping through suffocation. We need to learn how to murder each other well, so that murderous delights add to life's fullness rather than cause harm. I suspect Winnicott has something like this in mind when he speaks of the importance of the Other surviving the infant's destructiveness. The Other gains in otherness precisely in surviving. We need to survive each other's destructiveness to feel fully alive, part of learning how to live together. To some people killing and be-ing killed comes naturally. They bob up after intense interactions ready for more, as if the risk of undoing each other adds to life. For many, the sense of creative murder does not develop well. They withdraw or become too aggressive, expecting neither self nor other to survive or survive fully. Energic interactions are costly and trau-matizing. The knack or "feel" of coming through each other's im-pacts needs nurturing.

Bion emphasizes coming through the Other's destructiveness, Winnicott stresses the Other coming through self's destructiveness —two profiles of a dual capacity. We come through ourselves and each other and the quality of coming through depends, partly, on how well we kill and are killed. There is an art of coming through impacts, a capacity easily abused and exploited, but important if we are to work well together.

MORE ON SURVIVING MURDER AND
COMING THROUGH DAMAGE

For Bion murder is part of psychic birth, a kind of being murdered into life, a process of discovery. One learns it is possible to survive murder one is sure one cannot survive, a learning necessary for growth. As aliveness grows toward an apex, murder comes to meet it. If one holds back out of fear, murder grows in menace, an impassable barrier. Arrested or avoided death becomes a stagnant ele-ment in life. Bion invites us to practice getting murdered, ultimately being enlivened by it. Murder is a passageway, a divide: one cannot feel all right if one cannot come through it. Or, rather, coming through it enables one to feel all right in a new way, a way that en-compasses more of what one dreaded. The quality of self and per-sonality feels different depending on whether, or to what extent, one is a pre- or post-murdered being.

The murderous superego plays a special role in being the object that stops dreaming. Bion and Winnicott both emphasize the role of dreaming in processing feelings. To emphasize the fact that we do not really know much about how we process feelings Bion coins the term "alpha function" to express semi-unknown ways that feelings, sensations, or thoughts undergo storage, digestion, and use. Raw impacts of reality are "beta elements," which alpha function nibbles away at. Alpha function helps convert raw emotional impacts into feelings the psyche needs for growth. It transforms beta into alpha elements that feed psychic digestion.

The murderous superego is a kind of beta object registering cata-strophic impacts that take the form of antilife tendencies—a beta ob-ject that can damage, deform and freeze alpha function. Dreamwork is part of the way alpha can function, part of the way raw impacts are transformed into a flow of psychic nourishment (e.g., impact gives rise to image gives rise to symbols gives rise to thought . . .). One might say the murderous superego is a representation that destroys representation, a registration that damages what is trying to encode it. Nevertheless, alpha function cannot stop trying to digest it. One reason dream life can be so scary is that it tries to work with damage while damaged itself. Dreamwork is part of a psychic digestive sys-tem that suffers from quasi-chronic indigestion.

One must process what cannot be processed with a processor that cannot process it. The affect processor must process traumatic im-pacts that damage processing ability. Alpha function, then, labors with a chronic disability, injured by the injury it works with. Yet it is driven to process damaging forces as part of the way it heals itself, risking further injury by seeking health. The impact that proved too much, too devastating, is precisely a key attractor. To assemble any-thing means to assemble what destroys one. In attempting to use, feel, create oneself, one puts together the moment of destruction. To dream the destructive force is already a bit of alpha work, no matter how halting or constricted.

The fact that dreaming destruction is a bit of alpha work against all odds is one reason, I believe, why Bion says the analyst must dream the patient while awake in sessions. Resistance is resistance to the real, which Bion equates with dreaming the patient. The analyst's anxiety/resistance is anxiety about dreaming the patient, making the patient real, taking the patient in, making the patient's life and de-struction part of one's psychic bloodstream. To constitute a living person within oneself is to constitute what is destroying this person as well. The analyst must dream what destroys the patient's dreams, and since the analyst may or may not be much better at this than the patient, the analysis turns on two people becoming partners in evo-lution, doing work all humanity must come to do. In other words, part of the long-term work involves becoming real to ourselves and to each other and the profound ethics this implies.

Alpha function must survive its own destruction, go on working, converting unbearables into useables. Recognition of how disabled, unevolved, and destructive we are or can be is an important step in modulating, even modifying, destructiveness.

Sensitivity comes with risks. Ozone dangers outside pale in comparison with damage done to inner filter systems. In the psychic realm, it is often better to sit with feelings and let them transform than to rush into action (the problem is not being Hamlet, but not being Hamlet enough—even Hamlet acted precipitously, betraying his deeper intuition). We cannot take for granted our ability to feel or know what to do with feelings. To feel our sensitive beings and endure the building of experience is a start. Perhaps, in time, we can better dream our feelings and feel our dreams, making room for the amazing and dangerous experiential field we are all a part of.

RHYTHM OF FAITH

In "Analysis Terminable and Interminable," Freud writes of depletion of plasticity and capacity for change, "psychical inertia," "exhaustion of receptivity," "psychical entropy," "fixed and rigid" mental processes and distributions of force. He feels theoretical knowledge is inadequate here and adds, "Probably some temporal characteristics are concerned—some alterations of a rhythm of development of psychical life which we have not yet appreciated."

His essay raises the specter of cases in which there is a preponderance of death over life drive, to the extent that psychic mobility is challenged. Freud speaks of individuals with too much or too little psychic traction. The rhythm between life and death drives is compromised, so that flow and confluence between alternating tendencies, such as building and breaking apart, is impeded. Freud evokes a sense of something wrong, stuck, or damaged in the timing and rhythm of psychic life.

Here I suggest that part of the rhythm Freud intuits has to do with a kind of psychic pulse, an opening-closing linked with death-rebirth (Elkin), breakdown-recovery (Winnicott), coming alive–being murdered–feeling all right (Bion). The basic rhythm takes different turns in Elkin's, Winnicott's and Bion's work. For Elkin one is reborn through a merciful Other after suffering boundless horror. For Winnicott trauma breaks personality as it forms, dread of breakdown persisting as an undercurrent associated with new beginnings. Therapy creates a situation in which horror and breakdown can be lived in a way that enables moments of spontaneous recovery. For Bion it is as if one is murdered every time one tries to come alive. One needs to dream the murder that stops one, a murderous force that damages dreamwork. Damaged dreamwork is like a bad digestive system. Analysis helps dreamwork to process destruction, so ability to be nourished by living grows.

In analysis the patient experiences the analyst variously as traumatic force or wounding object, supportive background presence, vehicle of wisdom and stupidity, auxiliary dreamworker, agent of faith. The experiential arc described here constitutes a rhythm of faith. For Elkin faith evolves and is sustained as the primordial self is nursed through despair and stupor, quickening into life with the Other's help. In Winnicott's case, the therapist is experienced as traumatizing and supportive in ways that jump start the breakdown-recovery rhythm. The outcome is less focused on trust of the Other (which seems to be taken for granted) than on building trust in one's own ability to come through the trauma-recovery sequence, an experience of one's regenerative capacity. Gradually one's experiential reach is able to encompass blends of intrusiveness/obtrusiveness/abandonment/support that is part of intersubjectivity.

Bion emphasizes a need to symbolize affective damage when capacity to do so is damaged. One must symbolize destructive processes that stop symbolization. Often one cannot take the necessary steps for fear of further injury. Yet, in part, it is in enduring and going through the murderous object that psychic birth evolves—a process of opening to the worst and coming through, repeatedly.

In Bion's rhythm, there is simultaneity of creativeness-destructiveness, as if the creative impulse maximizes destructive possibilities, yet one perseveres. One plunges over the barricades and never stops plunging. The therapist provides support in dreaming catastrophic elements that stop the flow of dreamwork, that stop dreamwork from working. At the same time, catastrophic impact is an important source of raw material for creative work. Creativity is obsessed with destructive forces. In dreaming the therapist as murderer and support, one has a chance of beginning to digest what is troubling one.

The attitude that opens itself to murder Bion calls faith. I think this faith has in it a love of life. It is passionate about living. It opens the heart wide and cannot stop opening. It is a faith that is stronger than murder, that makes murder fruitful.

The tension between faith and murder in Bion is radicalized: both persist maximally, simultaneously. To build a psyche is to be murdered and go beyond being murdered—perpetually, both feeding off each other. But it is not a simple iteration, more of the same. One never gets murdered the same way twice—if one is opening. The "all right" feeling, as well as the murder, undergoes development. Capacities do not stop evolving. In the faith dimension—the place of opening—one cannot step into the same hell or heaven twice. The everyday real does not stop bringing new messages.

Winnicott's primal image isn't murder, but breakdown and madness. He offers practice in an atmosphere in which recovery is established as part of one's basic rhythm, a recovery from oneself and others. Winnicott and Bion overlap in their interest in madness. The murder built into life is mad or has maddening properties. Winnicott tends to call it destructiveness, which he believes is part of aliveness. For Winnicott, the Other must survive my destructiveness in order to feel like an Other. Otherness is other, in part, because it is more or other than my destructiveness can reduce it to. For Bion, the self must come through the Other's murderousness and one's own—the two often indistinguishable (murderousness as part of the human condition). A faith rhythm develops by learning how to come through each other and ourselves. Mistrust does not go away—it shouldn't—it is part of reality-testing. Faith does not exclude other capacities but opens a larger sense of who we are for one another, so that we not only survive destructive aspects of aliveness but grow through the profound enrichment mutual impact can have.

CHAPTER 3 *Mysticism and Psychoanalysis*

Psychoanalysis is officially nonmystical or antimystical. It sticks pins in mystical bubbles. It understands mystical states as remnants of infantile experience, expressions of primitive drives and structures. Yet—as with so much in life—there are complexities and countertendencies. There seem to be mystical aspects to psychoanalysis, and there seem to be mystical psychoanalysts, or analysts tinged with spiritual interests. Freud would have viewed this as regressive. He saw religion as the last great hurdle in freeing man's mind for scientific inquiry. Men resort to religion to assuage a sense of helplessness, a heritage of infantile dependency. One wishes for a good outcome in what is a very fragile and rocky existence. Beatific promises soothe our fears.

On the one hand, mystical states may be related to what Freud terms "primary ego-feeling," a sense of all-embracing, limitless I-feeling, including an "intimate bond between the ego and the world around it." Here there is expanded boundary, sense of infinite inclusion, "oceanic feeling." On the other hand, Freud notes, "Mysticism is the obscure self-perception of the realm outside the ego, of the id." Here the ego is more contracted, separate, "shrunken," taken aback by what is outside it.

P. Federn, working with psychosis, picked up on boundary issues in Freud's thought. He was fascinated with the observation that the *I* contracts and expands, including more or less of the world, body, mind in its movements and identifications. The I and not-I keep shifting. Even the I and me-feeling can drop away as consciousness ticks on.

One can somewhat rework Federn to speak of an originary cosmic I-feeling—everything included in its boundaries—a boundless I-feeling that comes up against the hard knocks of life and contracts in response to pain and learns to deal with limitations. A kind of practical I oriented to space, time, social life and mental and physical boundaries grows up. We are challenged to learn to work with cosmic and practical I-feeling.

Federn portrays the psychotic as one who has difficulty accepting spatial limitations, especially the fact of having to be where one's body is. He portrays a primary boundless consciousness that has to squeeze into a time-space body and world—and not everyone welcomes this challenge or is good at meeting it. The problem Federn points to seems to be different from Freud's formulation of first and foremost a body ego; in fact it seems to be somewhat the opposite. The psychotic, as Federn portrays him, is not someone who has been embodied and opts out but more of a pre-embodied consciousness opting not to start. Apparently the issue in both cases revolves around one's reaction to pain and attitude toward limitations.

Freud depicts a state of shrinking cathexis, withdrawing first from object, then body, then mind—a series of contractions. Federn depicts a state in which consciousness refuses or is unable to extend itself to body boundaries and social and physical limitations. Both begin with an ego that includes everything. However, Federn's inclusiveness does not include physical reality qua physical. It seems more a vague sense of everythingness or everythingness/I-ness without acute distinctions. The fact of physicality comes as quite a surprise, with a threat of essential wounding: "You mean I'm only this?" To somewhat rationalize Federn's psychotic's reaction: "No. I refuse to be only this. I'm not going to get small enough to play the game."

Someone who feels more well-being through and through may welcome the chance to get into her body, a contraction which is also an extension, opening new worlds: "You mean I'm also this?!" An unpsychotic person may welcome learning about the world, its limits, the materials she has to work with. Her drive to explore may win out over what she must give up or re-vision, including pains and difficulties that are part of the admission ticket. For a person who feels good in her body, physical reality may be a field of dreams.

It seems for Federn the ego is first and foremost a mental ego, and Freud's oral-anal-phallic-genital phases are ways the mind gets into the body. It would appear Federn arrived at this position by studying

Husserl, for whom the transcendental ego or attitude has a certain privilege. His work with psychosis, and study of Husserl, came together with his incorporation of Freud.

Elkin's work raises overlapping considerations. He wonders what world the infant must live in if the sense of self and other emerges prior to awareness of physicality as such. It appears the infant smiles in response to a face and is sensitive to mood before it knows it has a body. Elkin argues that body-image development can be read in terms of growing eye-hand-mouth coordination, but that self-other awareness, expressed in the smiling response, is earlier. What must the world of self and other be like prior to awareness of materiality?

Elkin depicts a drama between a sense of self and other that follows contours of mood or spirit. Self may arise in relation to a void or background Other, the latter supporting self without self's awareness of being supported. Examples might be infant Jesus blessing the world on Mary's lap or cross-legged Buddha facing the Void. Bad times come and break up this nice feeling. Say, hunger hits and pain, then agony disturbs, devours well-being. A favorite imagining of infantile disturbance for Bion is the sense of blood surging from nowhere and rushing through one's head or brain without a frame of reference for it. The infant is plunged into dread, perhaps screaming in rage to offset the terror. The boundless, immaterial Other may now be experienced as insensitive, inscrutably menacing, abandoning, persecuting—perhaps a primordial devil.

If the agony mounts and becomes unbearable, the infant may grow numb, stuporous, pass into oblivion. At some point, the infant's mother brings relief. The caretaker tries to fathom what is wrong and mend things, and consciousness blooms again. The light of primordial self and other re-emerges from darkness, this time with more emphasis on the bountiful Other, whose merciful intervention enables restoration of aliveness. God restores my soul, my spirit returns from death.

I think something of this pattern remains as a basic organizing sequence, a rebirth pattern informing emotional life. Some or all of these phases may be traversed at different times. Disintegration-integration, fragmentation-wholeness, death-life: loss or stuporing out of primordial consciousness and renewal of joyous appreciation with help divine. The psalmist's utterance, "Yea, though I walk through the valley of the shadow of death, . . . thou art with me," expresses a nuclear vision of this emotional thrust.

Throughout her work, Marion Milner dipped into mystical or spiritual imagery to organize central aspects of her experience. She may or may not have been a mystic (she probably would say she was not), but mystical concepts (if that is not a contradiction in terms) permeate her formulations. In her semi-preanalytic diary writings, in looking for a pattern to describe what for her were the most significant moments in her day, she appealed to the "dying god" image and emotional or psychic or perceptual resurrection, a coming to life out of nowhere, a sudden blossoming of consciousness and significance.

Her sense of heightening of consciousness and aliveness spanned many dimensions and regions of being. She spoke of elusive body feelings, such as awareness of one's own toe from the inside, an awareness of what it feels like to be physically alive moment to moment and have the kind of consciousness that can feel and expand on the sense of aliveness. This includes proprioception, kinesthesia, tissue aliveness, mucous membrane sensation, the feel of skin, and a vague but very real whole-body sense. For me, the latter often is allied to a dark, inchoate, chasmlike sensation in the center of my chest below my heart, perhaps related to the solar plexus. It is a sensation that tells me, yes, no, this way, that way, a kind of inner body-English that semisteers, evaluates, processes, registers—very much part of what makes me feel real.

For Milner a heightened sense of being spans the inner body feel and perception of the outer world: light, color, sound, forms—the is-ness of things. She doesn't choose between internal and external. Each may take center stage *and* permeate the other, contributing texture to one's sense of creativity. For her, the primary sense of generativity has an orgasmic aspect, and creativity symbolizes vicissitudes of its generative sense. She connects primary generativity with pregnant emptiness/void of Eastern and Western spiritual experience, dying-rising god images, and the nuclear "I-yet-not-I" feeling voiced by St. Paul. An orgasmic I-yet-not-I kernel breathes through body sensations, a heightened sense of physical reality, person-to-person encounter, and symbolizing activity, including a generative sense of self and other coming into being and partially dissolving.

Milner describes a broader, more open focus than the narrower task-oriented, causal, means-end, instrumental, practical orientation —a wide, unfocused sort of attention. She moves between "sudden moments of intensified perception of the outer world" and "inarticulate images of the depth mind." In expressing shifts of awareness that are important to her, she spontaneously blends psychoanalytic and spiritual imagery, traversing body-world-imagination-perception-attention-thinking. She quotes Traherne and Blake to help sing what for her is a very vital sense of perception as luminous and even part of imagination (for Blake, you will remember, messiah *is* imagination). As it turns out, our body is a very imaginative body indeed.

I. Matte-Blanco was a psychoanalytic mystic, although many may feel it safer to emphasize his logical, intellectual aspect. He distinguishes two modes of thinking, one moving toward division, the other indivision. He divides the pie by attributing asymmetrical thinking to consciousness and symmetrical thinking to the unconscious. An example of symmetrical thinking might be: to believe that all members of a class are equivalent—say, all women are mother. Another example might be that since you and I are people, then I am you and you are me. Of course, the fact that I can formulate you and me as being the same is a tribute to asymmetrical work being done: I am saying you and I—making distinctions in order to assert sameness.

The deeper we go into unconscious being, the fewer distinctions we make. We rely on consciousness to create a sense of space-time and awareness that I am not you and you are not me. To unconscious symmetrical thinking, all women may be mother, but in space-time reality, individual women must not be reduced to this. Matte-Blanco's work abounds in wonderful descriptions of the interaction of these two modes of being. as he shows how we are constituted by a psychic bi-logic.

We sense infinite depths through space-time and self–not self divisions, infinity everywhere. We tune into finite-infinite meldings and select where to put the brakes on, our points of focus. We slide up and down scales of divisibility-indivisibility and discover yields of alternative views. Psychic life is ineffable and, as Matte-Blanco puts it, the infinite is here to stay. There is a "perpetual co-presence and intermingling of timeness-spaceness and timelessness-spacelessness or, more generally expressed, heterogeneity and indivision, which constitutes the very essence of human nature."

If the deep unconscious is timeless and spaceless, it cannot, by definition, be experienced, since consciousness, by definition, employs asymmetrical logic that aggressively divides. Yet we incessantly voice intuitions of unity, "'imprisoning' the ungraspable indivisibility in some structures we know but are not able to express fully."

At the end of *Thinking, Feeling, and Being*, Matte-Blanco concludes, "I consider the awareness of the indivisible, and its search in human manifestations, to be of primary importance for the understanding of human beings." There are "aspects of ourselves that do not refer to the external or internal world nor to an intermediate 'area'" but are "located nowhere."

Matte-Blanco, in his very creative way, plumbed and reworked depths of processes that, partly, gave rise to the Council of Nicaea's formulation of a triune God. It seems to me that Matte-Blanco was in mystical communion with intuitive realities the Council of Nicaea put its stamp on. I suspect that for him, the latter partly functioned as a notation, a lead into realities to probe, taste, amplify, and deeply love and live—the primordial indivisible-divisible.

Bion's use of mysticism emphasizes shatter. Shatter with many faces. He depicts the birth of the psychic universe as a big bang, an explosion into consciousness. It is as if consciousness represents an increment of experiential intensity too great for the organism. Organism explodes into another level, partly too much for it. The theme of excess, a psyche too much for itself or for body, runs through Bion, as does, correlatively, the theme of insufficiency. If we are too much for ourselves, we are, also, not enough.

In important ways we remain embryonic, unborn, premature, and immature all our days. We are in the position, too, of possessing or being possessed by capacities that run with or without us. Passions and cognitions have lives of their own and run away with us, so that we are ahead of and behind ourselves at the same time. Thoughts tick automatically; drives inhabit us and we may or may not find decent enough ways of relating to our experiences.

It is as if Bion says over and over: look, look, we are here, experiencing—we *experience*. Consciousness is dumbfounding, shocking. We are ALIVE! What do we do with ourselves, our experiencing, our shocking experiential aliveness? How do we relate to our experience?

If Federn is preoccupied with shifting boundaries, Bion seems preoccupied with shifting intensity. We are more alive or dead at any time—not only bigger or smaller. And more: Bion conceives of a moment in which we are maximally alive and maximally dead at the same time. A state of maximum-minimum emotion. How do we support such a state if it is real, or is it just a hypothesis, or a hypothesis of something unseen that someday we may notice?

A particular scenario Bion repeats is the difficulty encountered when a mind that has grown up to deal with survival becomes interested in truth for its own sake—for example, issues of psychic integrity. Ancient Greek literature documents tensions between abstract, personal, and communal truths, and between all these and practical survival drives. Is it better to die for truth and integrity or live a lie? The death of Socrates is an epiphany. Or, again, when Pontius Pilate says, "What is truth?," Jesus shows him. The problem is as alive as ever, even more so, since genuine nourishment and emotional, spiritual, and social toxins often indistinguishably fuse.

In Bion's work truth is both nourishing and explosive. The mind can't grow without it. Yet it can blow one's life away. Truth nourishes. Truth shatters, even kills. We are hungry for truth *and* truth is dangerous and must be handled with care. The latter is one reason why we have learned to test truth in many ways. We learn to take it in a bit at a time, turn it this way and that, see what it looks like from many angles, develop variable approaches, methods, a sense of context, common sense.

Bion used the terms "mystic," "messiah," "genius" to call attention to heightened aliveness, consciousness, truth, faith. He somewhat keeps terms open in meaning, akin to functions that take on different values depending on relations they express. Mystic surges or breakthroughs can come in terms of consciousness of sensations, emotions, thoughts. For example, the writer of the Song of Solomon was a sensory genius, a sensation mystic. Meister Eckhart was a "detachment" genius: he saw, experienced, intuited a sense of reality that seemed beyond sensation, yet the objectless purity he expresses makes one's spine tingle. The demand to go beyond everything one is or thinks or imagines can be absolutely heavenly.

In *Cogitations* Bion has diagrams beginning with O, issuing or fanning out through beta and alpha into music, religion, sculpture, poetry, painting, and presumably science and even psychoanalysis. Well, believe it or not, there are scientists who make tie-ins between scientific proposals and mystic vision. If Newton were alive, he almost certainly would be one of them. Isn't it odd to think, as Freud noted, that old Fechner's "other space" grew out of madness and mystical vision that his psychophysical concern with thresholds was meant to express and quantify?

Bion had his eye on a religious force that could give rise to the love of God or the death pits of Ur, the mass suicide of Jonestown, and the frenzy at Waco, Texas (whether on the side of the government or the rebels). He puts a marker not on institutional religion necessarily, but a religious force they fan out from. Blake, as do the Upanishads, speaks of a central intuition or sense or vision or imaginal point (no bigger than a thumb, say the Upanishads) that religious specifics grow out of, mask, elaborate in different ways.

Religious sensation permeates impulse, thought, vision. It can arise from fulfillment or sacrifice of impulse. It can be transitory or affect one's whole life. Tolstoi depicts Ivan Illyitch on his deathbed, seeing his wasted life in a moment's ineffable vision that nearly makes up for everything. What if such moments occur throughout a lifetime? What if they contact each other, link up, spread, so that more and more aspects of self taste them throughout the day?

There is an ancient link between heightened moments and sacrifice. "You are here and I did not know," says Jacob on his first journey into exile. He builds an altar to commemorate his awesome realization. The Bible devotes a lot of space to describing places of meeting, moments that count. Some are transitory, some meant to be permanent. The Temple, with its Holy of Holies, was to last forever. It was replaced by the temple of the soul, prayer, good deeds.

Prophets spoke of a good heart and justice as the sacrifice God wants. From sacrifice of animals to sacrifice of self.

Sometimes it's sacrifice of pleasure, sometimes sacrifice of pain. On the order of Ecclesiastes, there is time for suffering, time for joy, time to give up suffering, time to give up joy. Each state has its season.

An overlap between spirituality and psychoanalysis involves a vision of destructiveness. There are moments one sees how bad one is, the injury one inflicts, endless depths of destructiveness. Bion framed this moment by positing a force that goes on working after it destroys time, space, existence, personality—an outgrowth of Freud's "force against recovery" and Klein's "destructive force within." Winnicott expressed how wonderful it feels to find oneself and the Other surviving this backdrop of destructiveness.

There are a number of moments involved here, possibly aspects of the same moment:

1. One sees evil and weeps, tears at the garments of soul, rips soul itself, trying to get the bad stuff out. One repents, makes reparation, mends one's way, tries to become a better person. But destructiveness does not stop, and repentance is endless.

2. One sees evil and collapses in terror. There is no end, no remedy. Injury continues, no matter what precautions are taken. We are traumatized traumatizers. Terror of who we are and what works in us is paralyzing but gives rise to thoughtfulness, reflection on our condition. We work against impossibility and with grace, luck, and persistence exercise of self opens self.

3. There is new appreciation of self and other upon discovery of continuing on after experiencing the worst. Unconscious mutual forgiveness plays a role but so does growing awareness of infinite gradations of experience. Areas of self keep opening after all seemed lost.

4. Immovable dense spots one gave up on begin to give way. Impacted despair, depression, compressed balls of terror/hate loosen, dissolve a bit, get partly digested or disappear. It seemed impossible this or that clot of hate or loneliness could ever leave or lessen or find a place in a larger whole. One would be saddled with it forever. What a discovery to find some of it gone or taking less space. One breathes

more freely in places where one felt suffocated. Surely, heaviness will come back. But one knows something else can happen.

There are many ways to envision the unconscious sense of attitudinal and emotional rebirth that play a role in structuring experience. So much "rebirth" is premature and short-circuits growth possibilities. Still, biblical affirmation that the lame will walk, blind see, dry bones live point to areas of collapse and unhappiness that have a chance of changing.

Psychoanalysts and prophets have faith in new beginnings. You can start again, in one way or another. As I grow older, there are experiences that are less available to me, but others open up. Outer layers of the soul fall away like dead skin, and feelings I scarcely imagined possible or did not know existed swim into view.

Personality is uneven and, like a tree, can be partly alive and partly dead at the same time, some aspects ready to bloom, some already vanishing. Since soul space is spaceless, a single "area" can be simultaneously alive and dead—maximally-minimally and infinitely graded.

I would like to say a word for pain, although I'm aware my suggestion is not for everyone. There are people who vanish in pain, done in by it. For some, to stay with pain is to risk falling into fathomless depressive weakness with no way out. Nevertheless, in my twenties I spontaneously discovered that going into emotional pain as completely as possible often led to very real, if momentary, reversal. One might, in acute agony, see stars. Van Gogh's starry nights are ecstatic results of the agony journey.

There are other possibilities as well. Staying with dire agony as fully as possible can obliterate consciousness. One loses consciousness in the pain. One may "see" white or red or black, but not a pure white or red or black, something more porous, grained, textured, somewhat liquid, capable of giving way as one goes through it. Sometimes I've felt an inner point or vagina or womb opening to radiant light. Such moments change one's perspective, uplift life. Light suffuses bodily secrets, touches sick spots that long for healing.

I see light in many faces. Sometimes focusing on the light helps me endure what is horrible about a person. It certainly helps me endure what is horrible about myself. I've been hitting my head against walls for decades, clenched fists of self, dead spots, frozen spots. Light surrounds and permeates clots of self, like water in crevices, and sometimes miracles of opening occur.

Recently I was with a man who was doing better. He looked more solid, toned, able, his creative work moving along. I was absorbed in his strength and accomplishments, enjoying the session, when I became aware of light seeking bits of depression and despair in his expression, collapsed areas I hadn't noticed. Light gravitates to sore spots, massaging them, decompressing and decomposing them, partly dissolving them into—where? I do not know. The Rosh Hashanah sea?

A custom called tashlich that is observed on Rosh Hashanah, the Jewish New Year, is to empty one's pockets or throw bread into living waters. Rosh Hashanah is seen as creation's birthday, the world's birthday, and many gestures of cleansing and renewal are associated with it. There are jokes that go along with feeding the fish one's sins, but the overall sense is that the water can handle it. The water will metabolize our toxins.

A lot of trust and faith goes into this, a background connection between God, the water, and, for a psychoanalyst, the unconscious. God is not simply nature in Judaism, but God gives us good things, like water and renewal. The gesture of relying on the water to help digest what one can't handle symbolizes our dependence on God. You get to an important moment of letting God do it. Not just a semiangry, "You got us into this, you get us out," although that is fair enough. It's more an opening, a partnership with forces that support you and give you life.

There is a scent of faith, I think, in J. Lacan's reworking of Freud's "Where it is, I will be." A kind of following the scent of the unconscious: "I'll be where it is" or "I'll go where it leads." Lacan reworks Freud's writing on the burning child dream. A father dreams his child tells him, "Father, can't you see I'm burning?" In "actuality," the child lies dead and a lamp has tipped over, endangering his body. He comes to his father in a dream and alerts him that there is an actual fire, not just a dream fire.

Lacan touches the endless ambiguity of the dream. A fire threatens the boy's corpse—literally. But the boy's words burn a hole in the father's heart. The fire burns through the heart of loss, self-reproach, unspeakable guilt—simply, the unspeakable. It is literal fire, but also a blaze in the field of the unconscious. Like the burning bush, it burns in the navel of the dream, yet the navel is not consumed. In a way, it is a Naomi and Ruth relationship: I will follow you into the field of the unconscious, the field of dreams. I will disappear into the navel of the dream. Where you go, I will follow. We will not stop burning. We will burn our way to new beginnings. Yet, Lacan hints rightly, the father, like you and I, will never recover. We can never recover from being human.

In the 1960s there was a lot of talk in the United States about trusting the unconscious. This fit in with Freud's use of religious language to express creative processes in the Fliess letters, an emphasis on letting the horse lead, free association, free-floating attention, creative drift, the creative unconscious. Jack Kerouac's *On the Road* put free association into practice as a way of life. One should live very like a patient free-associating combined with Buddha analyst's openness. Kerouac tried to do what Walt Whitman talked about. He piped the electric roads of the United States, surrender to *it*, to aliveness as such, a kind of deification of Life. How shocking to find Kerouac propelled to destruction as violent in its extended way as Marilyn Monroe's or John Kennedy's. The man who idealized spontaneity ended his days living, of all things, with his mother—Oh my God—on Long Island, drinking himself to the grave. How can this on-the-road man who was all travel, all spirit, end up a mother's boy, a spiritual stay-at-home?

Psychoanalysis knows these reversals, mother's body soul breaking father's spirit bones, the pull back and down, dissolving boundaries, eating God's backside, dropping into the abyss, the black hole's arms of light. Bion might appreciate the connection between deification and defecation. Deified self and defecated self. Body electric meets evacuated self. Freud tells Fliess that psychoanalysis is akin to ancient mystery cults, in which one moves from being submerged in mother's bowels to the light of higher consciousness, the name of the Father. Lacan defines madness as collapse of the triangle, points of light collapsing into the density of attachment sucked into itself, attachment nulling itself.

Today we are wary of polarizations and collapse of polarizations. What if the problem includes but is deeper than tensions between sexes and generations? What if we can't keep up with toxins we dump inside and outside ourselves? What if unconscious processing is overwhelmed and immobilized by the mental, spiritual, emotional toxins it works with? Freud hinted at this, late in his life, when he said that psychic structures—id, ego, superego—were irrelevant or useless in the face of the pull of destructiveness.

What if warp runs through the structures? What if unconscious processing is warped, traumatized, damaged, frozen, mutilated? What if unconscious processing cannot process or works in deforming rather than transforming ways?

Can society digest the indigestible? What of the streets littered with homeless spirits, depleted, evacuated, homeless spiritual stay-at-homes in surgical shock—society bleeding to death in its own arteries? So many beings indigestible to themselves.

We try to control artifacts of indigestibility with medication. But where is the medication that can control a furiously mad homeless man who slices his arm, then tears off the doctor's sutures, and runs spouting fountains of blood through the emergency room—aiming at papers behind the desk, at orderlies, interns, nurses. Aiming his spouting blood like a fireman's hose, hoping to spread the sickness that will kill him. And his sickness? A physical counterpart of abuse that wore him down to the point where only blood can tell the tale. Where is his psyche? "Blood everywhere." Here is my blood, my sickness, all the power I have left.

The Bible tells us the soul is in the blood. In Judaism, we do not eat animal blood because it is disrespectful to the animal to eat its soul. But we cannibalize each other's spirits. We grow by eating each other's souls. This is the message: not literal blood, not literal language. We are soul eaters, spirit metabolizers: the spirit giveth life.

The man spurting blood with precision about the emergency room falls back on the only language left to him, an ancient language, a language that tells us we are killers. He tries to kill his killers with the keenest weapon he has left. Even as lights dim, an acute mind works the body. There is precision in what we do to each other.

Does the blood-spraying man bear witness to the collapse of the mother, the collapse of the father? Has the name of the Father failed to stem the tide? Is this the end of the Yahveh line? Little Yahvehs running around, Yahveh remnants, breaking children's and wives' and their own bones, beating disintegrating chests. What local groups of Yahvehs were the blood spurter's personal and social traumatizers? All pale compared to an image of God drunk on annihilating wrath, righteous rage, turning multitudes into fertilizer, abandoning yearning souls. What do we see when we look into this God's mirror?

I think we need to acknowledge how pulverized we are, and how pulverizing—acknowledge pulverization as a fact. Christianity tried getting at this by confessing that we are sinners in need of help. The results have not always been sanguine but it is a start. Pulverization calls for compassion—a connection that needs much practice and is all too easily lost.

Shirah Kober Zeller, a New York analyst who links psychoanalysis and Kabbalah, once said her path is devotion to the sacred broken heart. What might she mean? I've heard her speak of God as mad and brokenhearted. We are here, in part, as God's analysts, helpers, healers. In mystical Judaism much is said about putting God's name together, the implication being that we put God together by putting His name together—a variant on getting Rumpelstiltskin mad by putting him together with his name.

Fusions of goodness and rage: apparently we, or at least some or many of us and maybe God, are stitched together this way. God needs our help to become whole. Does this mean He needs our rage, a rage for healing? As a group, what do we do with our rage and wish for wholeness?

Perhaps Shirah Kober Zeller means God's heart is broken because ours is. We are in the broken heart business, often a heartbreaking business. Shirah's God seems to say that brokenheartedness may not be short-circuited prematurely. If the sacred broken heart is everywhere, can the joy of mending be far behind?

Crushed psyches—psychic pulverization. We go on anyway much of the time, one way or another. Fairbairn depicts a wholeness split seeking to be whole again. So does Winnicott, in a way, with true and false self, psyche/soma. But what if the psyche is crushed, bits ground and mixed like spices, hard to tell one from the other? What if psyche undergoes incalculable alterations and mutations in the grinding? Not just broken hearts—crushed hearts. Pulverized psyches searching for voices.

Deformed, crippled, mangled, crushed, malignant, encrypted, walled off, suffocating, collapsed, frozen, rigid, diffuse, radioactive, dead, empty, hollow, warped, traumatized, mute, exploding—who thinks of healing all this now? What can warped and toxic psychoanalysis do? Psychoanalysis grows by analyzing its traumatizing impacts. It grows by analyzing how it is destroying itself and the patient. Psychoanalysis tries to cure itself by more psychoanalysis. Psychoanalysis is quite mad, but that does not count against it.

A psychoanalytic belly laugh is starting. Psychoanalysis laughing at itself. Psychoanalytic laughter, psychoanalytic fire. How does Alice get out of the psychoanalytic rabbit hole? By waking up or by her author going to sleep? Can she find that hole again when her author wakes up? Crazy God, crazy world, crazy helpers, crazy partners to each other. Is homeless God our home? Homeless bits of soul on the streets of the psyche. Home everywhere. Homelessness everywhere.

What about "unstained white radiance," good objects in the womb, fetal, embryonic goodness? We are inserted in a sea of destructiveness and white radiance, a sea of goodness. We have a love of beauty, truth, goodness. It gets very complicated. There are beatific moments: a thing of beauty is a joy forever. Hell, purgatory, heaven superimposed and indistinguishable—all together, all at once.

For many years we believed in an incorruptible soul, a pure soul singing of life to God. What do we do with our pure soul link to God and what we go through and become? Weren't ancient mystery cults about refinding consciousness as immortal mindspirit? I swim in an eternal sea of awakening. No, I fly; I fly. No end to Orpheus-Apollo.

The Omaha Beach landing scene, in Steven Spielberg's movie *Saving Private Ryan* depicts horrible moments with reverberations beyond literal horror. American soldiers in landing barges were decimated by German guns. Many could not begin to disembark. They were blown away as barge doors opened.

It seemed almost a matter of numbers, more American bodies attempting to land than German bullets able to keep up with them. More bodies than bullets.

Wave after wave of soldiers landing, getting slaughtered—depicted in ghastly detail. Yet soldiers began to get through, to establish beachheads, to develop positions, and gradually prevail. Bodies everywhere. Slaughter and sacrifice.

There was virtually no chance that the first to try to land could survive. Yet there had to be the first and second and third waves. There had to be enough waves of bodies for the job to get done, enough live bodies to thread through the dead.

Human beings like ants. You keep crushing the ants and still there are more that keep coming.

Which live, which die?

Sacrificial slaughter. Some get through. Enough get through.

Generational waves. We keep coming, building, reshaping. Incessantly.

The movie spans the horror and the triumph. Mass and random slaughter is steadfast. Death is an anchor, whether it comes quickly or slowly. Bodies blown open, insides gushing out is a constant pole in the movie's depiction of reality. If you can't deal with bodily insides in your face, you deal with nothing.

In one scene a dying soldier tries to tuck his guts back in. I understand he was trying to live in the face of disbelief. But I could not help feeling—perhaps my idiosyncrasy—he was being modest. He was trying to tuck himself in before dying. A little like covering nakedness, or closing an opening (our need to close a corpse's mouth). An act of modesty and dignity before death. Modesty and dignity belong together.

Life keeps emerging.

The movie ends with a sense of goodness coming through. Evil is uncompromised and uncompromising. Goodness may be fragile, ineffable, but no less real. More real, perhaps. Is it only sentimentality —Hollywood, after all—that goodness is more true, more real than very true and real evil?

A compelling case for goodness is made because evil is not obscured by it. Goodness does not blot out evil or substitute for it or escape it.

The Jewish New Year begins by dipping apples in honey, challah in honey, reminiscent of mannah in the wilderness, life's breathless sweetness. Through all the destruction and possibilities of destruction, a field of mercy, a sad, sweet, joyful, ecstatic field, keeps beckoning.

Without minimizing destruction, evil, horror, the Bible keeps saying in one or another way: "Your miracles of everyday are with us / Your wonders and benefactions at all times" and "From the stream of Your delights / You will give them to drink. / For with You is the source of life / In Your light shall we see light."

A field of mercy opens up, heavens within. We taste it, bathe in it. A flow opens between us. This is real too, as real as hell and bullets.

Perhaps some of us are lucky enough not to be forced to delve too deeply into ways we damage ourselves and each other moment to moment and over time. Awareness extends to good that goes on too. Winnicott attends to a sense of the Other surviving our destructiveness or, perhaps one should say, the Other surviving our fantasy of destruction. We know the power of fantasy. For the infant, there is no great gap between destructive fantasy and screaming and kicking and falling into stupor and muscular paralysis. And for a screaming parent or a distant analyst, the gap seems small as well.

The issue Winnicott fingers is close to us. Can you survive the worst in me? Can anyone? Can planet earth survive us? Can we survive each other and ourselves? How destructive is our destructiveness? We keep learning how destructive we can be, and there are many facets to such realization. Winnicott adds to our sense of who we are by amplifying ways we *do* survive each other, even if such survival is only partial. Quality and spirit of mutual survival adds or takes away from feeling and being real.

A burning question that arises from reading Winnicott is how we and our world survive a baby? Does anyone know what to do with a baby? Who knows what a baby is? Winnicott sees destructiveness as part of our sense of aliveness. Do we really know much about modulating destructiveness while keeping aliveness alive?

Parent and child undergo repeated breakdowns, times of madness. We keep learning about qualities of coming through, possibilities of "spontaneous recovery." Perhaps therapy is, in part, the business of learning more and more about spontaneously recovering from ourselves.

Mysticism and destructiveness go together. There is an urge to rip off mental and emotional clothes, tear our minds out, get to the bottom of ourselves, find something we cannot doubt or take another view of. But as long as we have minds, we may take another view. Flies have a lot of outside eyes, and we have a lot of inside eyes. When I wrote "eyes," I wrote "yes" by mistake. Mysticism says no, no, no, to get to yes, yes, yes.

Mystical father, mystical mother, mystical baby, associated with destruction, associated with life. We have a desperate need to get below categories that filter experience, to get past our own makeup. You see this with certain animals—a dog, for example, trying to get a little past what dogs do, reaching emotionally past themselves, lifted by a person's longing. We try to get past our minds and bodies to the heart of life—hit the home run, score the touchdown, not just a matter of material success, not just saying I'm good, I'm good, but touching the thing itself, the thing that makes this all go. Can we, ought we stop doing this?

For some of us, psychoanalysis has become part of this sweeping through things, this pressure of discovery. Waves of psychoanalytic schools are outgrowths of the pressure. Psychoanalysis is not one filter, but many filter systems. In moment-to-moment encounter, an analyst may rip off filter after filter, not only getting to the edge of the psychoanalytic unknown, but jumping into the unknown itself— for his or her own sake, but impelled by the needs of a patient, a pressing, anguished person slipping through known filters, in danger of perishing or never being born.

So many sessions involve crises of faith. Not simply will a person live or die or whether life is worth it—although these are desperate and crucial matters. But with what tone or spirit or quality will a self exist or, if one does not believe in self, then whatever core attitudes and approaches to life animate a human being's existence. In the course of an hour, an individual traverses areas of collapse, despair, disability and may sink or come through in better and worse ways.

Kleinian writings used to sound a bit like morality plays. Will internal good objects prevail or be spoiled by hating, contemptuous aspects? A kind of good and bad object war. I think it a good reading of an ancient story, a *Star Wars* of the psyche, amplifying Freud's sense of psychic acts as variable amalgams of life and death drives. To this was added the need to recognize emotional truth, good or ill, hoping one could survive the truth about oneself, and that truth would nourish growth.

Bion seemed to say, as time went on, that faith enables truth to appear, and a good deal depends on one's attitude, including one's attitude toward truth, for example, whether compassion plays much of a role, or whether truth is used as a murderous tool. This can be a delicate and complex matter, but difficulties of being trapped between truths that kill and lies that poison may pressure us to continue evolving.

In *Toxic Nourishment*, I write of, among other things, failed suicide and miscarriages. Attempts to kill oneself sometimes relate to miscarrying oneself as a baby or to ways one's growth was aborted along the way. You'd think it easier to kill yourself than give birth to yourself, but both are riddled with complex states and tensions. Suicide is a kind of miscarriage of life, a lack of faith in the baby self. Wounding has gone too far, and one buckles under. Often what is wounded is naive faith, and one is unable to journey through to something more complicated. It is difficult to believe that life can be so bad, and radiance so bright.

There is a sort of semiconscious/unconscious arithmetic to life and death. From one vantage point, death is subtraction, life addition. To kill oneself is to take away from life. Minus life. Of course, this can be revenge for feeling something has been taken from one, resentment over losing one's chance at living. One dramatizes loss. One imagines something satisfactory about achieving an end point, a limit. To add oneself to life is to admit the gift is real and suffer the indignity of living. Perhaps it is more dignified to say no thank you, and kiss the pain goodbye. There is humiliation in living, and only death can save one's pride. Perhaps this is why pride of self is religion's point of attack. Insofar as one frees oneself of self, everything looks different. Addition and subtraction vanish. There is no longer any great war between being and nonbeing—they feed each other.

They are each other. To kill oneself is to throw away the possibility of this freedom. It represents victory of a negative slice of self. Whether such a victory is ultimate, no one knows. To me it appears almost always a symbol of defeat.

In a journal entry, the year before he died, Bion affirmed, "the fundamental reality is 'infinity,' the unknown, the situation for which there is no language—not even that borrowed from the artist or the religious—which gets anywhere near to describing it." We patch together what filters we can for our infinities, our bits of life. Pain and radiance are clues. They tell us we are alive and, if used well, keep us reaching. They are points of entrée to infinities we taste. For thousands of years we have been developing languages for pain and radiance, and there are more threads to pull.

In a related formulation, also near the end of his life, Bion says, "Many mystics have been able to describe a situation in which it is believed that there really is a power, a force that cannot be measured or weighted or assessed by the mere human being with the mere human mind. This seems to me to be a profound assumption which has hitherto been almost completely ignored."

He uses the terms "power" and "force" repeatedly in these late passages. Unknown infinite power and force, expressed in Yahveh, Jonestown, and glistening through nets cast by Emerson and Freud. Power and force are one set of terms, "relationship" another. Bion writes of Buber's I-You, "the significant thing is not the two objects related, but the *relationship*—that is, an open-ended reality in which there is no termination (in the sense that this is understood by ordinary human beings)." Power and force, on the one hand; relationship, on the other. Two languages? One?

An open-ended reality in which there is no termination. This sounds a little like psychoanalysis. As it must, as Bion addresses psychoanalysis and personality as parts of being, forms of life—in which unknown infinity, power, force, relationship moves. We situate anything we know vis-à-vis inner and outer horizons of the infinite unknown.

Are we still evolving? Has the infinite unknown closed walls around us, put us on hold? Probably yes and no. For one thing, there are moments of evolving in sessions. Let me share two of them. Maybe they're old hat, things you know. But I feel something important in them, something asking for voice.

Gary was depressed for some time. He could not work, could not play, could not be with his girlfriend, could not be with himself. He was sinking. This state had been mounting for years. Depressive subcurrents came together and gathered force, but he did not totally die. He spoke bitterly of ecstasy in his head. In a way, he blamed depression on ecstasy. Nothing was good enough for the ecstasy in his head. Nothing matched his private high. But mental ecstasy did not save him from embodied depression. On the contrary, it furthered depression.

He missed sessions but kept coming. He told me everything—problems with girls, parents, creativity, jobs—everything he could think of. I know many people today would have suggested medication.

Then one day he quietly said, "I snapped out of the funk I've been in for a while."

"How?" I asked.

"A couple of things. I had a good day with Julia on Saturday. That made me feel better about a lot of things, instead of worrying about our relationship, just to have a decent day.

"I'm not worrying about the ecstatic thing in my head. I'm doing a lot more. That's been good.

"That got me thinking about other things, the difference between imagining and living a life. Also, I'm finally playing music, gigs in out-of-the-way clubs where there's no one I know, just other musicians, less pressure, more fun, before going to places where there are people who I really want to hear us. I felt good about playing. Every part of my life is a little better. I'm applying for jobs too.

"I look at the last few years—a step forward, a step back. I have a terrifying theory. I have expectations of how life should be, how I imagine it was. Disappointments come, and I feel worse and worse. Then I lower the bar and feel better. That's the new day."

So Gary was lowering his sights, adapting downward? But I heard a put down in his voice and couldn't help wondering if his terrifying theory did justice to the whole story. I tested out what I was glimpsing. "That's a good description," I said. "But is it only a matter of lowering the bar, or is it adjusting the bar, changing perspectives, so life comes into view a different way?"

The cynical trace in his tone lifted, and he continued, "What's become a constant for a while is a sort of *humbling*. Shrinking yourself in certain ways. Shrinking your self-centeredness. I've been thinking about compassion recently. It can be a secondary emotion that affects us in the way we see ourselves, like empathizing with others because of our own pain, our own pain as felt by others. But it is also an *investigation*, not an emotion, but a way of looking at what's real, more a sense than emotion, related to this kind of humbling."

After a pause, Gary went on to talk about how some people at the gig thought he was European. Perhaps that meant he looked more written on by life, more complex, or just different. He went on to say he's been enjoying watching patterns of stock market numbers, the way they flow. He's begun to make some good investments. "I'm feeling better and don't know how that happened."

"You've been going with the flow?" I asked.

"Yes. I've been wondering if it is possible to observe patterns in my unconscious.

"Like the stock market flow?"

"Yes. One thing about being depressed is that I really do search for meaning in my life. What's wrong with my life bears down on me all at once, good and bad. Good if I plough through it, bad if I just slip. Am I so erratic? Is that normal?"

"What's normal for you?"

"That is normal for me, up-down. It kind of keeps something in focus. I guess maybe it's another investigation."

He spoke more about the stock market going up and down, and I couldn't resist mumbling that he went up and down with it and that he just went through a good sequence, down-up, although it took a long time.

"It's beyond my control," he added. "It just happens. There's got to be some patterns. Sometimes I see them, sometimes I don't. I don't know what good it does to see them."

"They go on working anyway."

"Right. I'm unable to compartmentalize. No, I can with good

things, I put good in its little place. I have a little place for good. Bad spreads."

"Radioactive dispersal."

"I feel it's organic. It's important to feel I can communicate myself to other people. Feeling bad helps me to communicate better. Although feeling badly makes me unable to communicate. It makes me more specific inside, but I can't broadcast. I shut down, turn off a while. But I wrote five songs during this last down time. But I couldn't play them till I came out of it."

"Each state has its season?"

He agrees. He senses patterns, rhythms to his flow and stoppage, although we don't know what they are. He meant by organic that there is a back and forth, something natural, if he could find it.

I did not know Gary would come in feeling better. He describes a kind of spontaneous recovery from a depressive spin, akin to coming out of a catatonic stupor or coma. I feared his downspin would last longer, since it had gotten worse for several years before he came to therapy. Neither he nor I knew what accounted for the upturn. He attributed it to a good day with his girlfriend—so it is possible feeling a good object blessing took hold. It is, also, possible the good day grew out of a change already working. My guess is the background support of therapy made it more possible for Gary to move from state to state. At the very least, therapy provides practice in experiencing transitions, since one communicates shifts of state moment to moment and listens to another's response. In therapy, hopefully, one tastes an atmosphere in which psychic reality is welcome.

I'm not against medication when it is helpful—on the contrary. And I'm not unaware of the importance of mood- and mind-transforming agents from the earliest times till now. But I'm wary of too easy reliance on medication and its exploitative abuse. I wish to recount another recent session, for in it a nucleus of faith cries for a hearing.

My patient was an able psychoanalyst—we'll call him Chris—who got the rug pulled out from under him by the trend toward "objectified" thinking. Chris spoke with angry disbelief and righteous horror and despair of what he called "not lack of faith, but conviction of no faith."

Chris was working with a boy who was warm and lively and feeling better about himself and life. Maybe he was a bit wild, but he was good-hearted and life-loving. Therapy supported his basic spirited nature, which had been tarnished by wounds and suffocating demands. A good deal of oppression goes into everyone's upbringing.

"He's a great kid," said Chris. "We were getting somewhere, things were happening. Then I get a call from his parents saying they referred him to a psychologist for testing and the psychologist said he has learning problems and is ADD and she recommends a psychiatrist for medication. Do you know that she never saw him? This was all done by mail—the tests, the scores, looking at school records. She never met Ken. This was all done by numbers.

"I called her and asked, 'Don't you think you ought to have seen Ken? You never even met him.' 'That might be helpful,' she replied. 'But the tests show he could be doing better. He's not performing up to his ability. Medication could raise the level of his work.'"

Chris was appalled. He went into a long, excoriating diatribe on our times, of which I'll relate only a little. "Did you see the Christopher Reeves's commercial on the Super Bowl? It's the future and there's a cure for AIDS, cancer, now spinal injury. Christopher Reeves walks out on stage to an ovation smiling. It was a commercial for an investment company! You can create images indistinguishable from what's real. Seeing is no longer believing—there's no assurance that what's being transmitted as an image of the world is an image of the world. The fictive shapes we create become indistinguishable from history. We've moved from mechanical reproduction of image to mechanical creation of image, insulated from true reality, from suffering experience—substitution of generated experience."

"*Brave New World*," I venture.

"Yes, exactly," Chris continues. "Tinkering with genes, synapses, images of the world, a solution to everything. We'll fix problems you didn't know you had. I feel dread of this, real and true dread. I worry for my kids. What sort of world, what sort of culture is being offered to them? Where does authentic experience get formulated and expressed? On another commercial you see poor yokels left out of our fast-moving civilization and an announcement that the advertiser just wasted two million bucks: what are *you* going to do with *your* money? As if everything but the high of making money is a waste of time. What were the yokel 'monkeys' doing wasting their time sitting on porches, talking, singing, playing instruments? What does e-trade create that's beautiful? Strip everything away to money and the drive for more of it? Instead of a sense of place and transcendence, we'll all be connected to a great poisoned breast; our little accounts will grow, and we'll get things, turning things of loveliness and sustenance to emptiness. I have to struggle to be myself in the face of this and in the face of my greed to want part of it.

"Yes, my patient could do better in school—he could be on top. But why should he reduce himself to that? Is medication going to solve the human heart? Ken has heart. He has something more important than being on top. He's doing well—he's doing well enough. He'll do just fine. What is this drive to operationalize him, to turn him into a machine? To make a higher cut?"

For Chris the obsession to get more by getting on top denudes life of living. The soul price is high. We have a new plaything, wealth for many, greater mobility, a more homogenized world—shiny new toys. What do we do with all this? How do we relate to it? We can't stick our heads in the sand, but do we want to turn off our depths in order to make competitive ability the ruling force in town?

Chris spoke of his dread of the spreading conviction of no faith, a kind of antifaith. He has faith in the boy he is working with, in this boy's faith in life, faith in what being alive feels like, faith in his work and that it is worthwhile to feel everything, to be what you feel and feel what you are. There is a mystical invisible point at the center of this affirmation, a heightened sense of life, of life's value—which is not simply one with the euphoria of financial value. For it is indeed a vision of financial success, a fear that he will not be on top enough, that drives Ken's parents to quell his emotional noisiness with medication, so that he can achieve better focus and catch the ring.

Who knows what leads to what? Perhaps an unmedicated Ken would make more money than a medicated one. Or maybe it's not a matter of either/or. No crystal ball here. We're stuck with making choices in the moment, one after another. And my patient cannot bear the choice he sees spreading, covering him with dread.

My patient's fear is less of physical extinction than of soul extinction. Is it true that we are headed for premature extinction of soul? It may look that way at times—but I feel otherwise. I cannot believe that a world that has produced Bach's music, Blake's visions, Beethoven's agonic heavens can be a spiritual crater. There are soul singers and creators now—even in psychoanalysis. Spiritual volcanos are ready. The history of fire is not over. Singers and fires may get smaller and smaller—but that was always part of human sensation, the greatness of the past. I suspect many of us have a basic feeling of gratitude and praise for the fire that never goes out. Were we all to be gone tomorrow, or even the next instant—gone as if none of this ever existed—one moment of illumined consciousness is all we needed. Of course, it's nice if there's more.

CHAPTER 4 *Half and Half*

"Well then, if you want to know," he said, becoming confidential, "last night I had a most enjoyable evening. People smoking, intelligent, friendly atmosphere, and *then* . . . ," becoming indignant in a noisy voice, "the waitress brought me only half a cup of cofee, and that ab-so-lutely finished it." Dropping his voice, "I couldn't do a thing after that. Not a thing." Almost whispering, "That finished it."

This is a typical Bion clinical fragment: a sudden change in experience, good to bad, with no prospect of recovery. The "spontaneous recovery" rhythm, depicted in the last two chapters, is missing or is not working well. The patient takes a hit and goes under. Recovery is not a possibility.

At least, that is what the patient *says*. The communication Bion describes is complex and finely nuanced, in spite of the proposed simplicity of outcome. The proposed simplicity rotates around a switch being turned from on to off. Life going on, then being turned off.

The turnoff hinges on an abrupt, unexpected happening. The waitress brings half a cup of coffee. How could she! How dare she! Does the patient think she possesses diabolic intent, or is she merely careless, indifferent, inconsiderate, insensitive? Whether mean or distracted, it is clear she does not *care enough*.

Our psychoanalytic ear hears echoes of a wounding nourisher feeding the formation of personality. A fusion of wound and nourishment runs through many of Bion's examples. A patient reports a good lunch, when a mug of beer is inexplicably thrown in his face; the delight of ice cream becomes the scream of deprivation, then no scream at all as the patient "dies" into the cold silence; a patient's mother "cuts off supplies" so he did not have enough money to buy food, let alone the mental/emotional food of analysis.

The cup is half empty rather than half full in a psychic environment where half empty means totally empty. Not totally full = completely empty, nothing at all, less than nothing. For it is not simply nothing, but a hostile, furious, even malevolent nothing, a devastatingly insulting nothing. The patient feels insulted, and insult instantaneously spirals into devastation. Perceived insult = assault = devastation. Experience gets negatively infinitized: less than everything = less than nothing. And less than nothing is infinitely worse than nothing.

It is possible that the whole event was hallucinated, in which case the insult was not simply "perceived" but constructed and infinitized. It is my sense that the kind of state or attitude Bion is expressing is of a constant hallucinated insult going on forever. Insult as an Eternal State or disposition. It is, in a sense, irrelevant whether the event actually happened or could happen, or was hallucinated or otherwise "made up" by the patient or author. Which author? Whether the patient's, Bion's, or my imaginative elaboration of whatever is being described, expressed, found, created: imaginative elaborations of something very real. You, I, Bion and his real or imagined patient are co-authoring something of significance now.

The half-empty cup example conveys a sense of finality. Absolute finality. In certain forms of schizophrenic and depressive experience absolute finality becomes a sense of doom. Often in psychosis an individual feels he has made a fatal mistake, or failed to act bravely enough in following the True Path, that he has sealed a bargain with the devil and is doomed forever. Change is not possible, although a longing for salvific change never quite goes away. The sense of doom and salvific longing are strange attractors.

At the doom level the psychotic's tone is tinged with hysteria, panic, is deadly serious, yet also mocking. This is buried in Bion's example, in which the tone is lighter in a blackish sort of way. I think I hear the mocking, the contempt, the reference to repetitious damnation. But the passage has a "funniness" too. Bion's tone? The patient's supercilious attitude toward what he is purveying as disaster?

Bion's examples almost always refer to catastrophic shock. Disaster at the beginnings of personality formation is implied. A half-empty cup or breast or feed-that-went-wrong hints at much more than a bad or unsuccessful nursing situation. In part, it hints at something missing, not there in life itself, and the capacity of life, even as it nourishes, to wound. This is so in the best of situations, how much more so in the worst.

Bion's "levity"? He was a very serious man, but I can't help but feel a lightness in his tone as he processes this little bit of psychotic thinking. He catches the "confidential" pull into "intimacy." The schizophrenic can be off-putting, but for those with a certain sensibility he has an aura that draws one in, as if he has an "in" to truths you need to know. It is an invitation to intimacy Bion is very familiar with. He knows the ropes.

He *could* say: the waitress is the unsatisfactory breast, wounding mother, disaster always about to happen and ever going on in psychic substrata. The patient reports it in a way that makes him sound a little on top of the trauma he is indignant about. He tries to gain a higher ground on it. "You know, of course—this absolutely finished it—her behavior, what could you expect!" Yes, we know, Bion knows —disaster waiting, ongoing—and it happens to *you*, poor patient, who reports it incredulously, with a mixture of hysterical naiveté and disdain, the same old thing.

But the patient *is* reporting the ongoing disaster of his being, his life, a sense of disaster that has hardened around him, molded him, encased him, that he cannot find the outside of. Or, perhaps, he has become all outside to find a way of living with it, as its reporter. Throughout *Cogitations*, Bion returns to a psychotic individual he calls X, and we might as well call the patient of the half-empty cup X. It is the same knot, attitudinal affective cluster, twist of mind and heart that Bion returns to, a psychotic element in our lives. Is it an accident that Winnicott writes of madness X—a shock, disaster, catastrophic impact, as personality begins to form, a deformation or warp and injury that exerts a pull on attention all life long?

Winnicott says we have to make contact with madness X in order to feel real. Bion's patient seems to have sewn many layers of unreality around X, cotton padding, but it still sticks him, more dagger than pea. Shakespeare's *King Lear, Macbeth, Hamlet* are daggers trying to stick through the cotton padding, driven expressions of X. Bion's patient points to it, cannot speak of anything else. But it is a contact many times removed, sealed, contact meant to blunt contact. In a way, he is staging the disaster that ruins his life, makes him unable to live. He puts on a show partly for Bion, partly for himself. He gambles on Bion as a collaborator, someone who gets it, someone on the "in" of X. I remember how astonished I was as a young worker to discover that the schizophrenic who spoke so intimately to me spoke the same way to everyone else.

Nevertheless, a real disaster is being conveyed. A disaster as great as soul or self or world destruction, an apocalypse now, then, ongoing. A forever apocalypse. It is as if personality dies and comes to life semimummified, embalmed, semi-undead enough to keep on reporting (not bearing witness), saying over and over, repeating: something terrible happened to me and keeps on happening. It is sort of the reverse of Winnicott's "ongoing being," more an ongoing SOS, disaster in progress: I have become a crustacean or insect, an exoskeleton to live with it—and that is part of the disaster. But the underbelly is still somewhere sensitive, the black box in the crash still weakly signals. The half-empty cup tale—the story of sensitivity wounded, unable to respond. The patient reports sensitivity dramas without the ability to go through them. He points a finger at wound and wounder and says: "Look what you've done! Look what happened to me!" He shuts down, stops there. When he says, "That finished it," he refers not only to the momentary sequence, a transient closing off and recovery, but also an underlying sense of finality that closes off recovery of life. He repeats over and over the moment of closing down, a moment going on forever, incessant finality.

Cure, partly, involves moving from reportage to bearing witness, testifying. Someone must tell this tale so others feel it. Someone must feel it in order for us to embrace it as reality, not something to mock. Hamlet tells Horatio to tell his tale. Faulkner's tale told by an idiot perhaps, signifying nothing perhaps—but the story is about our feelings, not simply nothing. Do our feelings count? I think Bion's half-cup episode says yes, quite a lot.

The half-filled cup (worse than nothing) episode shows, partly, how important feelings are by what does not happen to them. They are not taken in, suffered, processed, digested, but rather spewed out. Bion's patient keeps telling his tale—I fear more like Faulkner's idiot than like Hamlet—not to be deeply affected and changed by it, but to get rid of it. He speaks to show off the injustice of his life and slough off dis-ease by inflicting his exhibitionistic outrage on the listener. Speaking as infliction rather than transformation. He is unable to suffer through the disaster he feels but endlessly attempts to discharge it. Part of psychoanalytic listening conveys the deeply felt message that the pain you speak of is real, more real than you or anyone, so far, can bear. Indeed, you—we—are real. A silly, banal message? A dagger sticking through the cotton?

CONFLICTS WITHIN CONFLICTS

Bion traces a series of linked conflicts ever present in work with psychosis. His terms tend to be binary: pleasure principle–reality principle, frustration evasion–frustration modification, narcissism–socialism. But like the *Tao te ching,* each is in and necessary to the other. When things go too far awry (nearly always), tendencies work against each other, split, proliferate, diffuse, reverse, attack every which way. We will tolerate, if not quite accept, some of Bion's simple dichotomies to see where they can get us. But remember, when we speak of the X of psychosis, madness X, we speak about ourselves. It is a way of locating psychotic dynamics that permeate our lives.

A good place to start is with Bion's notion that every dream somehow fails. He writes, "The dream is an emotional experience that is developmentally unsuccessful." It tries to satisfy both reality and pleasure principles and achieve frustration evasion and frustration modification at the same time. An assumptive basis of this vision is that there is something in the psyche that is not satisfied with anything less than total satisfaction of all its tendencies. Thus functions that are deeply cooperative and work together become antagonistic, at odds, incompatible. Perhaps Bion is saying that incompatibility is there from the outset and that the infinitizing capacity maximizes different aims.

Another possibility is that conflict between functions is part of the way psychic life prospers. Having a makeup with many "opposite" tendencies ensures variability, color, plasticity. Bion was fond of noting that we can always gain another "opinion" or take on a situation by appealing to another of our capacities or dimensions (the world as "known" through vision, hearing, proprioception, kinesthesia, synesthesia, many forms of intellectual analysis, intuition, feeling, endless combinations, etc.). The capacity for conflict is an asset, although it can run amok.

We are ever envisioning new turns of conflict with ourselves. A sense of conflict runs deep and changes terms. In the present text under consideration: pleasure *and* reality, evasion *and* modification. Dreamwork wrestles with both. Wishes may be partly fulfilled in dreams, but they also are fraught with dread, a sense of persecution, mishap. Fulfillment is aborted, and reality ticks on with wishes trailing in its wake. There is, too, a tendency to work with our tendencies, a hunger for the facts of life. In this mode, we try to endure what is necessary in order to work with ourselves. Frustration modification involves tolerating tension, life building on itself, whereas evasion involves discharge, evacuation, intolerance of tensions, getting rid of ourselves. Both movements are part of our makeup and not necessarily mutually exclusive. For example, often we push away, say no, before taking in and saying yes.

Bion warns us that talking about these things is no easy matter, since pleasure is part of reality and vice versa. So-called opposite principles inform each other. There may be a tendency to wish for only pleasure, but knowing good and evil lures us on, at times beyond opposites, beyond pleasure-pain. Even if we fail to solve unsolvable knots, hitting up against our walls opens unexpected passageways.

NARCISSISM-SOCIALISM

Bion brings out a bind the therapist finds himself in when working with psychosis. If he seems empathic, the patient may think him crazy. Empathic understanding is taken for complicity: "You're on my side against the world." Or, then again, "If you can understand me (no one else does), you must be as crazy as I am." On the other hand, if the therapist adopts a viewpoint too far from that of the patient, he becomes another insensitive representative of a cruel, indifferent world. Bion notes that a basis for this bind is the conflict between narcissism and socialism in the individual.

The psychotic patient has a sense of what society demands, although he may be unwilling or unable to meet the latter. The analyst is expected to live up to society's standards yet break them in order to foster a special, exclusive intimacy with the patient. He must meet standards yet enter a conspiracy against them at the same time. Sensitivity to the patient's "narcissism" may be mistaken for catering to it, since a certain amount of "molding" to the patient is necessary and inevitable if effective links are to be forged.

Bion entertains the notion that the analyst's dedication to the patient can have destructive consequences for the analyst, since the patient takes him to places society is unwilling to follow. As they enter the patient's idiosyncratic, private world the patient may increase demands for loyalty, to the extent that the analyst begins to look silly, mad, irresponsible, or unethical in the public eye. Loyalty to the bond or loyalty to society? The patient's behavior may attract attention of those around him, so that pressure builds for institutional care. How many masters can the analyst serve? Does he rely on his own intuitive judgment or give in to social pressures? The analyst tastes the conflict between narcissism and socialism that rips the patient apart. Something has gone wrong with the devotional element in human relations that creates binds that cannot be set right. I have seen analysts abruptly break off treatment when hostile dependency mounts. On the other hand, there are instances when the analyst's refusal to consider normative society leads to the fulfillment of the fantasy of shared ostracism.

Inability to "solve" binds—often they are insoluble—may lead an individual (or group) to try to rid himself of the capacity that gives rise to endless knots. If we are sensitive to ourselves and the world we live in, unsolvable conflicts are inevitable. At times, the best one can due is wait, let problems be, turn them over this way or that and see what happens in time. Waiting on a problem builds waiting ability. Tolerating difficulties builds tolerating ability. In psychosis there is a demand to right things totally now, a utopian vision that dooms therapeutic effort.

Bion's work bears testimony to the power of passivity, a much maligned capacity. Activity gone wrong generates psychotic spirals, somewhat like cancerous proliferation of active defenses. Defense against psychic pain leads to more defense against pain, defense against defense, as defensive operations themselves add pain. A psyche may attempt to uproot its own sensitivity as a solution to the pain it brings. That is, psychic life may try to cancel or undo itself, rather than be exposed to its own sensitivity. To wait patiently on what is bothering one may be a better solution than attempting to scratch irritation out of existence. When irritants involve tensions between one's own strivings, ridding oneself of disturbance can be costly.

In some instances, the patient becomes the carrier of irritants the analyst would rather wish away. If the analyst gets rid of a patient, hoping to make life more peaceful, a problem is postponed rather than solved. This may be necessary, even desirable under the circumstances: a patient's problems may be too much for the analyst. But sooner or later the difficulty will surface again, and again a choice will have to be made. There is a price to be paid for working with "insurmountable" difficulties, and a price to be paid for avoiding them.

When Bion writes that narcissism and socialism are part of our makeup, he is saying, in his way, that a double sense of self and other informs us, and we need to make room for both. Not so long ago, I remember debates about selfish and altruistic attitudes and their relationship to one another. Are both primary? Is one a derivative of the other?

The meanings and uses of "self" and "other" have much sediment. Self-interest, self-preservation on one end, sacrifice, devotion on the other. Me-first, you-first. Me-centered and you-centered threads fuse in daily life. Extremes of one or the other tend to catch attention. More or less imperceptible blends is the rule. Psychotherapy tends to emphasize repair of damage to self-feeling, but a changing sense of other is crucial in this effort.

To illustrate what he means by socialism, Bion recalls Aristotle's depiction of man as a "political" animal. A sense of debate, discussion, argument (if not dialogue), and representative voting is included in the obligations of the citizenry. Public duty is part of the freedom and dignity of being human. Social life is defined by complex systems of rights and duties.

The sense of the social persists in psychosis, although the composition of personality, ordinarily taken for granted in social exchange, becomes a focus of internal debate. A cacophony of shouts from capacities that ordinarily work together smoothly press for a hearing. Capacities not only work against each other, they splinter and work against themselves. Thoughts fight thoughts, feelings fight feelings, senses do not agree with each other. Totalitarian vision (the universe run by a devilish God or other paranoid fixations) tries to organize chaotic diffusion. Tyranny spreads. Every psychic bit seeks to tyrannize every other psychic bit. Any seizure of control is monomaniacal. The tyrannical attempt to unify diffusion exacerbates the latter.

In psychosis a kind of Hobbesian picture of primitive social tendencies gets filtered through mythic/cosmic vision, one against all. Yet there could be no parasite without host, no predator without prey. Internal violence is embedded in relational contexts. The social may be torn, deformed, and mythologized in paranoiac ways, but it never ceases to exert pressure. Every narcissistic triumph depends upon a supporting cast.

Bion points out that for the psychotic attitude, either the social or biological realms may be menacing. The individual feels he can be destroyed by either, and his feeling is not without reason. A woman may die in childbirth, a man in war. There are contexts in which men and women sacrifice themselves for society or for the species. In psychosis the problem is not simply heightened (it may be more brutally intense in everyday life) but fragmented, rigidified, and often inserted into terrifyingly boundless psychocosmic dramas. The latter are filled with threats of an annihilation that never definitively arrives but is on the horizon, always arriving (an annihilation horizon brimming with annihilation waves, approaching, receding).

The psychotic contracts with regard to the social, as an anorexic does with regard to food, with the special difficulty that the social is more pervasive than physical food. It provides emotional food one can't get away from, even if one is starving. One may hate the social matrix that informs one, but one cannot make it go away. One is always being force-fed. The model for social feelings is more like air than literal food. In this regard, one breathes against one's will. In the psychotic mode, to fight influence means to try to rip social feeling out of oneself, which results in a massive assault on sensitivity. Sensitivity attacks itself.

Another solution is to make the social part of one's narcissism. In his comments on the empty-cup example Bion writes, "The schizophrenic relationship is not with the analyst predominantly but with the analyst + himself. That is to say, it is predominantly a social transference—dualism to narcissism." It is a narcissistically oriented social relationship. The schizophrenic looks at himself through the analyst, imagining infinite regard coming his way. The destruction of this fantasy occurs simultaneously, often expressed through persecutors. Massive personal damage is placed a little farther away, coming at one from outside (always arriving), rather than as an ongoing explosion ripping self apart.

In mad logic there is a simultaneity of displacements: destruction near is experienced as farther away, destruction far away is experienced near. A certain interchangeability of here there happens emotionally. In Bion's example, the patient generates a full-cup/empty-cup situation in which the two conditions cancel each other out (which means the patient cancels himself-and-the-analyst out too). One reason half-empty is so shattering is because the patient creates a "full-cup therapy" out of a fantasy that combines and magnifies experiences of real interest with a wish for more. In mad logic opposites coincide: total fulfillment and total lack (my cup runneth over and is completely empty) coexist. Two boundless states go together, infinitely full–infinitely empty, maximum gratification–maximum destruction: no room for halfway measures.

At the same time, as suggested above, the psyche makes some attempt to apply the brakes and create boundaries. Massive core damage is sprayed into various persecutors or destroyers, who parcel out diffusion. Gratifiers involve mixtures of self and other, megalomania, control, helplessness, despairing hope, hopeful despair, rage, aspiration, loving ideal feeling fanned by flickers of interest and concern.

Therapy continues, hopefully not without result. Reality obtrudes on utopian-apocalyptic fantasies of total gratification-destruction and the attached attempts to bind them via idealized gratifiers and streams of destroyers. Although therapy is always in the process of evoking fantasies of something more and less than therapy can be, it is partly self-corrective. Its cup is something less than endlessly filled and more than endlessly lacking. Patient and analyst are pressured into taking stock of the process itself, getting their bearings, restarting, reshuffling, seeing where the analysis has landed after the latest shipwreck.

In spite of the tyranny of positive and negative totalities, there is, also, partial realization of myriad states in between. The ability to be disturbed is part of sensitivity. Evolution requires withstanding the urge to destroy disturbance and sensitivity as a way of solving problems the latter presents.

We are challenged to stand up to our own psychotic attitudes. In psychosis, as we have emphasized throughout this chapter, anything at all in the cup would be unbearable (short of complete fulfillment-destruction). In the psychotic attitude, it is impossible to bear what people *can* give. Partly because of trauma, partly because of spiraling deformation of ability to feel or use feelings, psychic democracy is lost or fragile. The borderline psychotic sense of never getting enough partly hinges on not being able to feel what is there, perhaps a lack of respect for what is present. The granting of respect to voices inner and outer calls for a mixture of caring flexibility and persistence, a sense that what is matters—and that how one approaches what is matters. "But I never got respect, so I can't give it." One prays that in therapy there is at least one person in the room trying to find and communicate the respect one dies for, even if, for the moment, it can no longer be taken in or used. A caring respect exerts pressure toward psychic democracy, wherein all votes count.

A democracy of capacities—no small order. Use of self melded with respect for others means caring for what little drops in the cup most of us can access, a love for the rainwater of the self our cups manage to pass on to one another.

Psychic democracy and tyranny are intricately, complexly woven, and each contributes to our lives. We do not like to own up to how much we owe to our predatory, dictatorial natures, our "lesser" selves in general. But it is the latter that support us in life until we can get to a place that asks for more. Work with the psychotic core brings out something central for our lives. The psychotic hears but does not listen. He is overwhelmed by shouts within that seem to come from everywhere. He needs someone to listen, not simply to make sense out of it all. Sense is cheap (sense is good, precious, but meanings galore swim in psychic seas). Beyond various psychic contents or meanings, he needs to see that someone *can* listen, that *listening* exists, in however faulty a mode. He needs to come to believe in listening. Passivity is important. It means, for moments, one is not trying to impose anything on anyone else or on oneself, and in that mysterious lack of imposition, things start to fall into place. A melding of individual-social beyond paranoia. Thirst for one's own and each other's cups.

CHAPTER 5

A Little Psyche-Music

In the 1960s psychotherapists used to speak a lot about trusting the unconscious, following the unconscious. Such talk resonated with Freud's descriptions, in his letters to Fliess, about letting the horse lead. He spoke of drifting, going with the flow, a valuation of passivity, openness, formalized in doctrines of free association and free-floating attention. Unconscious communication, unconscious resonance was in the air. Hans Sach's book title, *The Creative Unconscious,* embodies this feeling.

As psychoanalysis unfolded, interest turned toward psychosis, annihilation anxiety, psychic mutilation, grave damage running through the psyche, permeating psychic systems, where not only conscious but also unconscious processing was damaged. In fact, psychosis was important to psychoanalysis from the outset, and Freud's structural system is based on it. The id is described as a cauldron of seething excitation where the law of contradiction doesn't hold, out of contact with "reality." Hallucination is an early mode of cognition for the ego, which develops antihallucinogenic qualities. Hallucination not only returns at night in dreams, but even filters into over- and underestimations of self and other expressed in transference, idealization, denigration. The mad superego feeds hallucination with a delusion of being morally right, inflicting an endless stream of hate on personality, co-opting id/ego functions on behalf of destruction. In extreme instances—extreme but not infrequent—moral violence (i.e., destructive use of mean morality) becomes the great suicidal terrorist of the psyche, the ego deforming itself and becoming monstrous to conform with it.

Thus a kind of phenomenology of psychotic-psychopathic states informs Freud's structural concepts, which he developed to work with neurosis. The burgeoning of psychoanalytic interest in psychotic dynamics—from Federn, Klein, Winnicott, Fairbairn, Milner, Sullivan, Searles, Bion down to the present moment—involves psychoanalysis coming out of a closet. In a sense, Freud redefined the confrontation with sin as involving confrontation with madness. This is not to equate sin with madness or to call madness sinful. But it calls attention to the madness in sin, including blends of hallucinated lucidity, archetypal confusion, and the double helix of megalomania-impotence that conditions evil intentionality.

Near the end of his life, Freud went farther, and spoke of the personality's tendency to become stuck, even to undo itself, a kind of soul entropy. He links loss of flexibility, mobility, psychic traction with an alteration of the timing of psychic life, damage and/or mutation of the psyche's basic rhythm. Timing, rhythm—musical ideas. As if we're saying the music of the psyche is off. Not just music of the spheres, music of the psyche.

One possibility for a bit of this music, this basic rhythm, is the back-and-forth between injury and recovery. Elkin writes of a loss and recovery of primordial consciousness linked with death-rebirth dramas of the early self. Winnicott writes of breakdown and spontaneous recovery in sessions. Bion writes of coming alive, being murdered, then feeling all right. These are profiles of a basic rhythm or psychic pulse that can get damaged. When this rhythm stops, the psyche stops breathing. Parts of what we call character structure trace paths of strangulation and paths where freedom flows, mixed arteries of psychic flow and blockage.

The sense of rebirth functions as a kind of unconscious archetype or template that helps process the movement between trauma and recovery. Of course, trauma can overwhelm recovery, and, as Freud points out, there are all kinds of attempts at recovery. For example, Freud suggests psychotic hallucination tries to reconstitute ties to self and other in the face of traumatic derailing. Schreber's "blackout" (annihilation of self and world), is followed by self-other cosmic dramas. The ticking of the psyche goes on, although injury speeds, deforms, and magnifies it. There are all kinds of ways to partly abort and partly go through rebirth processes. The *quality* of *coming through* is hampered by our human limitations, fragility, rigidity and "necessary" compromises with evil and madness, whether materialistic or idealistic.

Bion reaches a general formulation of difficulties involved in basic unconscious rhythms when he writes of damaged alpha function. He coins the term "alpha function" partly to indicate that we do not know much about how we process affects, how feelings become real for us, how "emotional digestion" works. Yet he believes feelings and emotional meaning are the heart of psychic life. He chooses "alpha" perhaps because how affects are processed is of the foremost importance, perhaps because the way we process feelings plays a role in the way we process everything else, perhaps because emotional life is what makes life feel like life.

To get a sense of alpha work, we can liken it somewhat to dreamwork or primary process, involved in initiating the processing of feelings. There is a tradition in psychoanalysis that values what primary process or dreamwork contributes to affect processing. Noy, Rycroft, Milner, and Ehrenzweig—to name a few—are part of this tradition, in which emphasis is less on primary process as discharge than on what it adds to experience. Years ago most workers tended to see secondary process as the binder, but psychic work involving holding and reworking of feelings is already present in primary process. For example, processes Freud describes in Chapter Six of the dream book, such as condensation, displacement, symbolization, are already parts of the psychic digestive system.

Bion especially emphasizes the role alpha function/primary process/dreamwork plays in initiating the processing of catastrophic impacts, shocks that go with sensitivity. Processes involved in dreamwork often gravitate toward catastrophe and try to break down, rework, and feed these impacts into images, ideograms, myths, narratives, reveries, reflections, various forms of thinking and expressive actions. A general formula might be: impact gives rise to image, image gives rise to symbol, symbol gives rise to idea. But all such formulations are too simple. To add to our difficulty, Bion points out that dreamwork can be used both to evacuate and modify emotions, at once aiding the psyche to evolve and to get rid of itself. A source of confusion is that we can build and null life at the same time and do so at many levels of being. Often nulling is part of building and building is part of nulling. At a given moment we may not know whether we are creating or destroying. The biblical dictum, "By their fruits ye shall know them," can lead to uncanny problems.

I have used alpha loosely in conjunction with dreamwork and primary processing, but in Bion's writings they are not strictly identical. Alpha function is the broader concept, left open, as Bion put it, as a kind of nest where birds of meaning might alight. Thinking about what alpha might mean helps correct what seems to me a misleading tendency in certain parts of our field. For example, it mitigates against polarizing acting and thinking or thinking and feeling, body and mind, or concrete and abstract. It is not simply a matter of action vs. thinking or sensation vs. feeling vs. thinking, and the like. It is more a matter of how any capacity is being used.

An amazing tap dancer has alpha feet, a pianist has alpha hands, an analyst has alpha intuition at times. Of course, things are in movement, subject to change. A baseball player makes an alpha catch one day, and on another he is leaden and unable to move. Life is uneven. A pianist with great alpha hands and a heart for music may be unable to love a person—music reaches alpha function but people remain beta objects. Things get complicated. Often sensations are said to be examples of beta elements, but again it is a matter of functioning and use. Logical processes can be used in anti-alpha ways and sensations can throb with alpha life. Symbols can be used to destroy the alpha function they rest on, while sensations can stimulate growth (the writer of the Song of Solomon was a sensation genius). There are those who think abstractly but stupidly, those who think concretely but intelligently. What capacity and what portion of reality are involved is less important than how the capacity is being enlisted to light up the world.

As Winnicott points out, in psychoanalysis verbalizers may intimidate the less verbal, but that does not make them right. There are, however, plenty of opportunities for the less verbal to get revenge. In either case, the spirit of unconscious processing matters. We are unconsciously working with catastrophic impacts that are part of our experiential heritage, part of how we approach each other. When two people meet, an emotional storm is created, says Bion. How we relate to our sensitivity, our emotional storm center, what we do with it, is, partly, what alpha is about.

Words like "conscious" and "unconscious" tend to break down when we think about alpha capacity, since consciousunconscious thinkingfeeling depend upon and make use of alpha. Again, emphasis is less on conscious-unconscious than on use of capacity. That something is either unconscious or conscious is no guarantee that it is working well. There are, so to speak, unconscious and conscious evil and good spirits. Making the unconscious conscious is no guarantee of either goodness or health, if madness and sin permeate all psychic structures. There have been moments in my life when someone's unconscious being or actions touch my heart, while conscious attempts to manipulate situations or feelings can be chilling. A certain look or touch can transmit faith. It is a matter of the informing spirit, which spans categories.

Nevertheless, unconscious processing is important. Being a human being, a psychic being, depends on it. After all, consciousness can't do everything. For Bion, unconscious storage has special meaning. It means something is taken in and is important enough to work with. This point is brought out dramatically when he speaks of the psychotic's inability to let something become unconscious, or let unconscious processes do their work. Trauma has wreaked such damage that unconsciousness cannot be trusted. Unconsciousness becomes an infinitely damaging other. Not that consciousness is undamaged. But it works overtime and hardens itself to escape levels of annihilation that unconscious damage magnifies.

To use Bion's wry formula, if the neurotic has a hard time letting the unconscious become conscious, the psychotic has a hard time letting the conscious become unconscious—or perhaps more accurately, letting the unconscious work unconsciously. The issue for living is less causal location of disease than quality of connection, flow and interaction, between different processing styles and dimensions of being.

Both Bion and Winnicott place special importance on dreaming and other unconscious activity. In a way, they say that in order for something to feel real, it has to undergo unconscious processing. Dreamwork plays an important role in making reality real. The realizing of reality requires use of alpha function, including and, especially, unconscious alpha functioning. It is not enough to say we dream the world into being, but without dreaming feeling (as if dreaming were part of an unconscious affective circulatory system) the world would appear a schizoid vision. Trauma would have no fertile soil.

A theme that overlaps with Bion's generative and damaged alpha functioning, is Winnicott's sense of breakdown at the beginning of personality formation. The word "breakdown," like so many words, has double meanings. On the one hand, it refers to breaking, getting broken, a car breaking down, a mind or self or psyche breaking down. The sense of breaking is agonistic. Unbearable agony leads to obliteration, passing out, numbing out. One cannot stay in dire agony overlong without further changes of states, what Freud calls alterations of the ego, which reach farther than ego, however, involving mutations that permeate all psychic structures and, in some instances, threaten to undo psyche altogether. A sense of being damaged is a residue of radically breaking as one begins to form.

The idea of breaking as one begins to form is a powerful one. It leaves one imbued with the feeling that if one begins to form, one will break. This catastrophic dread may be part of any new beginning, any forming, and limes creative joy. Whether one creates something new artistically or begins further soulwork, anxiety of breakdown informs one's work and being. The feeling of breakdown as personality begins to form becomes part of our unconscious background that seeps into experiencing. Since we are supported by unconscious processing, we are in the precarious, if challenging, position of being supported by breakdown. Or, more mildly, what support we have is permeated by intimations of potential breakdown. The sense that breakdown is possible melds with transience and temporality and intensifies longing for the enduring and unshakeable.

Winnicott calls breakdown when personality begins to form madness X and says it is the most personal thing about a person. He depicts a double movement toward and away from madness X, an attempt to defend against it or to escape from it and an attempt to taste, embrace, and work with it. In a remarkable passage he says that moving toward madness X makes one feel more real, while shutting it out makes one feel more unreal. There is a dimension of affective intensity associated with madness X that is crucial for one's sense of being.

Winnicott adds to his compelling brew by saying that we can never reach madness X. What is important is reaching toward it. This is akin to reaching toward independence or dependence, partial, directional movements. It brings out important "facts" about the psyche, which I wish to amplify.

Actual breakdowns are partial breakdowns. The idea of a complete, total, breakdown is an idealization. In the 1960s psychotherapists had the idea of going through madness in a full, total way and coming out the other side. There were many casualties of this starry-eyed view. The smoke would clear, personality resurface, and guess who would still be there—mad me, mad you, mad human race. No amount of going through makes madness go away. There is no final mother of all breakdowns and coming through with all one's heart and soul and self once and for all. Winnicott ensures a modicum of sanity by emphasizing approaching and reaching toward rather than a lasting finding. He touches upon a sane or responsive openness to our mad selves.

However, the feeling that we *should* be able to go through our madness fully and decisively and emerge healed expresses threads of psychic functioning that need to be taken into account. For one thing, it points to a totalizing, absolutizing, infinitizing, magnifying capacity that spreads through experiencing. Not only are there actual breakdowns, there are ideal breakdowns as well. It is almost as if every experience has its ideal counterpart. Madness X, in a way, is a kind of Platonic ideal that empirical, messy breakdowns approach, reflect, shadow. The sense of the ideal is very valuable. Scientists conduct ideal experiments, construct hypothetical ideal conditions that provide insight into actual processes. The sense of the infinite can be awesome, inspiriting, as well as lethal. It motivates, stimulates, activates, invites, leads—and crushes.

Our unconscious background of breakdown melds actual moments of breaking (mixed, partial, variable) with our totalizing, idealizing tendency. Winnicott gives a list of agonies that are hints of madness X, the inexpressible breakdown at the beginning of personality formation. These include disintegration, unreality feelings, lack of relatedness, depersonalization, lack of psychosomatic cohesion, split-off intellectual functioning, falling forever, generalized panic, ECT-like shock. They point to original madness X beyond experiencing, perhaps providing entrées, dips, or tastes. Sessions may become organized around the pull toward breakdown and recovery, hopefully in doses that are, in the long run, semidigestible, or digestible enough.

I have known people who feel their breakdowns were not good enough. If only they could break down in a fuller, better way, their recovery would be better too. They feel they've aborted the process and sense darkly what might heal them if they dared. They persecute themselves for not being mad enough and failing to endure a more satisfactory obliteration. It is frustrating that breakdowns are incomplete and fragmentary, like everything else, including recovery. One cannot find refuge in being obliterated by disturbance or its lack. Obliteration is tantalizingly partial. Idealized obliteration wins for a time, but new efforts must be made to keep it going.

There is much to learn from Freud's fiction that a hungry infant hallucinates a memory of satisfaction. A hallucination with many components—good breast, taste, skin feel, nourishment, a filling feeling. Not just a satisfactory feed, but an ideal or beatific moment. Not just OK, but heavenly, divine. Perhaps a feed such as never quite existed anytime, anywhere, but which exists all the time everywhere as an omnipresent ideal moment in our unconscious.

Is it right to call this beatific capacity hallucinatory? Not all the time, perhaps—perhaps not essentially. Perhaps not even when it blots out pain, blisses out disturbance. Such ability helps us maintain faith in life, helps us keep going. Perhaps it becomes hallucinatory in function when it foists itself on us as the only or primary way of relating to experience, preventing pain from having its say, preventing alternative capacities from having a voice in psychic government. What I am saying is by no means adequate, but it does point to a capacity we need to make room for, turn this way and that, appreciatively as well as critically. Our totalizing tendency exploits a ubiquitous hallucinatory capacity, and, too, we hallucinate totality. But hallucination makes contributions to truth, as well as exploiting it dangerously. We are hallucinatory beings capable of channeling and relating to this startling propensity in a variety of ways.

One more thing about Winnicott's madness X. By saying madness X cannot be experienced, but only approached, and by saying it is the most intimate, personal x about a person, he is implying that what is most personal in our beings cannot be experienced. What is most personal is what is most unknown and unknowable. To say anything more about this would be to water it down. I really should leave it as a kind of psychoanalytic koan. But I hear my inner voice speaking and will pass its ravings along for fun and perusal, in case it helps anyone. I mean these remarks in a playful spirit, but they are earnest too, for these are life-and-death matters after all.

It is hard to avoid linking madness X with Winnicott's incommunicado core, ineffably beyond experience, important for what is most personal and intimate, the tone and texture of unconscious processing, the feel of a life. Shirah Kober Zeller links Winnicott's incommunicado core with Kabbalah's Ain Soph, the unknowable, ineffable infinite, which Grotstein (if I may titrate him a bit for my purpose) links with the Ineffable Subject of Unconscious Processing. We are at the gates of the unspeakable and unsayable but, then, we are always at these gates, and they do not stop us from speaking too long. At the same time there is a breathless moment that never says a word.

God shines in the human face. Is that hallucination? Or simply extravagance of experiencing, the fact of color, emotional richness? A patient of mine, Milton, says he is certain he did not see radiance in his mother's face. He saw tubes and holes. Yet his face glows. I experience his radiance but he feels black holes. He hates me if I hallucinate a better him, a him he has no access to. He has no access to his own glow. But I do not just hallucinate his glow—his radiance is real. But he cannot feel his own reality, except the lack of it, the agony of not feeling it. The fact of trauma and damage is his reality, his truth. Everything else is phony, unreal, deception. One must believe him absolutely before daring to think that there is more. Milton's damaged alpha function dreams damage and is a sample of ongoing, persistent damage, yet recovery is not completely absent. Milton and his life get better in spite of himself, a betterness he appreciates yet hates. He hates getting better, fears and loathes its unreality, knows it is real but cannot trust himself to feel its realness. This kind of trust has been mutilated. The ability to feel the realness of his realness gets annihilated as it forms, nearly a pure slide of one sort of madness X.

A friend from out of town recently sent me a poem likening the vanished World Trade Center to a "negative image," an image of what is not there framed by buildings that still exist, counterpart to a phantom limb or missing teeth. One sees and feels the object more acutely because it is gone, because only the space it filled remains. My friend asked how to tell which way is downtown, discovering the harrowing compass point or fixed star is an image of what isn't there. One guides oneself via a missing object. Milton describes a sense of being both positive and negative image of himself, akin to positive-negative hallucination, hallucinating himself as there and not there. In Milton's case it is more than presence-absence, for both being there and not being there are damaged beyond recognition. The World Trade Center is not just gone; it is mutilated, and the space that is left is mutilated. It is precisely this fact about himself that Milton relentlessly insists must be recognized.

This mutilated space is both material and immaterial. What remains of the World Trade Center is a fragment of hell. One feels the debris of souls in the burnt and collapsed ruins, spirit mixed with deformed rubble. The remains of the colossus signify the remains of the tortured dead, which will never be retrieved. Parts of bodies found represent the remainder of bodies never to be seen again. Not just incinerated bodies, incinerated souls, spirits, minds, beings. It is part of the poetic truth of our lives that sometimes the spirit of a being, his or her very essence, shines more brightly in death—as if we distill the truth we need for living from soul contact that death liberates.

Ancient burial places that antedate recorded history do not just express a wish to live forever, but grow out of an acute sense of the other's presence, more intense because it is invisible. Everything visible is invisible. What is visible triggers the life of invisible feelings. The latter coat the former, an unseen sea objects dip into. A sense of immateriality pervades materiality and, at times, when material life stops, intensity of spirit becomes more acute.

The economic spirit dominates our age. When a great economic signifier explodes and collapses, a hole is created for something more, something else to happen. That is why many of us cringe when we are told to go out and spend money in the face of death. As if money, any more than words, can fill the gap, as if money is spiritual sustenance. We'll show them. We will not let them break our spirit. We'll make and spend more money. I think what many of us are fighting for is that a moment of transformation not be missed. There is danger that trauma be trivialized, commercialized, politicized. It is difficult to take in pockets of synchronicity between mutilated unconscious and external devastation.

Life goes on. Children make connections, the psyche cannot stop creating. A man recently told me how traumatized he was by his father and how he has done his best to be a good father with his daughter. He goes to the other extreme. He is endlessly supportive, always telling her how good she is. A few weeks ago she told him she had gone to the potty, and he asked if he could see. She said yes, and he looked admiringly at a long, intact stool. "Oh, how beautiful!" he exclaimed. "Yes," she said, but she was not quite satisfied. After a few moments she added thoughtfully, "It's just like the big building that fell down."

One wonders what unconscious work she and her generation will be called upon to do. How like big whole feces big buildings are. She is already a transmitter for links Freud made between money, feces, waste, building, creating. Her father, longing to protect her from trauma that marred him, finds her psychic body disposed to catch the spirit of the age, working with materials life gives her.

Unconscious work never stops, no matter how stagnant or damaged. It is part of the activity of life itself, chewing on experience, knitting together, tearing apart, trying to make something new. The fact that we can't see it going on yet play a role in its transmission adds to the sense of the numinous that is part of the background of experience. It is important that what is seen becomes a part of what isn't seen so that it can be seen again anew. It is important that we protect the unseen and unseeable, so that vision can grow. Without fertile unconscious processing, the face of the Other has nowhere to go. Other souls seed us, but we must have soil for seeds to grow.

CHAPTER 6　*Alone with God*

No one knew how alone I felt or even that I had feelings. They had to take care of me, not love me."

Sarah was supposed to die three years ago, her body dissolving into a disease with no cure. Chemicals began to help less than half a year ago. She is weak but determined to see life through, in spite of hideous suffering. Chemicals cause more pain than the disease. Often she wishes for death. But there is a kind of faith, grit, and caring about God beyond anything that makes sense, which makes it impossible for her not to go all the way.

Where does this caring faith come from? *What* is it?

"There is a canary in my rib cage. It hops around ninety beats per minute. It has a story to tell, no one wants to know. When I was a kid, it bore my family's terror. Canary—lightning rod for terror. It bounced from one bar to another, absorbing terror from each person it came near. The heart terror of my family. No wonder it's nervous, speeding up, slowing down unaccountably.

"Now nurses tell me, 'You're not supposed to cry.' They give me more Zoloft. I want to cut down on Zoloft.

"I'm being poisoned."

"'No,' they say. 'Everything's fine. You can talk to me. Just don't open the secret door to your mind.'

"The canary can't breathe. It can't sing its story."

: : :

In therapy the canary sings. It sings through bars that don't go away. Bars need voices to sing them too. Who will listen? Who will *hear*?

: : :

The canary in her rib cage beats faster when doctors come. "The chemicals are working? You can bear it? Good. You can't bear it? You're doing great."

They cannot bear the canary's cry.

: : :

It cannot be the case that therapy is the only place where canaries are precious.

: : :

"I went to get my tonsils taken out and they took out my backbone.

"My mother didn't have a backbone. She couldn't move."

Her mother's body deteriorated. Doctors pretended she would get better. Sarah knew better. Where was the terror?

The canary was invisible in childhood. Now Sarah sees and hears the beautiful yellow flutter, hop, song. "It was frozen all my life, freezing my life." Sarah knows there is something to notice. She says that when there is something to notice, there is love.

"You're weird," Sarah comments. "You don't bat an eyelash when I say these things."

I don't bat an eyelash about things she doesn't say, too. I feel them creep into me. I tell them to you before I know them myself.

"Never forget!" This applies to lives everywhere, if we could see and hear. People think not hearing the canary makes life better. Sarah tells us it makes life worse.

"They took my backbone out instead of killing me," Sarah says. Her mother became ill before Sarah was two. "I think it brought them ghastly satisfaction to let me live boneless." When Sarah went into the hospital, her mother's body was home rotting. No one told her she was just having her tonsils taken out, a little part of her, that she was fine. Sarah thought they wanted to kill her. She felt she was dying, staring into light, they covered her nose and mouth; she died. No one told her what to expect, perhaps she wouldn't understand. There is lack of faith in communication in daily life, resistance to making and sustaining links. When she awoke, she thought, "So this is what it's like to be dead."

"It took time for me to realize I was only boneless. Now I know I partly died and bonelessness expresses my partial death.

"There's a spot under my skin to the right of my vertebrae—another set of vertebrae, an almost external backbone just under the surface. It's there to hold my real backbone up, a kind of prosthesis to hold my *self* up, mine and mother's. The canary sings this story too."

Sarah asks me to sing to her. I sing a Jewish melody I make up as I go along, sweet, heartbreaking, a special Jewish joy made of every heartbreak from the beginning of time. We hum a little together. "Ya ya ya, yeh yeh yeh," very sweet, and the humming is made up of syllables that mean God.

"No one sang to me like that," she weeps.

: : :

"When I got home I felt the warmth, faith, shattered heart of your song—a sun inside me. The whole universe was part of that warm shattering. The big bang—a breaking heart beginning the universe?

"There's a hole, not a sun, in my solar plexus. An impenetrable scream with horrible vibrations is in the middle of the wedge between my mother's and my screams. A scream that breaks your bones. The hole is as big as a cannonball. When I hear music, it tries to fill that hole. If I were better, music would spring from that hole, like the scream does.

"My doctors show the difference. One is visionary, speaking from abysmal experience. He's the one who suggested the chemical that works. He didn't go by the book. He made a leap. He said only, 'My heart feels this might work. Let's give it a chance.' The book treatments nearly killed me, left me in pain. The difference a voice can make. A heart moment. I hear the song, 'Your waves roll over me.' God-waves rolling ideas away. Deep to deep. Abyss to abyss."

: : :

"Trauma rips open a space, and the lens of abysmal vision grows over the space. You see differently. Waves roll over you, swimming in the abyss, floating. Abysmal ecstasy.

"When the ecstasy subsides everything is subtracted except nightmare. You're left being scratched to death with a scratched-to-death mind.

"I don't think my husband identifies himself as one living on Planet Madness."

: : :

"Darkness is equal in value to light on Chanukah. The point of the light is it never goes out. Darkness shines through it."

: : :

"Pain runs through me. No one knows where it comes from or how to get rid of it. I take drugs and get rid of myself, and the pain goes on without me. Nerves? Bones? Deeper than muscle. Music, tranquilizers, acupuncture help. Sometimes sex makes it better, sometimes worse. The pain can break through everything. Everything forms a nightmare image. My insides fall out. Something says, 'It's your fault you're in pain. If you were open, a better person, stronger in faith, . . . it would get better.' A demon eats experience, makes you feel you're false."

: : :

"You're a Kabbalist," Sarah says. "You work with shatter, shards. You find me, I find you in the worst places. You know where they are. You live them. You once said the breaking of the vessels is ongoing, mending cannot keep up. It's my secret—breaking beyond mending Sparks that can't be seen."

: : :

There are many stories in which you find yourself in a strange place, a deserted wood, a desolate town, a bombed out village, a rich man's mansion, your own backyard. You stare at diseases of war, poverty, wealth, habit and wonder, "Why am I here?" Always the same work is needed.

: : :

"I'm in pain," says Sarah. "Cold, awful pain, bone pain. Nothing can be done. What can freeing sparks mean when pain is meaningless? Pain just is. Are there sparks in the pain? Can one put God together from the sparks in the pain? A cruel soul alchemy. Do we need to put God together in order to be human? Sometimes I feel there's an ignition switch I must turn on in order to become a human being. Is God the ignition switch? Partly?"

: : :

"This pain is meaningless," Sarah tells me. "There are no sparks in it, nothing to redeem. A senseless waste product of disease. There is just me talking to you. This is a good place to be when I'm like this, when I'm vanishing."

: : :

"The pain sucks me in. I'm vanishing, but part of me is outside or I could not talk. I wish the pain would vanish instead of me. There's no end to vanishing. There's no pain without me. I think it keeps me alive so it can have a host. To be witness to my own vanishing is another kind of torment."

: : :

There once was a bottom. It was imagined there were fifty steps down the ladder of hell with redemption possible on forty-nine of them. Once the fiftieth was reached, the gates close, no way out. Now I know that much work takes place in the fiftieth level, which opens to another fifty, and another fifty—that work goes on in negative infinities: beginnings never stop. Hope in hopelessness.

: : :

"It does not comfort me when people speak of finding the center," says Sarah. "My center is spinning. The spin is the center. I hate it. This dizziness is one of the worst things in the world. If this were a different kind of therapy you might suggest I scream."

"It sounds like you're already screaming."

"Yes, and no one knows, only you."

: : :

Sarah dreams of tectonic plates rotating like Ezekiel's wheels. "My heart found God in the spin and a godforsaken place."

: : :

"Flowing is as bad as spinning," says Sarah. "Drifting is scary. All I see is ice flow. Whatever moves turns to ice. Spinning turns to ice. Ice spinning."

: : :

"I want to scratch the starry eyes out of heaven. I think I'd feel relief if I cut myself. In fantasy I do—but it is only fantasy. I've heard that cutters in mental hospitals reverberate to each other, emotional contagion. One of the cutters is leader, on top, the master cutter. A calm, cold cutter spontaneously organizing the others. They can be in different rooms, not physically in contact. But emotionally they resonate and cut in synchrony. Sometimes they compete—who is the most chilling cutter of all? They do this even when they don't know each other exists.

"It is chilling to think one can try to feel on top of injury by inflicting damage on oneself. Conceit and deceit of mastery, fantasy of mastery.

"Leaders cut the skin of our national soul in order to feel mastery. No blood comes out until financial or military hemorrhage.

"I read that in a convent nuns adjust their menstrual cycle to the mother superior's. Powerful force—rhythm of resonance."

ONE YEAR EARLIER

"I *am* something wrong—for having this immune system. The other voice says, 'Be aware of Mike's presence, the light on the building . . .'"

: : :

"Only now am I getting enough support to feel my mother's death. There was no support for any of us." Her mother was bedridden before Sarah was three, grew weaker and weaker, lingering through Sarah's childhood. "The constant dying, moment-to-moment dying, stretched over time. My father's immolation, the sacrifice he made to support her. He couldn't understand why I didn't want to see her. They [father, family, caretakers, doctors] would try to talk me into it. I didn't want to go to her.

"Everyone flees from the baby. The baby is a pariah filled with toxic aliveness. My mother needs intermediaries, helpers, people to take care of me. People come and go. She flees, kidnapped. She is terrified of being alone with me. Terrified of breast-feeding, terrified of wanting it."

I say something about terror encasing Sarah's unconscious. Terror permeates her through and through, the very subsoil and support of her being. Yes, she says and depicts her mother running away before she was sick, ill without knowing it. Always running to friends, events, dinners, parties. "She handed me over to others who didn't want me either. There was no one to spend time with me, hold me.

"In pictures she seems uncomfortable holding me, stiff, looking away with a distracted smile. She seems uncomfortable having a body. A body or a baby. Well, illness took care of that.

"Soon everyone was taking care of her.

"Maybe she wanted to love me but didn't know how. I know how alone she felt by how alone I felt. My father didn't have a clue. I made my own kind of renunciation, a kind of bleeding of desire, a loss of expectation, memory, desire to be appreciated. My mother was terrified to begin with. She was terrified to find me, of not doing it right, to be criticized. I was taken away from her before she had a chance. If someone had been there to support her, she wouldn't have died so soon, so ill, and I'd be less crazy. She could have had surprising moments. She could have surprised everybody.

"She didn't mean to poison me. The terror was poisonous. I knew it was a lost cause. The acid was spreading. There *could* have been moments of seeing, of heart-to-heart contact—one moment *would* have meant everything. Miracle moments of contact that never happened —they were pushed aside by busywork, pretending. On the way here I saw white kids breaking ahead of an old black woman getting on a bus. They had no sense of fragility, just I'm going to get there first.

My caretakers had that kind of energy, pushing me aside by the way they took care of me. A kind of taking care of to get rid of.

"I see a heart cracked. Mine? Hers? [mother's?] Now it is mine, a *yahrzeit* part of heart. It re-forms into a lotus. She is getting a transfusion. The petals are light beam needles linking all the transfusions in the world. They are threads of prayer weaving a boat passing from one state to another.

"People shouldn't think their prayers are unanswered if I die. They are like sunbeam fibers, some kind of transfusion. Trans-fusion. Not limited to me. If I die it's not whoever is sending them [prayer transfusions] fails. They'll change form into something else and help get me from wherever I am to wherever I'm going. They're changing from gold to black, not the color black, but something I can't see. Whatever they'll become is hidden, not given to me to know. I can feel it now as a kind of new warm shower, comforting, fruitful.

"If I were designing a mystical experience—ha, a designer mystical experience—that would not be it"—because she would want prayers to work now and save her, this her, this life. She speaks of blood drops, actual transfusions maintaining her on less than half a normal blood count. The first several series of chemical treatments failed and she needs transfusions once or twice weekly. The doctors know this can backfire. She is very weak, has stopped working. "How much can I lose and still be me? What me is still here?" She is fragile and feels the terror of life pushing her aside.

: : :

"What is there for an infant if it moves away from a mother? Away from mother's death to nothing? Madness?" Sarah pictures herself as an infant trying to get away from the dying transmitted through her mother's body. The body transmits states, body to body, psyche to psyche—we *are* porous. She could not defend herself against the death process eating her mother. A death picking up momentum, going on and on. She could try to look away, as her mother looked away in photos. She could tighten herself, harden. She could blot herself out with panic. As a little girl, she refused to go to her mother, a refusal that saved her but with terrible repercussions. Sarah cannot stop asking, "What happens to a baby that moves away from its mother?" *She* is one possible answer. To move away from mother one way means moving toward mother another way. Is disease a way of moving toward, a ghastly sharing, shared disease?

Sarah experiences herself as bloodless. Her mother's milk is a scream caught in her throat. "I'm experiencing depersonalization and making room for it. My other analyst wouldn't touch it. He wouldn't go anywhere near it. He left me completely alone, one of the most isolated people in the world. Ice—isolate. Completely alone. I held on a long time, under the thumb of the analysis, isolation a stranglehold." Sarah felt unreal much of her life, but not only unreal, often hyperreal, capable of very intense experiencing. "I don't have to be real or unreal here. I can be whatever. You don't force me to take sides, to stay away from myself. It's hard to understand you can be unreal and real. My past analyst couldn't take it." When Sarah was a girl, her father took her to a psychiatrist who told her to be a good girl and help Daddy with sick Mommy. In her twenties she found her own analyst who was nice to her, but did not want her to get too close to herself, fearing disaster and disability. He helped her stay afloat for many years by sacrificing a kind of contact with herself he felt was dangerous and sick.

On my couch, for the moment, Sarah is an imaginary infant that feels real. She knows she is in vision or fantasy but experiences a sense of emotional truth and wants to give herself to it and explore it. After moments of being a baby she reflects, "If I drink anything, I'll be cold, I'll freeze. I'm afraid to take in from the outside. I see my mother looking away, frozen—all her desires frozen, rigid, stillborn, aching. I become religiously precocious, filling myself with God. God came out of nowhere. I never heard about God in my family except in swear words or something to be against or make fun of. My eyes needed something to see, and I saw God. Some people invent imaginary playmates. My playmate was God. My analyst did not like to hear me talk about God, but I couldn't have survived without Him. To speak of God as a wished-for parent is fine as long as that doesn't wish God away. I grew up with a pain in my stomach, adrenal switches turned on or off too much. Holding onto God got me through.

"Now warm blood—finally, warm—can kill me. What gives me

life can kill me." Transfusions actually are dangerous. Now physical transfusions "mimic" her early history of emotional transfusions, life-giving transmissions that can kill.

I ask what she desires in a mother. "Absolute love," Sarah replies, then switches gears. "What a mess. I lived with this disease a year longer than I might have. A year longer than I should have. I'm having a birthday I wasn't supposed to have. I'm alive somehow. Still alive. If I make it through my birthday it's a big achievement. No one expected me to be here."

: : :

She had a lovely birthday party. With beautiful music. It was good even if she had to lie down for long parts of it. She needs a lot of rest. Bits and bursts of aliveness wear her out. She tells me all about the party, then breaks off, talks to God. "I want to meet You when I feel more alive."

: : :

Sarah dreamt of a small cat missing its left front leg. Yet it was sturdy. Another cat comes, a tough, strong cat. They get along OK. More strays appear. "What is this, a cat house?" asks Sarah.

I was frightened at first because experience teaches me a vanishing cat can mean imminent death. But far from vanishing, this cat endures and multiplies. One, two, many cats. Freud writes that many of something in a dream represents intensity. Sarah notes she is injured too and has a bunch of associations, including: doesn't have a leg to stand on (had to lie down at her party), has only one leg but makes the most of it, Rabbi Hillel asked to give the essence of the Torah while standing on one leg says don't do to others what you don't want done to you, a one-legged pirate, someone who comes through injuries and illness, toughs it out. Maybe, too, I'm a tough cat in the cat house of therapy, holding Sarah's toughness for her until she can confess her own. Therapy is very much about communicating sensitivity to sensitivity, but it is very much about communicating toughness too.

"It's the toughness of strays I feel here," says Sarah. I feel that toughness in my weak, weak body. A toughness runs through me."

"And strong feeling," I say.

"Yes, very strong feeling." She feels like crying. She's not strong enough to bear God's aliveness, but what leg she has will have to do.

Safety in numbers? What starts off with a sense of danger turns out well. Cats get along—sexual overtones—cat house, Sarah snickers. She is far from finished sexually. She links sex with music at her party. Small, crippled, sturdy cat coupled with big, strong one? All the cats are strong. She gets a chance in therapy to get a transfusion of strength to strength. Not a weak, dying mother with a baby, not inattentive caretakers. A strong, caring hand to reach and grab. Someone who loves psyches. Therapy cat house, better than ice house. Far-out cats here, strays, not in the mainstream but real, tasting what can be tasted. Suddenly her life is filled with cats her mother missed, and they arrived for Sarah not a moment too soon.

: : :

"Psychoanalytic time is like Sabbath time," Sarah says, "slowing down to see."

: : :

Pain runs through her body, nerves, bones. In such a state, she would have to blot herself out with pain killers to gain relief. She does not want to lose consciousness, yet pain is insistent, deadly. She knows it will pass—but in how long? If it gets extreme enough, aren't more drugs better, since pain blots out consciousness anyway?

"Pain of pain," she says. "What if I get to the farthest you can get and what you see is heartbreak—infinite heartbreak." She goes farther and farther into herself, and what she finds is not some beatific core of unblemished goodness. She finds more and more heartbreak. "I try to breathe out, waves crash, clots break, breathing cracks my heart. Cosmos breathing cracks God's heart. All crushed hearts in synchrony for a moment. There's no such thing as heart of flesh without tears."

"Acceptance goes with grief," I say.

"'I know you can't do this yourself,' God says. "'I give you this turning back to yourself, to me, out of mercy.'"

"But this mercy is heartbreak," Sarah replies. "The heart of flesh is tears [weeping, ripping]. Wholeness is only one side. The sacred heart broken—not all His ways are whole."

: : :

Sarah says, "I have an image of somatizing the destructive force, a force that tries to destroy everything." She is thinking of Bion's force that goes on working after it destroys time, space, personality, existence. "Somatization of my family's illness, mother a carrier, immune system with no teeth, teeth berserk, never stopping, breaking down everything until nothing's left, white teeth, bloody red."

I picture Sarah feeling this way as a baby, chomping, ripping, strength ripping through her, clenching, tightening, nowhere to go.

: : :

While she is speaking, pain comes. Everything stops. I point out soft shadows through the blinds, drops of sun melting on the chair, and ask if she likes it. Yes, she says. It exerts a counterpole to dying in her pain. Dreaming returns. Pain reaches a point of poverty, too much cost, too little for it. The truth of beauty comes through dreamlike shadow/sun. Warm waves spread in her skin, underneath, for the moment permeable to sun and shade, sharp points fade. This cannot always happen.

: : :

Sarah speaks of inner pain, outer light/shadows. "Light goes both ways." In-out, through.

: : :

Sarah says, "If I could ask for anything, I would ask for the ability to rest, to find a resting place even when there's pain."

"Relief from fear of dying," I add.

"I feel as if I'm going to die tomorrow and also not—the day or month or year or unknown time after. My body's some kind of ball, bouncing around. I totally lose energy, get a transfusion, bounce back, up, down. Meanwhile, doctors come with another drug, another maybe, no idea what it'll do or put me through, how my body will bounce. 'Let's try this,' they say. They don't want to hear about the sound of electrified sand pouring through my body when I move. Very few people can sit and hear the pain."

At least I sit and hear the pain.

: : :

God: "Why are you stopping me from being my merciful self? If you were different, I'd be different."

Moses (appealing to God's ego, if not heart): "How will you look in the Egyptians' eyes if you wipe us out?"

God: "I wouldn't like the God I see in Egypt's eyes."

Sarah's husband, Walt: "No wonder I'm how I am. Now I see how I am as I am." Sarah is thinking of the way Walt dressed down the head nurse for a mishap, his godly wrath. Sarah felt he went overboard and was too scary. Many is the time she tried softening her stiff-necked, stubborn man. She persists, and for a moment he sees the truth of his Yahveh nature.

Sarah (summing up): "God gets to be his own anti-God. No-wonder vs. wonder."

M.E.: "Does this tell you how we work?"

Sarah: "In the image of God." She can't stop laughing. She says something about feeling a lot better after coughing out bad stuff.

Walt says something about knots of fury and frustration, then exclaims, "Why are these nurses acting like idiotic human beings?!"

: : :

Sarah spoke of birds, horses. She was in the hospital for the weekend. She glimpsed maple trees, life from her window. She dreamt of horses. Religious feeling surged from her sense of nature, body life.

"Religion hasn't totally succeeded in strangling everything that gave birth to it," I say.

A holy feeling pulses without content and Sarah rests in it.

: : :

Sarah speaks of exploding parts everywhere. "I feel better seeing the fragments."

: : :

" . . . too much regarded by the eyes, and disregarded by the soul." Sarah speaks of the critical eye, the eye of judgment, her own toward herself, plus dreaded eyes of others, the eye that turns self to stone, in contrast with self warming soul. "I hear you writing the words down [she is lying down; I'm behind her]. They want to be recorded by somebody. They don't want to just disappear [weeping]. In this case writing is a form of regard. Yesterday I felt powerless with shame remembering my father letting his friend watch me bathe after I said I didn't want to be naked in front of anyone, certainly not a strange man. My father said, it's OK, he has a little girl too. He pushed my feelings aside. Your writing is a different kind of being seen, a healing. Something that my experience needs—to be recorded, a memory come alive. The opposite of my father and his friend. The seen word *protects* my privacy [experience is noted, responded to, not dismissed]. I don't get it but it seems true. It's a relief . . .

"Men coming into the bathroom. My wrath shoved into my throat, stuck. It starts in my mouth, goes all the way down to my belly—a very definite feeling. Stuck there, freezing. Now my belly is nice and warm, an amazing feeling. An alchemical transference of the spoken word into good feeling instead of rage-rape. To speak and be recorded feels like a good feed. If I could sleep, it would be a baby sleep. It feels like the first time my throat isn't stiff."

: : :

Sarah speaks of states she is going through, grotesque images, worse and worse, more neutral images, good-feeling instants. "Bless the image and just let it go," she says. "A real shift of attitude."

: : :

"No one can take it, the way I feel. Everyone wants me to feel better. I'm grateful for a place to feel miserable," she says.

: : :

Sarah dreams of a smooth log, no bumps. It is eerie, unnatural. She condemns herself for having unnatural dreams. She has a defective psyche, defective body. It's all her fault. Look, her dream is evidence she is bad, beyond the pale, on the other side, beyond help or redemption.

She then relates the smooth log to an incident with a nurse she has to get rid of. The nurse helped her for quite some time, but has gone haywire, paranoid, taking days off without warning, yelling, "I know what you're up to." Sarah knows what she has to do but must steel herself. She doesn't want to hurt someone who helped her.

"To not hurt people like Minna [her nurse], I'd have to become a bump on a log . . ."

"Instead of part of the bumpy road," I say.

To have no bumps, to have no flow. To be a bump on a log, lifeless. Sarah remembers going to school and how hard it was for her as a girl. She didn't belong, things went by her, she couldn't feel traction with life around her. She sees a teacher saying, "When you're dead enough, you can rejoin the class." A caretaker says, "Good girls button up." Good girls bottom-up, you mean.

: : :

"There is a baby allergen," says Sarah. "My family has it. People have it. It's psychic, congenital, contagious." People are allergic to babies.

Sarah compares two ways of dealing with scary feelings. The Bible has all kinds of purification rituals concerning natural fluids, ways to channel emotional attitudes about body. So many rituals concerned with keeping soul, spirit, self, tribe, body pure, keeping one's relationship to God holy.

This contrasts with a "love kiss through the eyes. They say you can tell a baby's name by looking into his eyes. The eyes are a home for the baby." How different from the critical eye that makes a baby homeless, the eye that needs to bind feelings in ritual chains, safe from emotional contagion.

"The love kiss of the eyes—in contrast to being yanked out of one's feelings, out of one's baby home."

And where the love kiss of the eyes is missing, defective? Where the baby is the object of dread? "In some horrible way a mother can dread possession by the baby, as by a demon. My mother, her mother, it gets passed on, being allergic to babies. You need a playful sense of self for possessing to feel good. It's OK, good—the self getting eaten by and eating the baby. It's different if one grips oneself in terror with no larger, creative self. The creative self creates the mourning/morning. Without it my thimbleful of courage becomes a terror grip."

Sarah goes on to reflect on the creative play-self dying, coming back, rhythms of going, returning. I reverie on the baby as object of dread, widespread baby phobia, baby as signifier of emotional life that throws one for a loop.

: : :

"I was terrified of horseback riding but acted in control. I hit myself more than the horse with an inner stick, a control stick. It was important to act confident. Camp was a nightmare. Beating my inner horse to do what it had to do, all those activities.

"Some kind of dream with a time limit. I have to go somewhere. I'll miss out as I'm in the bathroom changing my clothes. A ghost is tying me to the dream."

: : :

"God puts us in a schizophrenic bind. God demands you be able to do what's impossible, and you're punished for not doing it. This is my usual state, punishing impossibility.

"Two bulbs, Siamese twins. The one least likely to survive is the one we want to live, a good life feeling. The one likely to survive—the destructive, poisonous one—is the one we want to die. There's no way out of this contradiction. If one wants to do away with conflict, choose destructive judgment, which eats everything in sight. If we choose the God of compassion, judgment evolves into discernment, notation, evolution on God's part, which involves tension. Tension sustained, modified, not ended.

"*Vov* is associated with *tiferet*, solar plexus, heart holding *din* together, God of multitudes, hosts."

Sarah suddenly speaks to God, "I can't give you what you're asking me." She is quiet again, then concludes, "I vote for the God least likely to survive. If God gets raised from the dead, does that make it easier? God has a long way to go, a lot of work to do with Himself."

Sarah asserts that all-consuming judgment collapses the tension between judgment and mercy. Compassion ignites tension, requiring evolution of God and the human. *Vov* is a Hebrew letter (it sounds like "v"). It is a single straight, vertical line, likened to a backbone, with a kind of tear/flame/sperm-like head. It is the third letter in the Tetragramatton, God's unspeakable name. The backbone notion reverberates with the backbone serpent linking the *chakras* or energy centers in *kundalini* yoga. Sarah's imagery is Kabbalistic. *Tiferet* is the heart center in the sephirotic tree. One of its many functions is to attract and hold *din,* severity, judgment, as well as other sephirot (energy, mind, spirit centers, functions or capacities). Sarah feels *vov* has a linking function, in this case via *tiferet,* which she loosely associates with heart and gut, qualifying *din* or judgment. It is a vision of God and us as multitudes, made up of many mutually qualifying elements and functions, rather than monomanic. She is associating her illness with God's *din* gone wrong, aggressive energy turned against itself, rather than aggression needed to realize compassion, discernment, and evolution of personality. Sarah casts her vote for an evolving, dynamic God. What will God say? How much and what sort of God can her psychosomatic being take?

: : :

"My job: to absorb family terror and keep it silent. All these family members standing over me pouring this terror into my heart and not saying a word."

A FEW MONTHS AGO

"I got into this state seeing the snow; it's hard to say, it's— the snow and air were breathing. I became that air. Air that isn't air, that God breathes in and out. The closer to air I become the less me there'll be for him to touch." Him = God, her husband? She fears God's touch, if it makes her ill.

"I awoke with nail prints in my left cheek, a wounded animal, like a dog hurt by a car.

"I'm careful not to let this disease turn me into a lump. I'm stronger now than before I was ill."

Sex with her husband would peak and slide back down before orgasm. "Post menopause," she muses. The contact is frustrating but good, less fearful than God-contact. Human touch. She fears God in the night. In the night she's possessed. She gives herself to God; then a demon comes. She sees vampire wings, "Me inside its closed wings stuck. It invades, feeds on my unconscious life. My father would say, 'Sweet dreams,' and I'd say 'I hate to dream'; then he'd say, 'Sleep well, don't dream, but if you must, don't have nightmares.' Maybe I was seven or eight. Did I pray for me to be sick rather than my mother?"

"I've no recall of my parents ever in the same bedroom. I remember my mother in the hospital, in a sickroom of her own. So much sexual intensity—was it to get them together?" Sarah is thinking of her sexual intensity from an early age, wondering how much of it was attached to the sense of her parents' not being locked in as a passionate couple. How much of her intensity was a kind of cement to hold them together, her own intensity multiplied by intensity she imagined they ought to have? My speculation: the intensity of what was missing was aggravated by there being in fact a parental bond, a love couple persisting as a weak force for Sarah, but too weak to hold her fears, rage. Illness intensified a mothering weakness already present. Much family energy filtered through father's devotion to sick care. The parental bond, filtered by caretaking for mother, could not do its job of making the child secure. It seemed to do the opposite, escalating dread as Sarah cut off, developing the habit of being left out, pouring intensity into aspects of spiritual awareness, a solitary place of inclusion. What bonds there were seemed to make things worse.

: : :

She is a baby, a child in the night. A bat flies into her room, "opens, scoops you up, too bad for you." Something about greedy, it's greedy, she's greedy, punishment because of baby greed, maybe one gets wounded by greed, greedy for life.

I say something about the wounded baby part disfigured.

"Bats have sweet faces," she says.

: : :

Her next birthday party is magnificent. She dances until her ankle begins to give way. People think she is in better health than she is. She is vibrant, strong, responsive. What a wonderful evening. Quite a contrast with the year before, when she spent so much time lying down. Music and faces lift her, body moves with spirit.

: : :

"I'm cruel," she says. "You don't see it all."
I agree she's cruel and I may not know all of it.
She enumerates recent cruelties, toward friends, me, the way she treats her garden—a special brand of cruelty, cruelty toward flowers. It is not a matter of pardoning, but noting what's there: cruelty.

: : :

She speaks of feelings held in, a kind of inner pressure, a pressure becoming cruel mainly to herself. Going deep into inner pressure reminds Sarah of deep-sea diving, which used to be so freeing for her. "Inner pressure is cruel. Diving is a response to feeling suffocated. The pain mimics what could go wrong in diving. The pain pulses, mimics orgasm," she says. Cruelty.

: : :

"In my dream I snorkel instead of dive. I can't dive anymore. I have to stay on the surface. You try to show me how to put the goggles on but botch it. They get tangled, confused, upside down. They're the wrong goggles—for swimming, not snorkeling. Something always goes wrong. I lose a fin. I fear I'll swim in circles and be depressed. I'm not even sure there's much to look at in this water; it's murky. I try to hold my breath but can't very long. I'm not in as good shape as I hoped. I begin to feel the trip is wrecked. As I awake, I link the dream to terrible pain waking me, jolts in my legs."

: : :

"I wish I could rest like this outside session time. Since you're paying attention, I don't have to." She's referring to not having to be vigilant, since I am witness now and that suffices. She can relax into my care. As her mind drifts, she watches the watcher, a little Chagall-like reverie, figures over roofs, bringing up impending Passover. Like Chagall's life images in the sky, the Angel of Death comes leaping, hopping, dancing over rooftops of the Children of Israel.

She speaks of preparing for Passover. "That the Angel of Death is coming makes me more watchful," Sarah says. She bemoans the watchfulness which "is as old as I am and deeper."

She associates watching with the evil eye, endless rage.

"It never stops," I say. "Rage never stops flowing from the fatal flaw." I'm thinking of a flaw or taint or warp or twist or scar, the fatal flaw of self or character or who we are, a stain you cannot wash out. Rage flows from it.

"If I knew that, I could sleep and not keep waiting for it to stop," she says and relaxes into an even more restful state.

: : :

"I reduced the Zoloft. I was already taking half the prescribed dose. I halved it again. I'm anxious and angry again. It feels good."

: : :

"My husband's personality floats on rage. Mine floats on panic."

: : :

Again she wonders what good her life is, so taken with illness. What does she produce, what can she give others?

I say, "Your sensitivity has had a big impact on a lot of people."

She comes alive, feels good. She really has an impact on her friends, those close to her, those she meets when she goes out. Her words make one more aware of emotive possibilities. She has a natural tendency to awaken spirit. "It's all Torah," she says.

CHAPTER 7 *I Could Do It*

"I could do it. I could do it." Chris couldn't believe it. Years of self-hate, ripping self, ripping others. Tearing self to nothing, shredding nothing until what is left is the shredding activity itself.

Now, something else.

It began mimicking sacrifice, mimicking being human, making believe he was a version of what he'd like to be. Too good to make up for too bad.

What he did was try to give his wife a good weekend. She liked simple things, good things: taking walks, looking at stores, having sex, good food, dancing, gardening. To spend a weekend doing what she liked meant holding off obsessive exercising, countering anorexic pulls, countering the will against pleasure. Not tolerating pleasure but tolerating not ruining it for her.

He did not simply pull it off—it really happened. Beyond what he hoped or believed. "It was miraculous and excruciating at the same time," Chris said. "Vacation is empty, meaningless space. But I contained my anxiety. She had a good time, and I could do it."

It would be too much to say he enjoyed pleasure, joy. Yet there were moments, he had to admit, when pleasure, joy appeared. He could not say they were not there. His work was not to kill them. If he could not give himself to them, he could fight against shredding them. He had to be on guard. There's no nulling the annihilating force, but he mitigated the damage. That alone opened a clearing for a good time that escaped mutilation.

Chris knew about shredding good moments to avoid their disappearance, to "control" loss. This was different. He wanted to make believe well enough, to make believe he was not shredding life as it happened. And something real happened instead.

: : :

Five days later Chris says, "You look at me and think you see a person, a caring person, a person trying to care. You don't see I'm spinning at a fast rate. My contact with what people call reality is monitored. I'm not really in the experience. I'm committed to a life of caring behavior. I believe people are connected by love, the most precious thing we know about in the universe. But I don't partake of it.

"I'm supersensitive to my pain but not to the pain of others. I'm supersensitive to the pain of others, but something is missing. I'm excruciatingly sensitive, but I don't feel for another person. I look like I'm feeling and feel that I'm feeling, but in this feeling I'm not feeling. It's the most painful thing of all, to not care in the caring, to not feel in the feeling. Parts of self are extirpated, thrown away, crushed. Parts that make it possible to feel for another.

"Others argue, point to my struggle, the good I do, as if that makes it go away. If I don't detach, I enter total terror, but that's not what I'm talking about. My coldness is not only defensive.

"Neither of my parents had basic contact with elemental reality. I fit into place with them. Basic psychosis: out of contact with the essential constitution of reality, the living truth that there are sentient beings around myself. I can barely let myself feel how hate, paranoia, self-gratification replaced that basic connection. If you say it's defensive, you can undo defenses and get to love. But if what you call defensive has become the elemental reality, if elemental reality mutates —well, maybe you can get to connection, love if you keep going, but the pain is unbearable. A background pain filled with a low-voltage electrical charge makes it impossible to let down to feel connection. Terror of surrender, fear of loss, negativity—the voltage can spike anytime you dip into it. It's too hard. Impossible.

"Months ago when you said I don't have much to live on—that was reality. I felt you saw me. I was talking about how painful it was to see the beauty of the sky and sea and woods. Beauty is painful. The beauty of love, failed love. My father's love for me, my love for my kids. He got away from the pain of it and collapsed into his own gratification. He acted big and strong but couldn't sustain the pain of love. He had to gratify himself. I'm the same way and fight it.

"I can't believe in love with the stab in my gut always going on. He struck love down when it came. The stabbing pain took its place. I ended up not believing I could love. The pain overwhelmed me and I became cold and psychopathic like he was. He looked warm, acted warm—but when you went for it, the coldness came. He was out for himself, mostly indifferent when it came to others. Whatever warmth is in me is linked to psychopathic coldness. A maelstrom of destructiveness poured into the coldness that chilled the pain and now the chill and unbearable agony are the same.

"My father's valiums got him through my childhood. 'Why should I have any discomfort?' is what he conveyed. He might as well have said, why should I love in discomfort. He couldn't bear being frightened. He couldn't understand what being so frightened meant. Frightened by love or loss or hate or terror. Never admitted any of it, afraid we'd all drop down the shaft. Well, we dropped down the shaft anyway. He popped valiums, and we fell all the way.

"Can I really detach from my kids? Yes, I can. I really don't know who I am, how to live in the world. I'm at sea, wave after wave, bits of cellular life. My panicky cells work to restore some orderly persona to get away from that moment of reality, the basic reality I can't bear. I can think it but not bear it. Thinking is not much to live for. With my thinking I can look at psychopathic reality and steer so I don't get run over and I get along. The idea of touching people's true reality is excruciating. I fantasize a viscous fluid which explodes possible warmth spreading throughout my body. If I can have the fantasy of warmth, why not do it? The destroyer, exterminator is every bit as powerful or more. Maybe if you have warmth, joy at the beginning, you can fight off the annihilator. You're positive it [warmth, joy] exists and conscious balance can be maintained. Thoughtful balance can have meaning if it connects with faith in something worthwhile. But when love and warmth blow up . . . ? Explosive-exploding warmth! No one wants to believe the loving, joyous side can be exterminated. I'm not sure what's true, and truth matters significantly here. It's crucial if love exists or not. Good therapists can't tolerate this kind of destruction. But if you can't tolerate it you can't see your own destructiveness. How *can* you be receptive to destruction? Nothing less will do.

What has to happen is not possible. Maimed, crushed, mutated sensitivity must tolerate the destruction that destroyed it. No one can do that. And that is exactly what I must have."

For Chris, basic reality is something no one can stay in touch with. It is too traumatizing, ripping. Actually, he senses two basic realities, the negatively catastrophic one, destructive through and through, and a positively catastrophic one with a nucleus of love. Neither is endurable. For Chris, love is as devastating as destruction, perhaps more so. Love opens the possibility of greater pain, heightens what destruction can destroy. Yet to feel that love is not real is worse. Chris is stuck between two unendurable states superimposed on each other. At the same time, he plays the game. He acts as if basic goodness is real and quasi-psychopathically navigates the world. He knows how to get along, look good. But deep down everything is savaged by radical doubt and despair. One might think there is goodness if goodness is mimicked. But to feel that goodness is good is an act of faith, and faith is poisoned by hate.

Chris is trapped by hate, but the trap is both too tight and not tight enough. He complains, "I envy people integrated in their hate. My father's hate was more impermeable than mine, but he'd never admit it. He looked at my nice-guy act with contempt that said, 'I got your number.' He saw I was a murderous, sensitive monster. His hate made me feel my sensitivity. 'You're too sensitive. You need to toughen up.' Only he could be the truly sensitive one, the one with values who loved life and lived it. He was sensitive so he could manipulate people's feelings. I learned to navigate from him. I look like I'm empathic and paths open for me.

"I don't believe for a minute you can contend with this. Inside I'm pounding you, punching, ripping you to shreds, crushing you, grinding you till you're pulverized, not even bone specks, nothing. What I'm afraid of is not just the terror but the disorganization it brings. Only the rage, the hate has dependable structure, compression, coherence, composure—come, come, come, complicity, compliance. There's no escape."

Compliance and hate, part of the same structure, feeding each other, growing from the soil of deeper disorganization, signified by terror. Chaotic terror with waves of rage. Rage that becomes too solid, not solid enough, a prison of hate, with openings. Love is real for moments. There are connections with others and self, heart openings. Shutdown is fast but not complete. All the things people talk and write about faith, love, connection are not just words. He weeps that he has any of these moments at all, but they short-circuit and a scream runs through them.

: : :

For a long time Chris focused on connections between gentleness and murder, responsibility and murder. Great men who are responsible, caring—kill. British gentlemen colonized the world. The "father of our country" was circumspect about assuming power but capable of organizing the death of men when necessary. TV and Hollywood portray men warm at home, cold killers outside. Hot rage at home, cold murder in the world. Mythical images of a loving God whose wrath blows your skin off your bones. An insane God for insane men. At its core, life is built around madness, fundamental insanity. What makes this more galling is that Chris feels there *could* be basic sanity. There could be more sanity if madness was deeply recognized.

"And now there's all this dribble about biochemistry. Insanity is biochemical. So the insanity of the human race is biochemical, and everyone's going to be on medication? You're going to medicate insanity out of existence? I feel like screaming, `Why don't you speak to my experience?!'

"There are many kinds of concentration camps. My inner experience is a concentration camp. I've become a kind of commandant, a killer tyrant aimed at my own life and the aliveness of others. It's the only way I can deal with pain. Kill the pain, the torment, kill life. Tell me the ways we murder each other, all the soul murders, are biochemical. Biochemical, neurological, structural—that's the way we're made. What is amazing is we have the potential to transcend the way we're made. We have the potential to be other ways. We can be killers and saints. Ordinary killers and ordinary saints. You're telling me it's biochemical makes me want to call you a moron. It's biochemical that we're many ways, loving murderers. It's good to get this into articulated form but my neck is screaming, screaming, screaming shooting up the side of my head.

"I wonder if you feel as I do, that someone can talk back to his oppressor, then dissolve in insane rage. I stand up to my killer but throw myself into a wall, slamming back and forth not just out of rage but with the energy of madness, the force of chaotic feelings. The energy of madness fills me up till I want to slam into a wall. Maybe the pain of a broken nose can organize me. Psychic pain drives me crazy. The pain of smashing into a wall brings me a moment of relief, a moment where there's some organization, relief from unbearable chaos, rage. A hate so huge I can't embody it. It balloons outside of my body and I connect to a little bit of the balloon with my eyes. The balloon is everywhere, eyes connected with it. Can I bring it into my body? Will it cohere, congeal, make my body my own? So insane. Scream until I die, scream for eternity, scream forever. For what they did. World filled with what they did. I want my scream to stop people, blow them apart. My scream is the only potent force I have. My arms flap. The scream will go through everything, everybody, only if they see it, feel it and blow up—my only hope."

: : :

Chris tries with all his might to withstand the killer. He creates space for survival—barely. He weeps over his plight, can't believe this is the life he has. He shoulders it under protest. God must answer. Survival involves grinding everything into nothing. Only if there is nothing, is anything tolerable at all, although nothing itself is tormenting. The effort is too much, and he collapses into the energy of madness, rage/hate/terror beyond organization. Yet organizations arise—a balloon instead of a body. Chris fights to have a body of his own, each step taken with and against the energy of madness.

He affirms that the basic reality is connection, love. Alteration of the basic reality renders sensitivity insensitive and hypersensitive, mutilated, scarred. Destruction becomes the altered basic reality that he cannot get out of. He envisions a different life, seeing love through a glass wall. The destroyer finds it as fast as it forms. He slams against his walls to obliterate the destroyer and find moments of relief. He lives for those moments. What if destruction is the basic reality after all?

He speaks of concentration camps inside, not only outside. All kinds of concentration camps. He is like an inducted vampire, a victim who carries the destructive plague. Trauma is everywhere fueling destruction, and we try not to see it or find workable targets to absorb it. We cannot believe life is like this. We want to change the biochemistry of life. Put life on Prozac. He looks at me with love at the end of many sessions, as he heads out the door. He loves me for letting him pulverize me, turn me into nothing, for being there in the nothing. A nearly secret love. It does not stop the torment, at times adds to it.

: : :

"One thing I hate most about myself is wishing others ill. I know it's natural, part of hostility, part of longing. We're filled with opposites, love and hate. I feel how sensitive I am. Scared of getting hurt. Sensitivity dissolves into chaotic terror. Hostility strengthens me, tones sensitivity down. Sensitivity and injury go together. Hostility is a hardening technique. Wishing others ill dilutes their power to hurt me. I'm a tombstone engraved with past injuries. I bury sensitivity with hate. Yet nothing hurts me more than wishing others harm.

"It hurts to hurt others. I hate the satisfaction that poisons me when something bad happens to them. I'd rather die than have this inside me. But the point is I live and have to live with this in me, my face rubbed in things I'd rather not be.

"I want our soldiers to die. I want the heads on CNN, the White House, the Pentagon to be wrong. I want them to be shown wrong and everyone to know it. Bin Laden is inside me. A bedrock place, wishing they die as payback for their arrogance. I want them to be humiliated in their certainty. Where is their sensitivity? I can't stand it if they win.

"Inside me is my father's desperation cemented in smugness. It makes me want to vomit. When I was younger I wished him dead. Now that he's gone, I wish it again and again. I keep wishing him dead. This goes beyond imagining. Imagining can't go far enough.

"My mother is all edges. Barbed wire, squibs of feeling. I cut the wire to pieces. The instant she dies, I hope her eyes widen in horror and she knows. She'll go into the unknown knowing what she was, what she did, what it was like for me. She'll have to die knowing she is a killer. She maimed an infant's soul. This is what sensitivity subjects you to. You hate it and yourself and wish there could be sensitivity without so much injury. You look at what countries and groups do to each other. It's part of one circle."

Chris's hating himself for hating others, especially for wishing others ill, is a long-standing complaint. He takes it as a sign of his inhumanity. It is proof of a basic inhumanity that characterizes human beings. His sensitivity registers the inhuman in human affairs and recoils. To take satisfaction in the suffering of others—how can we stand it? How can we stand this side of ourselves! Chris wonders why everyone is not up in arms about it, shouting from every tower. Here is the great alarm, the great call to prayer, the hate virus that permeates us. This is what we should be talking about, this is what should be on CNN—not who's doing what to whom, but that this exists at all, that it permeates, that it dominates.

A special turn his unconscious takes here is that he feels bad about feeling good about bad things that happen to others after a secret love for me germinates. For the moment, he feels especially bad over glee concerning what is faulty, inept, lacking in me and bad things that happen to me. He secretly gloats that he is better than I am, but secret love torments him the more. Can I survive the satisfaction he takes in my inferiority? This moment translates into an emblem of what is wrong with humanity: a pervasive sadism with regard to being better or worse than others. Chris cannot take this trait for granted. It is a fatal flaw that must be worked with. He cannot understand why everyone does not drop everything to attend to it. What can be more important?

You can see his "basic reality" shifting from love to hate. He begins tasting secret love and feeling bad about his hate. Hate is a defense against the pain of love. Love is basic. As he hates himself for his hate, hate spirals and past a hairsbreadth becomes a starting point for hating not just the hate of humanity, but hating a humanity that hates. Our soldiers, our government, our news media, his father, his mother—there are reasons to hate, to hate war, to hate righteousness, to hate abuse glowing with innocence. But suddenly something shifts and his vantage point *is* hate. Hate becomes "basic reality." Love becomes persecutory, a lie—and the underneath festering increases, because love is also felt as truth. He ends with a renewed appeal to sensitivity. To feel one's own or anyone's pain is tantamount to glimpsing pain everywhere. Chris ends with a vision of oneness. What happens to groups happens to individuals, what happens to individuals happens to groups.

: : :

"I have no skin." Actually, he perceives layers of skin. Thick skin out, thin skin in. Thin skin out, thick skin in. Then, no skin. The Romans skinned Rabbi Akivah, who rejoiced at the moment of death that he could love God with all his might, with his totality, both souls, with good and evil inclinations. They skinned the evil out of him as an ultimate gift to God.

Chris was trying to skin the evil out of himself, out of all of us. The more he skinned, the more he found, although in less crude form. He became excruciatingly sensitive to an attitude of superiority that intensified when something bad happened to others. "At those moments I feel, 'I'm better than you because it didn't happen to me.'" But *he* happened to him. He cannot skin himself out of himself no matter how hard he tries. It is like being an animal caught in a trap, trying to free itself by gnawing its leg off.

For human beings, the trap and the trapped is the psyche. No matter how much it tries to get out of itself, or we try to get out of it, trap and gnawing continue.

Chris feels he is a failure because he cannot get rid of himself. He cannot rid himself of his share of human nature. He feels skinless and not skinless enough. How can he become skinless through and through? He feels caring and uncaring at the same time, so that caring feels like a lie and lying feels like truth. Caring on the outside, cold on the inside. Or cold outside and caring inside. Frighteningly sensitive and insensitive. A relentless way to live. Layers of skin, no skin at all.

One never knows where cruelty comes from. "I'm supersensitive to *better than* everywhere. Sensitivity glued to hate. I see *better than* at work and hate it. Layers of skin fold around it, defend it. The hate

I feel for the Enron executive laughing at California's energy crisis, mocking it, comparing it to the Titanic. Totally oblivious to the tidal wave heading his way!" Wherever Chris found a skin shield, a pretend mold, he found *better than* at work. Thus his commitment to the idea of becoming skinless, sinless. Ruthless tearing at the trap, the limbs of psyche.

CHAPTER 8 *Totalities*

"Rage leads to madness, confusion," Gershom says with a thudding voice that sounds like a hammer with a cloth around it. He pounds with his voice over and over, hoping to break through rage and open the possibility of love that is believable.

"Sunshine is cold. Sunshine chills." He becomes a five-year-old boy kicking in a coffin. He tries to feel the sunshine is warm. He knows it is warm for others. He kicks against the coffin. What is real is the rage of his body.

I ask if this rage is another kind of sun. No, he tells me, it is burnt out, a hole, a power linked with powerlessness. It runs on endless fuel, fills him, numbs him.

I feel a bright sun in my belly, then a dark sun. The bright-dark sun in my belly feels good to me. It is exciting, arousing, comforting. For Gershom it is horrible. His body explodes. His belly sun is a bomb. "There's no way to convey the *bursting* inside, hurtling me hundreds of miles per second."

Intense body becomes sexual, rage and sex uniting, feeding each other. Fury desecrates eros but turns it on, fuels, impoverishes, enriches. Richness of rage.

Gershom speaks of his fantasy of a totally available woman. He has had tastes of such experience in early promiscuity, in marriage. Total rage and fantasy of total fulfillment. He has had tastes of a totally available woman. Tastes incite rage.

Total rage is a fantasy. Body limits rage. There is more rage than body can keep up with. A baby's scream cannot exhaust the rage it feels. Rage is infinite, body finite. We lack concepts to do justice to this predicament. Gershom's body is exploding, and when it exhausts itself, Gershom continues to explode. Where is he when he explodes without his body?

Gershom was furious at women for not being totally available. He pretended not to know that total availability would not guarantee fulfillment. But he suspected. He had inklings that "totality" was a sham, a fantasy, a hallucination. A hallucinatory rager—his life in danger of being swallowed by hallucinatory excess. He had to fight to find a clearing, a thread, a break in dementia. If you met him, he would be mild and appealing, kindly, informed. He had good values. You probably would like him.

"It maddens me that my mother was near but I could not get to her," says Gershom. He felt his mother's sexual aliveness in his pores. She was not a very good caretaker. She was busy with worries about her body or in a daze. He could feel her body but could not feel *her*. There were moments she lit up with beauty. There were moments she was a good caretaker. When the light vanished, there was a void. Gershom felt a crater where a feeling might have been. He could not give up on feeling she was there if he could find her.

He tried to drive women crazy. "If I could induce profound desire, they would feel grateful to me for even more profound gratification." Fantasy of extreme desire, gratitude for more than total fulfillment. Mother would light up forever. "I was lucky. I married such a woman. A woman who lights up. But my other side comes and won't let go. Her satisfaction is not enough. I need to control her feelings. They must be there because of me. I turn them on, all the way on, keep them on, and I turn them off. Her body is under my control—totally controlled by me. It's awful having such a psyche. Such need for total domination kills me, but I can't let go. Are you supposed to feel that way when you're five years old? Like a demon inside, letting a demon dominate." That Gershom felt this way since he was a little boy was one reason why he was kicking in a coffin.

"Rage bursts/eros bursts. Void bursts through them. A baby's sensitivity needs to have a mixture of respect and love or it goes under and becomes inflamed. You can't pretend. You can know how to make money, look good, have amazing talents. But you can't fool a baby and get away with it. Try to fool a baby, you're left with hate.

"I've got to pee, piss the hate out. The coherence of rage disorganizes me. Having to pee disorganizes me. I can pee in my pants, diminish myself. You can't stay in the full force of yourself. You piss yourself away.

"I'm an infant. My father impregnates me with rage. His rage multiplies mine. To live this rage is madness. And if there's no other way to be? A feeling says it isn't so.

"I read in the newspaper that a teenage killer is sorry now. But some kids are just bad. The prosecutor is a hard woman who scoffs at his being sorry. To her he's bad and trying to wiggle out of it. She doesn't believe he means it. Her hardness matches his. Like a parent's rage matches an infant's. Some people get inside you through your rectum, worming up inside your body, and you see your body becoming not yours. You rage to try to make it yours again. You just have insanity. Nothing else.

"You cry to God, dear God, what did you do with me? You leave me pissing rage inside my parts like poison. From the neck up I'm a statue. I'm surrendering to the poison. No one cleans me.

"Part of my body is OK. Part of me believes you listen and hear. I believe you'd tell me if you thought there was something I could do. There's nothing to do except wait.

"I push away an innocent boy in me. Why don't I embrace him? Is he lost to me? Do I refuse to believe he's there? What could he do with this hole? Am I trying to save him from it? I'll take on the grief of missing him in order to protect him from what I go through? I wish you could see inside this hole, stick your hand in, your mind and heart in, and pull out that boy. I'm going farther and farther into a big sleep.

"I hate my father for leaving. Knowing my soul was in danger. I hate him for sticking himself into me, possessing me. I want to throw him out, sleep him off. He'll always feel superior unless I murder him. Only by murder can I be on top.

"No matter what I say, I seem a nice Jewish boy. I'll never get across what infuriates me. No one can feel it. No one feels the realness of my truth. I know you're trying. But do you really get it? My father could not face the truth about himself. I've inherited falsehood that never lets up. It runs through me like a critical drill. Falsehood. Falsehood. He felt the hardships of life justified exploiting people. Left traumatized souls in his wake and didn't bat an eyelash. Yet he thought of himself as sensitive. I'm his missing conscience. A warped version, ticking falsehood, choking on lies. I can't take an eye off them. This is no way to live. This is not what's supposed to happen, not the way to be a person. I refuse to be like him. I'm determined not to inflict such injury. I hold back. Work on myself always. But it seeps into my children. It damages them without their knowing. I fight it. My path is not to give in. I refuse to make believe it isn't there. I know it. My path is to see madness everywhere. To oppose it yet never get out of it. And those around me pay the price for my knowing, like I paid the price for his not knowing."

: : :

Two weeks later Gershom describes himself as broken pieces, rupture, with an island of hate in it. In day-to-day life, no one sees the pieces, the hate. "No one knows," he says repeatedly. I think of the spiritual, "Nobody Knows the Troubles I've Seen."

For Gershom "no one knows" means we are sealed off from one another. In some way he is in a sensory deprivation chamber, solitary confinement, unable to contact living souls. Perhaps this is what drives people to try to contact intelligent life in outer space, since we cannot contact each other.

"You're going to gnaw your way into my left side," he observes. "So much pain, death, terror. I can reach my arm out, touch it. My daughter's anger hurts. She pushes me away. If I get close it's really terrifying. Diaphragm tightens. I'm tempted to do what my father did, puff myself out over the tightness, or what my mother did, collapse into it. I look at death and never feel joined. I touch the tightness and abort myself, abort closeness, protect others from me, protect my children. There's not much protection from such forces.

"I can never spread out and inhabit my body because of sensitive sensations." Acute sensations now go up his anus and back. "'Don't have such thin skin,' people say. Like saying, 'It's only a dream,' if sleep experience frightens you. People dismiss everything." He breathes in-out, feels his breathing, murmurs, "I wonder, I wonder . . ." After a silence he remembers a dream. "You extend yourself. I bask in it. I see you're being good natured. Should I believe it? I fear you're faking. I'm hostile."

"In the dream?" I ask.

"No, now, thinking about the dream."

"You're suspicious of the dream?"

"There was good feeling in the dream. But now I'm not dreaming. Now I'm my hostile self."

"Self or mind?"

"Hostile mind thinking spiked thoughts, sticking you, sticking me."

"Protecting itself from the good feeling? From the dream?"

"My world's cracking, coming apart. There are no words for the feeling, the mix of grief, awe, fear. So many losses."

Neither Gershom nor I quite know what he meant by losses. Loss of dominance by hostile head? Loss of heart because it cracks when good feeling touches it? Fear of loss if he believes the good feeling his dream produces? Loss of dreaming if dreaming lies? Loss of me if I'm a lie, his lying twin? Loss we know nothing of? Loss preceding time, seedbed of time, loss that fosters time, time's medium?

: : :

Raw sensitivity under attack. Everything impacts. I'm piecing together remarks from several sessions: "Your voice, your look. Strip away everything and you're left with sensitivity exposed. Quivering. This morning I got up and hung on a bar, stretching my diaphragm. Sensitivity vibrating. Who needs a vibrator? The universe breaks apart the sensitive core. Sensitivity is the core, breaking and breaking, quivering.

"Where does attack come from? Raw sensitivity feels like attack. A sensitivity attack. It attacks itself to lessen its impact. It turns to pain to stop the quivering. It turns against itself to stop the pain. Bits of it break off, form malevolent amalgams to tone down the sensitive pulse. Mind breaks off, rises to the top, a top mind forms to regulate sensitivity. Things get violent. Top mind attacked by sensitivity. Top mind attacks back. Attacking the unbearable. Ripping, toning sensitivity down, wiping it out. You end up supersensitive and dead. Top mind and sensitivity hate each other. They can't hold on to the realization they are in this together.

"A universe with only deadness makes no sense. There has to be aliveness. But aliveness is unbearable. Aliveness is *too* alive. Trees, colors, beauty: *too* painful. Death ends this, settles over everything, the grief of ending. Death settles over everything now, tones it down. Aliveness, deadness—neither is bearable.

"My father was more adroit at co-opting my emotional than intellectual life. I still have some privacy with regard to thinking—yet it's thinking that tones things down. For me, privacy is deadening. Deadness is privacy. My father pressured me to feel certain ways. I resisted but not entirely, and when my feelings were giving in I'd be hiding in a private room of thought, watching. My thinking forked. One path unforgiving, relentless, hostile, critical. The other longing for real reflection, lucidity.

"Relief means deadness. I don't want to be dead. I see what's out there. I touch it, feel it. Feeling is too painful and quickly dies out. My wife says nature calms her, brings her peace. I walk in the woods and beauty burns me and it is too painful to talk."

He lapses into mute pain which turns into death.

: : :

Gershom is caught between two unbearables, aliveness and deadness. Between sessions death grows stale. His personality collapses into a degraded baseline of terror and hate, as chronic as death. It is what he can tolerate. It comes closer to say that no state is tolerable, not even collapse into hate-filled terror and terror-filled hate.

"It's one thing to be flawed, another to be rotted through," he says. "A piece of wood eaten up by water bugs. So little can be done. But in that space of what little can be done, I've done all I can."

And so he has. He gives all he has to many people. He never stops working on himself with all his might and glows as a result of this work. He has created a presence which he can't make use of from the inside, but which does good in the world.

"It hurts. My defenses have thinned to the point I know I'm avoiding feelings with people I'm connected to. A capacity to trace every nuance of incapacity. It's rare. People shrink from doing it themselves, this need to go just about anywhere. There are rewards. One is I don't hurt my wife anymore—not as much as I did. I can almost feel it's pleasant making love—it *is* pleasant. I can touch her without causing pain."

Gershom needed to cause pain, draw blood. To feel a woman's pain was important to him. Now he dares to try to feel her love. To feel his love. Love is almost plausible. "The love in her eyes rips through layers of pain," he says. He speaks of love as part of a supporting sea, everything else in it. He knows it's there, but is it there for him? He believes it is real for others, but every time his heart threatens to open, it rips. Melting tears him. "My father didn't know what sex was. He had a lot of it, but for him it was domination. He rationalized exploitation as being true to the call of life, life's imperative. My contraction mirrors his expansion. But I caught the disease, I'm like him. My wife is different. She teaches real opening. She offers another model. I thank God—whoever, whatever that might or might not be—for letting me know something else through my wife. My father pushed me into life but disfigured me, tightened me. I thank God my wife wants to touch my heart, even if it cracks." Gershom starts to tear, wipes his eyes.

For a moment, he is taken aback that he relaxed his grip on speaking, that words came with less control, and in this relaxation notices that he is seen—lovingly seen by his wife. "All my life I've used words like my father used women's bodies. To effect ends I want. Now I feel someone sees me as I really am, not as a reptile. I would have gone from one woman to another, looking for one whose beauty could calm my insides. I'd like to relax this contraction awhile." He speaks of his diaphragm as holding within holding. A muscle spasm is his being. Seeping through is someone seeing him as he really is—his wife. I don't seem to play much of a role, but it is doubtful he could begin to let her in this way without the background support of therapy. For Gershom, truth has been a hammer, a drill. His wife offers another kind of truth, beyond or other than psychic bloodletting.

As might be expected, by our next session rage and death became overpowering, drowning hints of thawing out. It was too much to let his wife in a little, to be touched by love. I thought of the man in Graham Greene's *Brighton Beach* who killed a woman rather than allow her to melt his armor. Better to pull a trigger than feel something. The theme for Gershom is more complicated, since he is driven nearly mad by his sensitivity. He pulls the trigger against himself, killing his own feelings. Love triggers rage. It's not even that he pulls the trigger; a gun goes off and he begins to die. His own rage kills him, blows him to oblivion, which he fights.

He has some moments of feeling better, fuller, his body opens. Rage flows through him, doesn't jam, coagulate, spoil. He feels rage more directly, less done in by it, almost warms with it, then his mind takes its desperate turn. Gershom speaks of a United States Senator who, while in the army, killed civilians as a by-product of war. "He said he once knew innocence, felt good, felt God was with him. That's nothing I knew. Noise spread through my body, no center. The only thing I have is rage. You must have contempt for me. I know I have contempt for you. I hate you for getting all the good stuff. You and the senator. Can you imagine him unhappy because he can't feel the good stuff anymore—he once had it?! I hear my mother saying she gave me good stuff. She claims she sacrificed. But I don't *feel* that. I wish it would end. It's too hard. If I change, people won't know and I can't tell them. If it was just me, I could find some way to live with it, go off alone. I'm probably fooling myself. I can't live with it. I can't live with rage poison seeping into children.

"I don't believe there's a lot of people walking around like this, even if the whole world is filled with insanity. People hush it. What could be is giving my wife and others pleasure. What is is a monster. There's no way out of this madness. I can't stand on one spot and meet one thing for one second. Trying to be a man makes me go to sleep like a baby."

His thoughts become sexual and he puts himself down. "A real man would want to give pleasure to a woman. I want her gratitude. I want her to pleasure me. I can't deal with her being absent or into her own body or self. I need to cling. My wife's love eyes decimate me. They threaten to make me come alive. The alternative is my mother's death eyes, not there at all, layers of deadness. She clothed us with deadness so we wouldn't feel real or feel reality. Die die or live die—death wraps itself around aliveness and deadens it. No options but different sorts of death.

"You can't make your body come together when these things are happening. Maybe if God took me in his arms and said, 'Now you can feel safe . . .' My Father tried and I relaxed in his arms, inside his body and got betrayed, usurped, pushed into, pushed out of myself and had to fight for my life. I just want to be dead. I just want to be . . ." His voice trailed off. "I'm in a waking sleep, wide awake fast asleep." The room was quiet. Gershom headed toward stupor, like an insect bound in a ball by a spider, a form of dazed hibernation.

: : :

Between sessions he worked hard not to attack his wife when he felt like melting. It was all he could do to force himself to stay present for extra instants. He could scarcely wait to start attacking me when session time came. He attacked to shore himself up in the face of melting. He read some of my writing and knew I was giving talks on psychoanalysis and mysticism and this fueled attacks too. He was convinced he was a better speaker. He saw me as hesitant, awkward, whereas he could compel an audience. That I seemed to be successful puzzled and enraged him and it was hard to know what to do with the fact that he was coming to me. Perhaps he'd be a better therapist for himself than I, if he could clone himself, a little like fellating himself, if only the latter worked. Meanwhile, he was stuck with me as well as with himself. Attacking seemed to go on and on, caught in its own momentum, sweeping "reasons" in its path.

"I pictured you as wimpy, with a walled-off spirituality out of contact with the world. Obviously you're not like me. I come on assertive, aggressive, a player. You're held back, doubting, tentative. Yet you get pleasure. You talk about ecstasy—you get thrills from your talks and writings. If I get such feelings at all, in milliseconds, they're followed by pain and fear of loss. It enrages me not being able to hold on to good. Are my own experiences unreal? Seeing you is terrifying, makes me contract. The you in my mind is not like you in your books or you in this room. I can't take in that you aren't as out-of-it as I think you are. You talk like you're in contact with life, the world. I don't expect it, don't believe it. It makes my sense of you unreal, my body tense with terror. I could shatter into thousands of little sparkling pieces.

"I'm dangerous and I've warned you and you think you're strong enough to withstand it. But I think you're a wimp and will collapse. I can't do this, act like this anywhere except here. No one could take it. It's too outside the normal. My wife says I try to take her apart. It's a lucky thing you talk funny, whine a little—or in my envy I'd have to murder you. Now I just want to be dead. I've no sense at all how to live in a world like this. All there is—terror of touch, fragments so intense they explode body, mind.

"Sometimes I enter psychotic places and feel a strange warmth, not a good warmth. It's like seeing flowers, sun, beauty, but with an intensity that has no name, an experience with elements of horror, unendurable grief, helplessness, terror, and something else with no name whatsoever, and rage and hate. I picture making the other moan, puncture, swoon. I'm afraid of rejection. The moment you set a boundary I'll shatter into millions of pieces.

"I'm right on the edge of talking in a voice I never use, I'm so used to trying to sound OK, pretending to be good. My father was right about me. He thought I was too good to be true. It's worthy to devote yourself to restraining your predatory instincts but this is my only chance at life. I don't want it if it's all fucked up. My kid hugs me, loves me, feels it all through in a way I can't. I want to dissolve, but you—you're dangerous, you could let go of me or get cold or protect yourself and release me into the cold. I never could talk about this—I couldn't do it. Dissolving is explosive. Contact blows me apart. I need this analytic setup. I have two desperate wishes: you tell everyone about this; you learn from this. It makes me feel equal, even connected, if you learn. I need you to say, 'You're good.' That's what I want. But when it happens everything explodes. It's not believable."

I, too, can collapse, explode, fragment in the face of impact. Perhaps that is part of why Gershom saw me as wimpy and semicollapsed. He needed to imagine there was someone who could withstand him. Perhaps, also, he needed the sense that no one could. Emotions must be too much for anyone, since they were too much for him. Could anyone stand being a feeling self? The ones who came closest to doing so in his life were his wife and child. He believed his child's hug, his wife's eyes, embrace. But his belief shattered him.

He could not reconcile the me in the room with the me in his mind. In his mind, my weakness, collapsed aspects, were magnified. How could this other me also be—one who loved life, who gave himself to living? He was tempted to reduce me to shards of my worst elements, but somewhat pulled back, protecting me, dodging me. How could I be so unreal and real at the same time? Would it be better if I were furious—my rage matching his rage? I was not exactly his explosive father or empty mother. But I was not without quivering mixtures of feelings and emptiness. I believe in the power of waiting—things happen when you wait that might be lost if you pretend to be just one thing or the other.

Gershom was shaken by what to make of me—an order of reality-unreality that irritated him. He may wish to murder me but feels I already am murdered. Since he does not have to murder a murdered man, his need to kill someone like me (at least in his mind) is frustrated. Yet something of me seems to have escaped total murder and still seeks life. Can murder ever keep up with life-seeking elements? Can murder ever be absolute? Perhaps that is the underlying movement of this therapy: life in Gershom arises, but he knows that life triggers death, the more life, the more death. He seizes on me to organize his doubt. Can we survive not surviving each other and ourselves? Sensitivity attacks him and he attacks it. Can an aliveness he cherishes, that he knows exists, survive and come through its own sensitive, attacking nature? He worries life cannot withstand him and suffers the more dreadful conviction that aliveness cannot withstand itself.

"I dreamt of a lot of men dancing with my patient, Lance, everyone enjoying each other. Rare for me to feel that way. I usually feel on the outside, a barrier between me and everyone. Now I'm locating a good feeling and want to say it's always there but I rarely tune into it. It's there but noise inside and outside blocks it. A good feeling mixed up with ill-at-ease stuff. A tingling mixing."

"The dream sifts a current you tend to play down."

"There it is, no denying it. It's good and for the moment I'm happy with it, but I'm afraid it will fade and noise will cover it. Can a dream last forever?"

Max goes through many hells—as, I learn, does Lance—although it is easing up for both of them.

"Lance returned from death," Max says. "He was alcoholic, drug dead. Stimulants numbed him. Killed him over many years. Trauma shredded him and what trauma failed to do, drugs and alcohol finished.

"He was raised in a cult—razed, I think. Crazed, demanding people, knew what's right for the world. Knew what's right for children! No sense of kids as kids. Children are instruments to propagate cult values. Lance was alone with his agony, grown-ups telling him what to think and feel, telling him he was in heaven when he was in hell.

"Drugs, alcohol—stimulants, painkillers, trauma killers. Kill what's killing you and you kill yourself. Drown your sorrows, you drown yourself. You know the phrase, 'drugged out of your mind'—exactly. He dragged himself into my office, fell into it. As if my office was another station for a long fall in progress. What surprised me was the way he spoke so humbly. Alcoholics Anonymous helped but he wanted more. Maybe I was moved by his desperation, his sincerity—a danger with addicts. Maybe I was moved because he felt so beaten."

"You admire his brokenness?"

"Envy it, in a way. All the hells I've gone through—I've not gone all the way, never let myself get that beaten. Life beats me. I beat me. But I've never quite given in to it. I've stayed a little to the side, some of me in reserve. Lance's voice seemed part of a demolition in progress, a hollowed out cry from inside the demolition. He was living somewhere closed to me."

"Living, dying."

"I feel his dying is a kind of living. I can't go down that far.

"As far as Lance did?"

"Yes, as far as Lance, that far."

"And wherever you both are now, you want more."

"We want more." After long moments Max added, "I feel I don't have the right to more if I don't go down as far as Lance. Yet he doesn't feel the right for more either, and he's been there."

"Neither of you has the right for more, but you feel he's earned it and you haven't. For you it would be premature, for him overdue."

"Premature more. Overdue more. They cancel each other. The result is the same: no more."

"No—more!" slips out of me. More is what we want! Meritless more, a form of grace.

"You mean whether I'm ready or not—more."

Max "got" it. The more that is ours whether we earn it or not, whether or not we deserve it. The more that is there. The more that is hard to take if we are just who we are where we are. The more that keeps us in life.

"Something unusual happened the night before the dream. I was dancing with my sister at a party. It was like a dream itself. We really enjoyed each other. I scarcely believed it was happening. So loose, fluid. It made me sad we've had so few moments together. Our lives have gone in different directions. Me a therapist, she in business. After dancing everyone looked good to me.

"Why did my dream turn this into men dancing with Lance? There was a moment I thought my sister male, angular, then she seemed open, vulnerable, happy. An instant vanished into a dream. Male elements, male to male, a male connection with my sister. The other night I saw a video of men dancing—*Zorba the Greek*. Everything went wrong that could go wrong—and they danced. They danced on the ashes of catastrophe. For the moment, my sister and I were outside trauma. We danced beyond catastrophe. Is it possible for trauma to fall away, to dance through trauma?

"My dream dance is a good feeling that survives catastrophe. I think of dancers in Matisse—life alive on a cliff. Lance's life survived steep cliffs—barely. Lance is a part of me that cannot dance, that stopped dancing or never learned to. For some people the dance of death is the dance of life or no dance at all. Someone like me who cannot be fully alive envies someone who can do anything fully. He dies more fully than I live. Death envy. I feel myself in his cry."

"Tell me more about Lance's cry."

"Sometimes Lance seems to be a kind of sensitive lump, clotted, immovable, thick. No matter how numb he gets, he is somehow sensitive. His sensitivity never dies, not for long. A bombed-out sensitivity that never stops crying.

"Lance is an injured soul. He tells me he always felt wrong. His mother's look made him feel nothing was right. She wasn't cutting, like his father. There was something oblique about the way she put him down. He felt pinned to her by something bad in him, a bug trapped in its droppings. Whatever he did was not what she was looking for. She was looking for something that wasn't there. To please her he had to become the thing that wasn't there. Nothing at all.

"He came alive with his father but it was the aliveness of getting killed over and over. His father was cutting and criticized everything. He set standards no one could live up to. He would come into Lance's life long enough to let him know nothing was good enough, then vanish into the cult's reforming activities. Lance used to say he got pressed by two different molds (mother and father), both wrong.

"Lance was obese when I met him. Slow, heavy. With a deep appreciation of beauty and the beauty of feelings. He relished the feel of little things throughout a day. Little things that led to big thoughts. Any change of feeling triggered reflections about the spirit of the day."

Max spoke about a connection between Lance's sensitivity and drink and drugs. The latter dampen and heighten feelings, increasing-decreasing sensitivity. Sensitivity is responsive to change in either direction. But this kind of "regulation" of emotional temperature does not solve the damage sensitivity experiences. Other people function like drink and drugs, food for feelings, to stimulate/soften the flow of reverie. When their input falters or causes him trouble, Lance can get rageful and abusive. His rages used to be worse. They've lessened but he has to watch.

"For a long time, I did not fully realize how rageful Lance could be," Max continued. "Therapy was a blessing for him, a place he could shine. A place his feelings could be appreciated. I so enjoyed his soft, slow, meaningful talk I could be lulled into forgetting how hard it was for him to be with another person in the way people really are together, when the focus is not mainly on one or the other. I looked the other way because of the contact with himself he let me share. He filled me with feelings and meanings. He filled me with himself. I didn't realize I was getting a demonstration of how others function to feed him feelings and otherwise are a nuisance. Feeling feed—that's all we're good for. Beauty, feelings, reverie, rage. But when emotional life is damaged, a Niagara Falls of feeling won't do the trick. Feelings fall forever but nothing takes hold. Nothing develops.

"My dream of Lance means he is inside me, part of me, meaningful to me. If I let him in, maybe he can let me in. All the men dancing with him—they're my feelings. We're together. I'm not shutting him out. I'm not shutting myself out. By making contact with him, I'm making contact with myself. I think the dream shows our relationship is developing in a feeling way, mine and Lance's, yours and mine."

Bion remarks that "anxiety in the analyst is a sign that the analyst is refusing to 'dream' the patient's material." The analyst is not letting the patient in. Resistance in the analyst is related to a refusal or inability to let the patient become part of one's emotional digestive system, to let dreamwork work the patient over. To work the patient over by dreamwork means, among other things, initiating or furthering the working over of traumatic impacts that wounded the patient's ability to digest experience. A function of therapy is to better digest impacts that damage the capacity to digest experience.

Max is surprised by the influx of good feelings in his dream. What he envies in Lance is his ability to be destroyed and survive destruction. Max remembers moments as a youth when he admired bums, wished he could be one, bum envy. They meant freedom for him, life on the road. Dread of destruction saved him, turned him into a therapist. He could taste severe destruction by proxy, through patients. Lance lived this side of things out for him, while he, Max, provided Lance a safe harbor over time. Lance gravitated to Max's being as well as Max to Lance's. They provided each other with tastes of experiences each needed.

"I'm beginning to digest his presence, so he can digest mine"—a principle of incipient mutuality. One could probably speak of homoerotic components between Max, Lance, and myself and of father-son feelings. These elements have their place and time. Now it is enough to appreciate that Max (partly through Lance, me) is dancing emotional digestion into life. A moment's grace that can spread. An inclusive moment, in which Max felt part of humanity, humanity part of him.

Max's dream dance and dance with his sister fed a network of feelings growing in him. Lance, in part, symbolized ways Max wasted himself and his chance at living, a life-destroying tendency that was opening to something better. While Max did not go down the tubes as devastatingly as Lance, he was plagued by a sense of something semicollapsed, a psychic lung not working well. The good feeling in the dream and with his sister did not cure his background sense of being semidisabled emotionally, but every bit of growth counts. Max and Lance were getting better together.

For Max, dancing was outside his usual activities. In fact, he did not dance in his dream. Other men and Lance did it for him. Nevertheless, an underlying sense was growth of capacity for living, where dancing and life go together. Dancing symbolizes life, an affirmation of aliveness. However, there are cases in which dancing and life oppose each other or involve subtle complications.

: : :

Rod was a dance instructor who sought help after the devastating breakup of his second marriage. His wife had been one of his dance partners, and together they founded a successful dance school. With the help of a relentless lawyer, she outmaneuvered Rod in the divorce settlement, so that she took the school and their apartment and he had to start from scratch.

He described himself as uncharacteristically passive in the face of the settlement. He just gave up. At the same time, he had an inflated sense that it didn't matter, he could build a new life easily enough. He was young enough, forty-four, strong enough, able enough. Inflation and deflation go together, whether in response to each other or fused. Without quite realizing it, Rod was partly breaking down. He thought people on the street were talking about him. He could not complete a task. He buzzed with anxiety when he went out and sat alone for days.

None of this affected his dancing. It was not that he came together when he danced. His dancing was more a unit by itself, together in itself, outside him, outside his life. His personal life did not affect his dancing, and the togetherness of his dancing did not make his personal life any better. Each ran on a different track.

His relationship with his wife also ran on different tracks. One track was nice, light, irrelevant—they would banter, make small talk, a kind of happy disconnection that got them through the day. The other track was mean, dense, tangled, explosive. A magnet pulled them to say the wrong things. A special magnet that pulls and pushes toward injury. They could happily disconnect only so long before the wounding force picked up steam.

Relationships set challenges. All must deal with wounding forces. Some people take advantage of familiarity by giving free reign to the wounding impulse. In extreme instances, the relationship gets sucked into, reduced to, the worst elements, as if it exists as an excuse for toxic, damaging properties. The relationship survives in a malignant key, tyrannical, parasitic, abusive. One gets what nourishment one can from toxic material, but the results can be devastating. Negative tendencies play a role in better, richer relationships too, but are offset by a greater degree of caring and mutuality. In one way or another, people "decide" whether a relationship is worth working with, worth getting through the bad stuff that is part of it.

Rod and his wife got along best when their relationship was superficial. Living together put too much pressure on their attempt to keep things trivial, and they were not prepared for the hurtful tendencies that began to dominate. There was not enough between them to get outside the pull toward injury and counter it with caring. When she dropped him, there was no place for the wounding force to go, and he began to feel the pain of what it did to him. He became food for his own wounding nature.

Up to that point, he danced above, danced away, the pain. Now dancing as a model for living failed him. There was the wounding force and there was dancing, but they remained outside each other. Since contact was broken or not established, dancing could not contribute toward healing the damage. It began as a good activity, but to maintain itself co-opted healthy areas, leaving little for other purposes. It was as if Rod put what health he had into dancing, and dancing sucked into itself what health he had.

Rod could not stand pain. He almost immediately wanted medication. I did not think this a good idea. I felt it important that he try to endure himself, build up tolerance for himself. Instead of the élan of dancing spreading through his life, it contracted into a smaller and smaller island outside his fear of pain. My bias that he begin to contact the pain, or at least give our relationship a chance to build before getting medication, increased tension between us. He was so unused to sitting and discussing personality difficulty that it was tempting to give in to him and take the edge off the pressure that was building.

I knew that medication helps make many individuals accessible to therapy and can be part of the therapy relationship rather than outside it. Maybe it would be wiser to go along with Rod and let his horizons spread after he felt better. Why my reluctance, this "power" struggle, this fear of "giving in"? I was surprised by the quick rise of tension, a tug of war that centered on medication but went beyond it. Was there a surge of "moral superiority" in my insistence not to give in to painlessness? A no-win situation. I was becoming smaller and smaller.

I decided to sit with the tension and see where it led. If I could not work with pressures that being with Rod entailed, how would he grow into the pressures he exerted on himself? My running would mirror and reinforce his running (dancing away) from himself.

As tension grew, Rod confessed he was a con man or, at least, that conning people was a strong thread of his existence. "I took the easy way, the path of least resistance. It was natural to teach dancing but there was more than teaching. It was easy to string people along. It just happened. Some people knew what they wanted and got it or found it wasn't for them. But there were others who—well, you found a way to whet their appetite. Some could afford it but there were others with little money who couldn't stop. Like potato chips or gambling, except with dancing you know you're going to get something and feel like a winner.

"I could rationalize I was doing something good for people. But the truth was I didn't really feel bad. I liked hooking people in. I got a spike seeing them get into it. It didn't matter if they had money, but it was better if they did. I could work them for more, and they could bring friends. I like the sensation of someone giving in.

"I've been doing this a long time. I remember winning a dance contest in high school and borrowing money from one of the kids. A bunch of kids admired me and I asked one to loan me bucks to go out after. I never paid him back. He kept pestering me. Boy was he mad. You should have seen his face, like he was thinking, 'How could this happen to me?'"

Shock, helplessness, disbelief, pain—for others, not Rod. He liked getting others to give him something. It was a thread going back to childhood. Friends learned not to loan him anything, but he always found new "givers." I would be very careful that he not run up a bill or that I grant special favors that might work against me.

He was winning, engaging, friendly, light. Awkward, thick, "loser" elements in myself gravitated toward him, as if his ease and confidence soothed insecurity. His winning self made me feel better. Dancing with him was a kind of balm. How lucky a god like him shared his body with me. While I enjoyed thoughts like these, he spoke about providing happy moments for unhappy people. He helped a crippled woman dance with crutches. With him she had moments of joy. She so wanted to dance but didn't dare. After a few months with Rod, she danced at her office party—the crutches part of her movement.

Another woman came to Rod while recovering from a mental breakdown. With him she felt she could dance and would not break down again. He released her love of dancing and made her feel whole. When she broke down again he visited her in the hospital. She told him she wanted to get better so she could keep dancing. In her broken state she could picture the joy but not feel it. He spoke with doctors and staff and arranged times to dance with her in the hospital and her joy returned.

I said something about goodness. He set me straight. "Yes, there's goodness maybe, but for me—and maybe you can't get it—my pleasure is pulling the strings. It's not that she feels good—it's that I make her feel good. It's not simply feeling bad. It's that I make her feel bad."

I am sitting with ways he makes me feel good and bad. He can see pain in my face and that gives him pleasure. He can see joy in my face and that gives him pleasure—as long as he feels it is because of him, that he controls it. What he cannot control is how I am working with these feelings, what I am learning. He cannot control the invisible work within. He cannot control what he cannot see, and what he cannot see he shuts out.

Childhood fragments. Rod's mother: friendly, social, into clothes, making a lovely home, feeling good. She admired and supported Rod from the outside in—his cute looks, winning ways. She made him feel good in his body as a performer. She did not have much patience for trouble, breezing past it, winking it away with comfort. She did not give him (or herself) much room for feeling bad. Maybe it was a kind of blessing that there was enough pleasure to tune into, so that pain could be averted. Pain was treated as transient, swept into an encompassing pleasurable horizon. This sounds healthy enough except "pleasure" tended to be skin deep. Rod does not remember being gripped deeply by anything, no surge of passionate significance, no throb of meaning. He was happy enough going from day to day.

Father: Mostly working, mild, flowing with whatever was up, supportive of wife and son and daughter. But again, the supportiveness was too easy, not really coupling, taking hold of what it supported. There is no doubt he loved his children, but somehow the love did not grab hold of them from the inside. It was just there without seeking too much back. There are difficulties when love is too demanding, but also when love is not demanding enough.

Sister: three years younger. Rod and she went their different ways and were not close. There was a certain amount of teasing, fighting, and surviving each other, but mostly they lived parallel lives with their own friends and concerns. Sometimes they did things together, provided background comfort, another kid around the house. But they seemed mostly out of contact with each other, bent on going their own ways.

Rod coasted through school. He was not invested in it. He got some recognition as a fast runner when he was young but gave up track when he discovered dancing. He never took dancing seriously as a vocation or as a creative possibility. It was something he was good at and enjoyed. It was not something he worked hard at or felt driven about. A lack of drive characterized his life. He had an easy-going approach to things.

After college he considered going for an MBA but went in and out of jobs instead. He gathered enough experience to go into partnership in a business, but in a few years broke away. Starting and stopping was a pattern, and he left a train of angry people in his wake. The other person in the partnership lost money when Rod walked away. Rod didn't mind dropping everything, letting it fall as if it never was. He didn't mind the messiness, chaos. The other person minded. He assumed Rod was a responsible person until it was too late. Rod discovered life had many playgrounds and moved from one to another. A bad name in one didn't hurt him in another. He had convincing "reasons" for what he did.

He drifted into the dance business after a number of failures. He once hoped to make more money than teaching dance provided. Being a dance instructor meant being a failure, but defeat might turn into something sweet. Dancing gave him an opening. He always enjoyed it. He was not going to be the entrepreneur of his dreams, but not all doors closed. Then he made the awful discovery that dancing lost its fun when it became a business. It gradually became boring and mechanical once it turned into something he had to do for money.

Scheming was automatic. It was easy to get people to extend lessons, to do more than they wanted, to bring friends. His wife opened branches. He was good at filling them. But there was not much joy in repetition. He already was halfhearted before the demise. His wife's greater will and energy left him behind. She dropped him as he dropped past business partners. She expanded as he contracted, and he crumbled.

His crumbling did not motivate any great soul-searching. All he wanted was to be put together and become the same self he always knew. Yet he was bored by the person he always was. But the threat of disintegration was too frightening. If talking did not make him better fast enough, maybe medication would. It was not his scheming life that bothered him, but the fact that his scheming life broke down. He was not in an ethical crisis and did not want to be in one.

While listening to Rod speak, it dawned on me that sincerity can be more interesting than scheming. This thought surprised me as there are so many quips about sincerity being dull. Now it seemed enlivening. Few things are more thrilling than tasting self and others in openhearted ways, seeing and living what experience unfolds. Sincerity, perhaps more than anything else, brings one to new places.

Sincerity concentrates intensity. Its heat and density can burst experience open. There is dull, even fatuous sincerity (Polonius) and fierce sincerity (Hamlet). The latter sweeps up a diversity of currents —including irony, rage, sweetness, deprecation—and twists and melds them into unsuspected compounds. The former reaches true heights at times, but as a chronic attitude sags and droops into monotone. For Rod sincerity exists to be exploited, something to manipulate, sincerity servicing dupery.

Sincerity and scheming commingle and feed each other in the greater scheme of things, contributing to enrichment and survival. In Rod's case scheming usurped the balance, dancing over or through rather than with life. Dancing life away rather than dancing toward life. While I was thinking these thoughts, Rod began to describe what it was like to con someone, the painful look on the sincere one's face, the sense of triumph behind scheming eyes spreading through underside of cheeks, lips, and mouth (as if licking lips with glee). Coupling triumph and giving in—repeated until shattering.

I stared at my sincere and scheming sides, amalgams, stratagems, tones. Sincere-scheming. Back and forth, fused. I felt a sense of awe and strength beholding their beauty, integrity, ability. Infinitely loopy, ropy selves. Terrifying incapacity in capacity, capacity in incapacity. One's try at living.

Look of pain–look of triumph. Welded deep. Through the ages. Triumphant one slicing, sincere one in pain. A smile resplendent with weaponry crushes the sincere face. Cutting never stops. Killing sincerity is relentless. Neither force yields.

Psychologist: two sides of a coin, parts of a system within the self, within society. Division of labor. Without letup. Rod shows me something in small letters some people write in capitals. To see one's pain in someone else's face, to see one's pain as someone else's. Rod animates in others a missing capacity in himself. This is not to say he *can* be in touch with his own pain but chooses not to. This is not to say he chooses to let others feel pain for him. It is not clear that he could feel his wounds if he wanted to. He inflicts others with what he cannot digest, creates in others what he cannot make his own. A look of pain inside his heart. He smiles at its absence with a heartless shrug, bringing disaster closer.

We hold each other's wounds, are each other's emotional digestive systems, although we never more than partly succeed. Rod is estranged from this kind of mutuality but is part of it anyway. Society is one great emotional digestive system with so much indigestion. The look of pain, surprise, astonishment, anger, helplessness, fury: the partial shock of trauma. We keep trying to digest it.

Sensitivity only partly born, drawn to the grimace of alarm for further birth. Too often another stillbirth. Rod tries to give birth to heartbreak that eludes him. The coupling of heartlessness and heartbreak. A coupling we cannot make go away with all the medicine in the world. Some surprise will shatter us.

Will Rod ever feel what he makes others feel? When the look of pain inside his heart threatens to see him, he dances away. He likes seeing himself through the other's painful eyes, not his own. Sincerity is a tool to find that pain; then he smiles and looks away, looks the other away. But Rod also makes others feel joy, like a god bringing pleasure or pain. A god above it all, tasting wider being by proxy.

Not the suffering god who shares the wounds of the world from within.

Where does therapy come in? One more con to betray the eternal wound, to get above or around it, to say it does not matter? Does Rod come for help in playing sensitivity down, to make believe it is not sacred or hellish? I am beginning to feel wounded by Rod's wish for therapy to go away, to render me superfluous. He wants me to help him reestablish control without really going through anything. A strong voice in our culture whispers, "Well, what if he is right?" Society enlists therapy as an opiate, painkiller, an alternative addiction —but also as a corrective, a balance, a voice for sensitivity. Failure of sensitive voices to connect with sensitive hearing increases momentum toward shatter.

Shatter both awakens and hardens. Hardening has not gone so far in Rod that he is indifferent to his own discomfort. But there are few signs so far of awakening and it is unclear what therapy can do.

CHAPTER 10

Not Enough

Doran tells me he felt angry at his wife when she took his hand during a dinner out. He had been complaining about lack of affection between them, felt she starved him. Now he recoils from her, he says, because she is not his "fantasy" woman, the one he really wants.

She is a hard worker, supplies the larger share of their income, supports his dreamy enterprises. He resents her superior earning power, yet needs her, loves her, appreciates what she has done for him. They have been married a long time and have no children. They are a nest for each other.

He recoils at his weakness and gets a sense of power imagining a better woman. His wife can't compete with his hallucinated woman's beauty, excitement, affection. His marital nest is surrounded by a hallucinatory aura of something better, something impossible.

The woman of his fantasy exists nowhere but makes him angry at his wife's touch, makes him recoil. Therapy gives him the chance to notice the connection between hallucination and irritation.

"If I met this woman, I don't think I'd leave my wife. She is so attractive because I don't know her. I value my life with my wife. It's a good life. I don't want to mess with it for a fantasy."

"But you're angry with your wife," I say.

"I'm angry at who she isn't. Maybe at who I'm not. I've never been able to be successful. I'm not who I hoped to be."

Doran speaks of weakness in his parents. They got by, did what they could. They weren't exceptional. He thought he would do more. He had a decent life, good experiences, but hoped for more. Currently he produces musical events and documentaries, makes a decent living, not spectacularly successful. It's a mystery to him why his career never takes off, fizzles, remains in the lower middle range, as if there's a missing x, maybe drive, fierceness, strength, cunning. He's nice, approachable, but can't push past a certain ridge.

He is mad at himself for not earning his wife's touch. Whether she is affectionate or not, she is in a position of power. He cannot let her reaching out be part of unmerited grace.

He is stuck not being the person he wished to be. No matter how much his wife and he do or do not touch each other, it will not matter, since they are both wrong people. Neither is a hallucinated being of desire.

"In fact I'm lucky to have her," Doran says. "My life would be grim without her. We're watering holes for each other. I might slip away chasing chimeras or wither."

His recoil at her touch at dinner? "It sounds crazy, but I was afraid a beautiful woman at another table would see her touch me. A fantasy woman in the restaurant I might have an affair with. She would see my wife touch me and think, 'Well, he's taken. I'll move on,' and I'd lose my chance. My wife fills the space someone 'really great' might occupy. Getting angry at her keeps possibility open."

There are moments when his wife carries the hallucinatory beatific moment. She can be beautiful, radiant. Love rises between them. Touch flows. When they first married it was more that way, but such feelings have not died.

It is frustrating not being who you want to be, not being with the person you imagined. Yet Doran's life feels good.

: : :

One afternoon after Doran left I sat with good feeling pulsating in my chest, radiance ticking, triggered by Doran's good feeling, despite discontents. Free-floating infinite fitting in my chest. It takes many forms.

It is in faces, skin. It can become erotic, throb through insides of body. When I feel it, I am content.

It may take the form of a semisolid golden ball. Golden light surrounds and begins to liquefy it. It *can* liquefy and take shape again. Golden ball, light, liquid are some forms hallucinated beauty takes.

For Doran, it partly attaches to a fantasy woman or his wife. He plays wife and fantasy against each other, but sometimes they fit together. The fantasy woman does not have to answer to reality. She is reality—an imaginary real. She attaches to different women Doran glimpses. If he is with one for a while, it slides onto someone else. It is part of sensitivity. As long as Doran is sensitive, there is someone somewhere who can make him glow.

Free-floating glow, free-floating infinite. Where will it show up next?

How much of one's life should one spend chasing it, catching it when it comes?

How much of one's soul should it take over?

: : :

"I'm always thinking of someone else," Doran says.

Slippery gold.

: : :

Diotima coaches soul to move from good objects to Vision of the Good.

One can get torn apart by objects drenched with goodness.

: : :

Free floating infinite, radiance, gold? Pulsating self?

: : :

"Without fantasy women at the restaurant, there would be no golden self."

"Is it all fantasy?"

"Isn't fantasy real?"

: : :

Is this what Freud meant, that aim is constant but object shifts?

Maybe it's a variation. He meant constant aim is discharge. By sleight of hand, broaden it to satisfaction. In another quick move, blend in bliss or ecstasy, radiance, light, glow. Erotic gold. A long way from discharge?

Unless we say we have the sort of equipment that discharges light through light.

: : :

"I'm talking about beautiful women, and you're talking about inner light?"

"Would there be beautiful women without that light?"

: : :

What would we be like without that light?

Where could we go to get away from it?

Can one hide from it in a restaurant, going out to dinner with one's wife?

Taste buds open to more than food.

Light dances around the tables.

"Does light hide in fantasy women?"

"No, it comes at me through them. You feel it inside you, faces, skin, eyes, bodies. Splattered by light, dancing from table to table, mouths opening, eyes sparkling. I reach for one, it slides into another, each slide a kind of homecoming, bouncing along from one homecoming to another."

: : :

Light does not cure anger. Anger is part of sensitivity too. It is not a matter of getting less angry or rooting anger out. Something else happens. Personality broadens, deepens, has more room. Anger does not occupy as much space, more goes on. One develops other interests. For one thing, feeling the ebb and flow, waxing and waning of light becomes more interesting. One becomes adept at letting it spread through one's body, one's feelings, one's being. More able to let the light one sees in others impact, seep in. One gets a little better at working over impacts and letting impacts work on one, so that one gets something more out of living.

One gets something out of being angry too. Instead of it simmering in the background, building resentment, or becoming diffusely explosive, one can feel it spread like light. Anger has its own light, angry light, its own nourishment. Doran did not seem to get much from his anger, not enough. I had the feeling he wasted his anger and, in some way, wasted away from it.

Over many decades I've developed a kind of knack for letting anger spread through me, surges, throbs, pulses, flows. I imagine it in my tissues, organs, skin, muscle. Surges of might. Once it starts, it can last a long time and become quite pleasurable. It wasn't always like this. When I was younger, I got headaches, stomach problems, backaches. I could sense constriction, holding back, narrowing. It is not simply a matter of letting go, exploding, although that might help for a time. It is partly a matter of catching on that there is more, one can experience more of oneself, that there is more to body than meets the mind, more to mind than narrowness believes.

I wouldn't expect a patient to jump into anger and feel at home. It has taken me over four decades of learning to work with feelings to barely qualify as a beginner. My way need not be Doran's way. But there was something stillborn, flaccid in Doran's anger. Even if he screamed or exploded, something did not carry force. He could not feel the impact of his anger on himself; his tissues did not feel the impact. Anger failed to convert to might.

It is not that Doran didn't get angry. He knew anger but did not get its full benefits. It did not fill him out. It's not simply that he sat on himself or held back. It's more that he kept his anger small. Pulling his hand back from his wife at the restaurant narrowed him. It grew out of a small feeling that made him smaller. Here the link between feeling and action diminished him and diminished his wife. It diminished reality. It grew out of hope for something better, a hallucinated fantasy woman, a kind of beatific vision, something that might expand reality if rightly used. However, I wonder if it didn't short-circuit growth of the real (real feelings, contact with feelings, the work of feelings) the moment he drew back. Hallucinated impossibles break what is.

Small feeling, feeling small: "You're not what I want." "I'm not what I want." Holding hands, connecting, letting feelings build— broken by smallness. Smallness heightened by grandiose vision of heavenly women. Anger that breaks rather than makes contact. The idea that marvelous women could be his brought out disappointment with his wife, himself, his life. His small life, which felt good. His small life, which he partly condemns. He ought to be equal to his visions.

He is angry at not being big enough for his hallucinations. Anger at self that spills onto others, anger at others that spills onto self. He cannot fill his hallucinations, and his anger cannot fill him. Or he cannot feel the fullness fully enough. There was much about his life that Doran appreciated. He was not all grievance. But the stream of grievances persisted, mainly centering on himself—he is not enough this or that. I began to wonder if he was aggrieved because he was less than he wanted to be or small because aggrieved. Did grievance keep him small?

With encouragement, Doran let his focus drop into his body's interior, where he placed or located his sense of grievance somewhere in his gut, a bit above stomach pit, a bit lower than solar plexus. All this was somewhat indefinite but a start. Through therapy he was learning how body feels to him from inside itself. With support, he took soundings of grievance, what was it doing, where.

"It seems to pull my gut around it, compressing into it. Stomach tight, squeezing. Maybe to cocoon the grievance, insulate it? It also feels like a force pulling from grievance itself. I'm afraid of damaging myself if I stay in contact with it. Perhaps there's damage I don't want to know about."

For a moment I get an inkling that grievance is a strong force, exerting pressure on body, self, personality. Does Doran feel power in him through grievance rather than anger? I encourage him to sing his complaints, say what it's like to be him, from the grievance spot.

"It's not like I hate myself; it's not so simple, even when true. It's like I don't fill myself, as if there's a leak in myself, but not an obvious leak. No place the blood pours out, no hemorrhage. More a slow leak into surrounding tissues, disappearing before I can find it."

Grievance exerting force on body, self, personality. Distorting, pinching, gripping. Is it, partly, a sign of awful processes leading up to it, forming it?

Doran comes up for air, pauses, then goes back down toward the grievance point. To get to it he swims through self-loathing, depressive coatings, complaints about his own deficiency. He also complains about the inadequacy of others. Others share his lacks. Deficiency links, unites for moments. Then he is alone again and his insides are ugly.

He spends the next months telling me how ugly it is to be him. Human insides are ugly. He asks if it is this way for me too; he senses it is. He can see on my face what he feels inside.

"I stick my hand inside my gut, my chest, push it around, feel worms, bugs in my organs, snakes, beetles, spiders, things you can't imagine. The mind can't get there—it festers, a sick thing creating sick things. It never stops. Puss, bile, blood—it stinks—putrefaction, maggots grow there. Metastasizing through psychic organs I barely sense and will never know. Most of me I'll never know about. Layers of sick stuff, dense, vanishing. We make myths for clarity. Once you wade into this morass there's no compass."

He looks at me, sees worms, bugs, snakes, spiders, infection.

It is scary, but he feels stronger. After repulsion, fear, anger at the bad stuff that makes us up, weepy anger at who we are at the ugly swamp level, strength grows and I can feel it. He is puzzled at the intermingling of light and ugliness but feels both. Mind is uncertain about what body feels. Body fails to keep up with experience vision multiplies. Bodymind cannot encompass what life generates through it.

Doran begins to look stronger, as if he exercises more, trains, lifts weights, runs. But the firmer, fuller look comes from psychic exercise. Something glandular, cellular may be happening, but it has to do with psychic glands and cells. Doran crawls and soars. He is picking at, digging in clots of grievance.

"The sense of never getting enough, having enough, being enough. I felt that all my life, ever since I remember. I felt that about my parents; they weren't enough or they were too much. On rare, rare, moments, they were just right. There *are* just right moments. Sometimes I think these just right moments have seen me through. Swimming when the water turns golden and bursts with sunset colors. Everything all right, this *is* life, the way it *should* be. Bad things come back, ugliness comes. Experience eaten by worms, stung by scorpions. I go limp. It's awful. I start to die. I die and never fully come alive again, never fully recover.

"I pick this stuff out of me. I lance a blood bubble and things creep, fly out. Disgusting. I smell badly. It goes on and on. I'm this infested thing. I didn't know how bad it was. I tried to make believe

I was better. My insides always had this rot. One puts a good face on. I get by. People like me. It's a relief not to pretend I'm better than I am. I'm always pretending. You can't get rid of it, can you—the rot or the pretending? But there's a way I'm not pretending now. I've gotten a glimpse of this side of things, the stench, the sting.

"I begin to feel grateful to you, slice you with a razor, rip you. No blood comes out, you are bloodless, you are nothing, made of wires. I laugh. You exist as a nothing for me to bathe in, to grow in. You are a petri dish. You are cultivating new kinds of germs."

"Psychotherapy germs?"

"Ha, psychotherapy germs. Infesting the world. Now I know I'm crazy, but the truth is only a small part of the world cares. Most people don't care about this. Most people would run or mock it. I was a scoffer, an interested scoffer. Am I a believer? Believer in what? It works, it's alive. Insides are alive. The ugliness, the beauty—alive. It goes and goes. I'm in it, it's in me, not only outside. I'm not only outside of me, outside of you."

"Were you ever only outside?"

"It felt that way, all inside, all outside. I was not in touch. Could be fooling myself now. All this slides around. But I feel it, feel something. Not sure what but want to let it happen."

We have gotten to a point of waiting, feeling something and waiting for more. It is another kind of living, respect for what is implicit.

As time goes on, he tells me he is getting more inventive with his documentary films. People are noticing; his creativity is having an impact. I do not want to associate gain in therapy with success in the world. Success may or may not happen. I would not want materialistic success to be taken as a signifier of psychic growth. Doran speaks about impact, feeling himself more, feeling his impact on others and on himself. A filling out. Feelings filling psychic veins, stronger psychic heartbeat. Not superman, just a little more color. Psychic flow creates more color and apparently new film possibilities.

In several places Bion writes about loss of blood as an image of loss of feeling or splattering of common sense. Unstoppable bleeding expresses injury to thinking and feeling processes. Injured thoughts and feelings bleed. Sensitivity bleeds.

In one example, Bion pictures blood being restored to the patient's circulatory system, implying growth of feeling-thinking, psychic circulation. Bleeding or emptying represents one set of dangers, filling another.

Often we reverse or invert images of feelings connected with states of affairs to make the intolerable tolerable. Thus blood restoration may signify hemorrhaging and vice versa. In the moment Bion attends to, murder/being murdered is the desired/dreaded result, whether at the apex of loss or reconstitution.

A psychotic patient sees blood mounting up his sleeve. Bion suspects his patient is experiencing murder or being murdered in reverse, that is, the return of life, or life after murder. It may also be therapy has enabled return of life, circulation. The patient now is in danger of living, the blood of feeling-thinking filling him out. Perhaps he hoped deathwork to be completed, only to be tricked by living. After all, to go to an analyst risks quickening. There are times in analysis when deathwork cannot keep up with lifework. To risk living is to discover new ways of dying.

Bion notes the point of entry into life (for a deceased or mutilated psyche) involves meeting the murderous superego. Growth, connection, synthesis takes place over the horns of a murderous object threatening disintegration or worse. Here is somewhat new meaning given to dying in order to live. The moment of growth heightens murder-dread. Growth threats stimulate death threats.

The psyche must process what threatens to kill or maim it, even while what threatens it damages ability to process and repair. That is, one needs to process what damages processing. This is part of the cruelty of therapy, egging the patient to do what can't be done. Part of the benefit of therapy comes from support given to whatever fragments of processing become possible. Something happens in the face of the impossible.

More specifically, to put oneself together means putting the murderous superego together. Any synthesis of self entails assembling a murderer. It is a murder that has no end, but one develops in the face of it. One makes room for murder in birth of self. It is necessary to create room for life-murdering tendencies, since aliveness murders. It is a basic part of Bion's vision that murder and birth are conjoined, that to be born is a kind of murder, not just of the Other, but the self. To be born one must pass through self-murdering tendencies, one must survive oneself. Therapy gives support to people trying to survive themselves. It helps one learn to murder oneself more productively, to live through murder more fully.

It is possible to try to outflank murder, to get around it, to hide, hoping it will go away. Often the only thing one can do is play for time, wish oneself away, hope troublesome tendencies disappear. One survives at a cost, since sneaking away from oneself has a weakening effect.

There is another kind of playing for time, a waiting *with* time. It is better to face one's murder, fully experience it. But waiting may be enough. This waiting is not sneaking away and hiding, but more like Job discovering destruction. One can do nothing but wait, experience what one can experience, and question, until every last shred of self is ripped away. Resources may develop to work with more. Meanwhile, a slightly more wisened faith is born by living through what must be lived through. Sitting through the worst without unnecessary defense is a necessary moment.

One may be more frightened by having blood than by not having blood. In the former, one risks trauma all over again; in the latter one has been flattened by trauma and is protected by hopelessness. In one case, fear has done its work and keeps on working, but one is more or less used to it; in the other, fear starts anew on planes life moves toward. To live one must be murdered by life. Bion writes, "At the point when his blood will be fully restored to his circulatory system he will experience being murdered. And then he will be all right."

I think this a point where Doran stalled. He tried to constitute himself as a creative nourisher without taking into account perils of nourishment. He was shy about dying at the breast, risks in feeding and being fed, the dangers of nourishment exchange, creative as well as personal nourishment. He repeatedly spoke of his parents' low energy, sometimes with resentment, sometimes just as a fact. His grievance about life kept returning to this. If they had had more force, he'd have more force. They were not enough. They did not fill him out. They were not filled out themselves. He imagined himself fading at the breast. Not because there was no milk but because it flowed so weakly. Nourishment was in danger of thinning out, fading away. The nourishment of being held, encompassed, sustained, penetrated, and inspired trickled on the border of oblivion.

"I picture myself a baby in my mother's arms. Encompassed by love, caring, tenderness, goodness. Her feelings flow into me. But she can't take my active energy. She is good with me if I am not so energetic, if I am quieter, softer. It's not that she's bad otherwise. It's just that her energy doesn't rise enough to meet mine, or she somehow doesn't find me when I peak. She is better when I ebb or am more level. She doesn't exactly draw back when I rise; it's just that she doesn't meet me, and I fall back to the calmer, quieter mode she modulates. Maybe I feel oversoothed. I can't break through the soothing and feel my force.

"She's adjusted to a lower output; maybe she's naturally that way. Maybe I'm naturally that way too. My father also is on the low-keyed side, not flat exactly, but not bursting either. We are definitely not a high-energy group. But we do things; we're not inert. It's not like we stare into space all day. My wife is more high-energy, and I like that. She helps keep things up.

"Now I'm in my mother's arms and feeling kindly, low force. Low, steady flame. I can't say that's bad but I feel frustrated. I want more output. I appreciate she's not stamping me out, but I'm not fully coming into myself either. I sort of stay a slow, soft idle. I want my engines to rev, roar. Nowhere to go with that. My blood is flowing slowly, my breathing is so quiet, I can hardly hear or feel myself.

"I get the idea she is murdered or partly murdered. Not that she's dead. She feels. I feel her feelings. What can partly murdered mean? Is it I'm angry and feel I've killed her? Yes, but more. It has to do with her too, like she's gotten used to being murdered, accepted being partly murdered for the life she can have. I come into life a new baby and haven't had to accept being murdered yet. I expect more aliveness and get a half-murdered response. Not dead. She's not an emotionally dead mother, just a partly murdered one. That's different. When you feel murder, when you feel murdered—it's not deadness. Her being partly alive makes me want more."

Murdered mother—murdered baby. It's not that anyone murdered anyone. It's more the way life works. Maybe Doran is just describing what it is like to be a low-energy person in a high-energy world. When he arrived, his parents were already worn down by life, doing their best. He felt supported by their goodness, let down by their lack of drive. A child can get wounded by parents being too driven, successful, highly charged. Doran felt less wounded than deficient, as if lack of vitality seeped down to him.

Exciting women elsewhere had what his mother lacked. He was not ruined by a seductive mother, but sagged not feeling her sexy enough. Simple depressive goodness was not good enough in the big city. On the other hand, he longed for flashes of fierceness his father could not provide. Life experience taught him how traumatizing paternal rage can be. But such rage was missing in his family. He was spared brutal onslaughts. He would not want to be abused but felt what he got was too tepid.

From time to time Doran opined, "Their blood wasn't hot enough. Wind didn't fill their sails." I thought of Bion's blood images, connections of energy, feeling, processing. Breathing and bleeding, air and blood, rhythm, circulation, in-out. Bion's image of blood returning to the circulatory system is somewhat analogous to inhalation. Intake of milk connects with filling up, being emotionally filled, then comes digestion, going on being, getting hungry, waiting, needing another feed, emptying following filling, breathing out after breathing in. Now a thermal image, cold-hot. His parents weren't cold-blooded, but low-blooded, not as hot as his imaginings wanted.

What is missing? The climactic moment in Bion's description above is getting murdered (after filling up), then being all right. Can Doran's grievance partly be that his murderous superego is too tepid? Has he come to me to undergo a fuller, better murder, so that the all right feeling feels more all right? Dropping toward oblivion is different from being murdered into life.

It is as if Doran is complaining about a mutual impact deficiency. Some of his grievance is not feeling his own impact on himself and others, and, in an important way, theirs on him. Part of human interaction involves going through mutual disturbances. We upset each other, recover. Get murdered, feel all right. His unconscious infinity machine needs something to chew on, not just hallucinated women. He needs to feel his blood rising in moment-to-moment interactions, emotional give-and-take. Doran has a hunger for intensity and has sought out a fairly intense therapist. His discovering bugs in his belly and stinging and pinching things in his psyche is a little like Jack Horner digging into new sorts of pies. He seeks therapy to get a taste of what it is like to be murdered by aliveness and survive.

CHAPTER 11 *Sensitivity and Vulgarity*

Author's note: Human sensitivity expresses itself in low and high ways, running the gamut from vulgarity to spirituality, which, far from being mutually exclusive, fuse and feed each other. As implied in the interview that follows, sensitivity uses body parts and functions for self-expression, to both reveal and hide itself. Sensitivity generates body symbolism to express the feel of life and also to dampen, ward off, or channel the latter. The aliveness of life can be awesome but also overwhelming and even destructive. Thus symbolic imagery and thought both heighten and tone down aliveness. We modulate energy through meaning. Vulgarity is a common emotional currency. It involves a kind of hardening we undergo in the face of our sensitivity, a way to negotiate and survive the latter. In time, we have to grapple with the downside of self-hardening processes and take the risk of gradual opening. Vulgarity, too, is part of passionate expression, a way of noting, as well as masking, opening in progress. This chapter is based on an e-mail interview done by Robert Marchesani for the journal *The Psychotherapy Patient*. The journal issue in which it appeared has also been published as a book entitled *Inhabitants of the Unconscious: The Grotesque and the Vulgar in Everyday Life*.

ROB: The first thing that comes to mind is a kind of free association on the work vulgarity. That's an interesting slip. I just wrote "work" and was about to go back and delete the "k" and write "word" when it occurred to me that in doing the work of psychotherapy we might be doing some kind of work of vulgarity or on vulgarity. The vulgarity of the unconscious? Comment?

MIKE: An interesting slip indeed. Most slips are hostile, but I'm not sure this was. Confounding "work" and "word" sounds pretty rich in meaning. In the beginning was the word. The creative word. And vulgarity trades—usually in hostile ways—on physical creativity. So many swear words have to do with sex, genitals, the activity of "making" babies, or "making" other things. When I was young I used to say "fuckshit" a lot. Now, if you take that apart, it can be pretty ugly. Like—disgusting—fucking shit. As a matter of fact, that used to be a pretty popular slang phrase, "I don't give a fucking shit." So much vulgarity refers to body parts, functions, often mixtures of birth and aggression.

I did some writing years ago (collected in *The Electrified Tightrope*) on the asshole holding the body together in the realm of meaning. There is such a thing as circulation of meaning, not only blood or air. Meaning flows or is more or less blocked, even impacted. Impacted meaning, knots, clots. The phrase "loose-ass" pertains to the circulation of meaning throughout the psychic body. So many top-bottom words for body parts and functions funnel bidirectionally through anal referents. In psychoanalytic body part/function equations mouth = asshole = vagina. But there are prick-asshole slang fusions too. And lots of permutations. Various body parts may fuse with face too, so there is top-bottom flow or blockages. The anal area seems to act as a conductor for the flow of meaning, front-back, top-bottom. Insofar as there is blockage, backup, clogged meaning, it is no accident that anal tropes are the most expressive for self-hate and psychic damage.

ROB: One of my first patients expressed what seemed to be a popular vulgar expression in my own childhood, always expressed in moments of extreme frustration and in the absence of any other available language: mother-fucking son of a bitch. After reading Sophocles' *Oedipus Rex* and Freud's reinvestment of the Greek classic, I could never again hear such language without thinking the obvious—that child inserts itself into the mother, much as the father did to create the child, only the child does so in language that is sometimes hostile to the impossibility of the fulfillment of the desire. So this was the language of the people, all right. The people of the inner city. Tongue can be cut (as Passolini shows in *Salo*) and ass filled, but it is done either way, from within or from without. One can bite one's tongue or clam up and say nothing of one's vulgar thoughts, or be ridiculed or punched in the mouth for being vulgar. One can fill up with shit as is the natural course of our digestion the way God/nature made us, or look for ways to fill our asses—to be fucked, literally or metaphorically. Hence, many come in feeling fucked up. What fucks us up? Why fucked up?

MIKE: It's quite something that fuck-up means mess or messed up. Again, the multidimensionality of meaning, fusing sex (front-rear) aggression, awkwardness, messiness of body functions, the child making messes, human fallibility, stain, warp, pain and pleasure. To be a fuck-up is a comment on one's character, one's very essence. But no one really knows how all this evolves and what is going on or what it means. We are making up stories, getting ideas.

I do want to point out a couple of things clinging to bits of what you've said. You write about the child's hostility with regard to "the impossibility of the fulfillment of desire." I suspect "fulfillment of desire" is always a fantasy or contains a fantasy aspect. Most sex we actually have does not come up to unconscious ideal fantasies. The child may fantasize sexual fulfillment no parent achieves. Let me exaggerate to make my point: fulfillment is, more or less, always hallucinated fulfillment. This makes envy and competitive hostility especially nasty and unyielding: someone is getting the really good stuff somewhere, because what I get doesn't quite match up to what I imagine getting is. After all, Oedipus does do what you say the child wants but can't, but what good is it—it made a big mess. Little child, little mess. Big boy, big mess. The adult is as delusional about fulfillment as the child, only he has the power to wreak greater havoc. He actually is in a position to carry out his dreams while awake—so watch out!

What I'm saying is that where human beings are concerned, fulfillment isn't just fulfillment. It contains hallucinatory abundance (or deprivation). We end up pedaling our bikes awfully fast to reach promised places (look what happened when the Hebrews got into the Promised Land—it always happens). The notion of heaven within you is a try to work with this conundrum.

It's partly a matter of catching on to ourselves. Something like, "Ah, so this amazing beatific experience—it's a capacity, given to me, inbuilt, something I can taste. It's something I can feel. Now I see it is there all the time, part of experiencing, rising, falling, peaking, fading, informing all. Now it is gone, never to appear again. Now it is coming back, rising, filling me with tears of joy." But I do learn there are people and things and sights and sounds that trigger it more than others. Create it. I learn the fact that I carry this bliss is no substitute for the joy that new, previously undreamed of experiencing brings. We do create and are created by the unimaginable happening between/within us. But now, you see, I've developed symbolic categories for this kind of exploding (including the category of exploding all categories) and that does make a difference. I can be annihilated by joy and keep on learning. But I am older now.

Psychotics often have a nostalgia for their "prepsychotic" personalities and lives. Things were better then. They idealize the time before breakdown. But a closer look shows that things were pretty bad then too. The idealizing capacity says, this illness is an accident, life was wonderful once. If only it can be that way again. The human race has something of this nostalgia. The golden age. Things were better when—idealizing some window of time or psychophysical function. Now, it seems, we idealize aspects of the present or future more than the past. This does not mean we are getting less psychotic. Maybe we're just a bit bored with idealizing the past and are looking for new hallucinatory fields. This leads us more and more into the present, as fantasies of the future (e.g., utopia/Armageddon) lose valence. Quite soon the present will have to carry quite a burden, quite a hallucinatory surplus.

As your description goes on, you refer more and more to trauma, disturbance—things going wrong, the ouch of things. This seems to be the underside of idealization. Cut, bite, stuffed, attacking, self-attacking, etc. Fusion of ideal hallucinated state or object and mutilation or something ripping, stuffing, or whatever form the injury takes. As if we tear ourselves down as far as we can tear ourselves down (tear—tear, rip, and weep). A double tendency: ideal wholes, shredding. Dialectic between vulgar and refined partly reflects this doubleness. We are inserted into a psychic field that has the cutter in place, ready to rip whatever illusion we fabricate about ourselves. A shark in the psyche zeroing in on garbage. But it eats good meat as well.

ROB: If you look up "vulgar" in *Webster's Thesaurus*, here's the progression of synonyms: 1. vernacular (conversational, spoken), 2. public (general, popular), 3. coarse (crass, crude, gross, unrefined), 4. obscene, 5. barbaric. It's a degeneration of sorts from the Vulgate to the most uncivilized aspects of humanity. In *The Exorcist*, the demon creates a mess out of its host, turning her language and body into something grotesque and obscene: "Especially important is the warning to avoid conversations with it. We may ask what is relevant but anything beyond that is dangerous. He's a liar. The demon is a liar. He will like to confuse us. But he will also mix lies with the truth to attack us. The attack is psychological, Damian, and powerful! So don't listen. Remember that—do not listen." It seems to me the demon defeats the priest on this psychological front. Damian lost his mother, who leaves him lost in a sea of guilt for abandoning her to an old age home. That's how the demon gets him, this priest who was also a trained psychiatrist. She becomes his mother in a hallucination! The lie swallows the truth that this possessed girl is not his mother. He loses the old priest to a heart attack, which may also symbolize the loss of his faith. In a mad reaction, he beats the possessed girl and demands the demon enter him, which leads to his death. In *Electrified Tightrope*, you describe a faith in O as Bion described it. Absolute truth. Absolute reality. Later in the book, you devote another chapter to "Demonized Aspects of the Self" in which you introduce baby mind. Now, it seems to me that there is something in the human being that is degenerative, maybe when the shark you speak of goes too far, devouring garbage and good meat. And if one identifies oneself with garbage, then there is even more trouble with the demon/shark. Given the range of the vulgar—the levels of vulgarity within the patient and within the therapist, it seems to me that the therapist's job is to keep the focus of the O in the space provided by the therapist, even in the midst of sharks and demons. In fact, the O, when seen as a space, a drawn object, an "O"pening, can become an arena, a coliseum for the barbaric to fight their "bloody" battles, which, if we were British, would bring us back to "fucking" battles, inferring, quite possibly, violent sex battles. Maybe some computer games serve that need in a safer way. I've seen a few academics playing the popular "bloody" game Quake with great delight! So psychotherapy may have developed the paradigm for virtual reality.

MIKE: I love your comments. You bring me to the edge of what it is possible for me to say. But I'll jump in anyway. First, I don't really see therapy in terms of space or spaces, although I sometimes slip into that mode, and it is useful. I used to see it more in terms of time, although now I'm not sure. One of the things about Bion's O is its unlocalizeability, ineffability. It is located nowhere. It manifests, for example, as emotional reality of moment. In *The Psychotic Core* I wrote of a "containerless container," "spaceless space." Something like the time of experiencing. We may find the spot in the brain that triggers joy, but that is not the experience, joy itself.

After the fact, I found correlates in Dewey, Whitehead, Lacan, Bergson, and Husserl. Dewey described a kind of arc of experience, the rise and fall of perception-emotion-awareness on seeing a painting. A moment of experience may have a developmental arc akin to the unfolding of emotion in a play, building, rising to climax, dénouement, subsiding, afterwaves. So much experience gets aborted, tension unsustainable. I now suspect the experience of aborting experience is inevitable, common (a meaning of vulgar in my dictionary). Aborted experiencing may be more common than sustaining buildup/unfolding of emotive moment and sequence. And is certainly more common than digesting experience. Most experience remains undigested, some perhaps indigestible.

Whitehead, too, speaks of experiential pulse, and Lacan, in expressing unconscious life, speaks of "pulsations of the slit." I happen to value the vaginal reference in Lacan's image of opening. It dovetails with facts of my life. At some point after sexual intercourse, I felt my heart as vaginal opening. Now I can relate it to prophets speaking of circumcision of the heart, especially turning a heart of stone to a heart of flesh. For me, I guess, it began by identifying with a woman opening, and opening has become a central theme in my life. In *The Psychoanalytic Mystic* I related Bion's O to, among other things, Opening, Orgasm, Ohhh, Origin-Omega. Opening-originating. Lacan speaks of transference arising at the point the unconscious closes, transference signifying the reality of the unconscious in its closing, loss of flow. The analyst, when he is psychoanalytically O'ing, is the speaking unconscious, opening the flow of feeling-meaning, pulsations from the slit.

The "unconscious speaking" can have an orgasmic element, *jouissance* currents. Milner writes of creativity being a kind of symbolic orgasm, creativity orgasmically symbolizing itself, its process of generativity. I've written that the arising of the sense of self and other has this generative orgasmic aspect. I feel the Bible associates such arising with singing a new song and the psalms do end with blowing wind, banging percussive instruments, dancing, shouts of joy. Words like banging and blowing really do sweep up so many dimensions of being. They express an ever new sense of self vis-à-vis the living God, and more.

Back to vulgar as common. Swear words seem to be some kind of common emotional currency. Common in many ways. A common language, common denominator. Swearing is related to oaths—taking an oath on God, swearing on one's children (this used to be common). Here swearing is associated with sincerity, really meaning it. This used to be a much more powerful phenomenon than it is today. So much so that the "Kol Nidre," sung once a year at the beginning of the Yom Kippur service, abrogates oaths and false oaths made during the year. This was once so prevalent God had to put in a special commandment about not taking His name vainly. Which can be broadened into watch out about using God for your vanity—it might backfire.

It is a quick leap from swearing as sex-aggressive-procreative fusion, to divinity, one or another way: the way up is the way down and vice versa. Ascent-descent works both ways. Of course, here I've fallen into spatial language, as inevitable as it is misleading. For the facts we are pointing to have to do with something felt, which space cannot encompass. The joyous blowing and banging and dancing in the psalms of David are consistent with the psalmist's expressive actions elsewhere in the Bible. King David's sister criticized him for vulgar tendencies, especially tearing off his clothes and dancing exuberantly with common girls. In one scene he did this with uncontainable abandon when bringing the ark of God into what would be Jerusalem. At moments, David united eros (here love of women) and love of God, body, and soul. Such unification is a *mitzvah*, a high good, a *simcha*, a joy. His sister was punished with a case of leprosy, so she learned her lesson, and eventually the leprosy was cured. I think there is a way—David demonstrates it—that low-high (David had heartfelt ways of promising, arguing, swearing, exalting, lamenting with God) unite in high spirits (also a fecund word).

In the Bible low-high undergoes all sorts of permutations. A mystical view says the spirit of the Hebrews descended to the minus forty-ninth rung in Egypt. Had Moses not succeeded just at that moment, their souls would have been lost, consumed if the minus fiftieth level was touched. Still, a spark of holiness persisted, enough to begin the ascent once more in the wilderness. False starts, setbacks to be sure. But they reached the plus fiftieth level when Moses saw God on Mt. Sinai with such intensity that no Jew lacks God's voice in his or her soul to this day. If Egypt was the furnace (that's what rabbis called it, referring to the baking of souls), what must the Holocaust be?

ROB: Just your use of verb tense is telling in your question. In the very last episode of Oprah 2000, she showed what's happening to women in various countries in and around the Far East. Genital mutilation, murder for the slightest slights, and acid attacks on young women, virtually girls, whose families refused to oblige the men who wanted them. The rationale: if the men who wanted them were denied them, then they would set out to damage the "property" of the family. This, of course, being the ultimate act of evil demand. The girl was disfigured so that no one would want her, so the assailing men believed. On camera—in her own words and endearing gracefulness, she embodied the beauty of a princess. At the end of the program, Oprah said that there is another Holocaust going on in the world as we speak. "And you can no longer say you don't know about it."

Your question made me contemplate Hitler's Aryan Race. Here you have manic ego racing to create a perfect race while at the same time defacing the races of millions, literally, taking off their faces with gas and skinnings and fire! Hitler created a furnace to consume his own grotesque projections. But since I cannot find language strong enough, (without becoming vulgar) I can only say that he committed suicide too late.

MIKE: I think you are saying something very important—important for the evolution of the human race. Oprah is right on the money with regard to oppression of women. Oppression of any person or group—but the notion of equal rights when applied to women exerts especially intense social/psychological transformatory pressures. These pressures and counterpressures are active on many fronts. There has been a long-standing "tradition" of trying to solve problems by violence. We now know a good deal about what goes into this psychologically but, in one way or another, the "violent" method of solution is still dominant. For example, I felt a good deal of psychosocial violence at work in the last national election, which ended in a sense for many of what I might call "election trauma or rape." In the end, votes weren't counted in the name of purity of "standards." On the face of it, each side felt the other was trying to "steal" the election. So much public back-patting about how we don't solve problems by violence—look at our peaceful transfer of government. This obscures one sort of violence substituting for another. No gunshots or bombs. But psycho-social-political violence, harder to catch, slipping into blurs of talk, fuzz of images, manufactured sentiment.

It is my opinion that nothing has led to more wrongs in human history than a sense of right. You describe the righteous rage of the defacer or slaughterer of impurities. This happens in subtle (or not so subtle) ways in marital arguments, child upbringing, institutional maneuverings—and in psychotherapy. The one who feels right—this rightness is a powerful force. It justifies aggression, manipulation, controllingness, seduction, force, stacking the deck—all sorts of attempts to bend the other to one's will or vision. In extreme cases—not so unusual, as you point out—it attempts eradication of the "wrong," eradication of individuals or viewpoints, feelings, thoughts, or groups wronging one.

I think this rightness involves hallucination, and that hallucinated states play important roles in our behavior and thinking. Not only do we believe ourselves right (the Other wrong), but somewhere we hallucinate ourselves right and too often are taken in and governed by unconscious hallucinated self-identifications (or identifications with "our" cause).

Hamlet shows something of the dilemma. He must kill to avenge his father's honor, the warrior's code of honor, passed on since antiquity. He hesitates, I believe, because he knows deep down that destruction will not solve anything—it will not really remove the stain or undo the rottenness, whether of a country, soul, or mind. Murder cannot purify the spirit. It will not solve the problem of our humanity. Murder cannot blow our disturbing beings away. Hamlet's hesitation is a gift to us—germs of a new ethic of indecision. I think psychotherapists have long gravitated toward Hamlet because of the missed opportunity he represents, an opportunity he transmits to us. Psychotherapy is built on attentive waiting, an informed art of indecision. It values what the dominant culture leaves out. The dominant culture idealizes decisiveness as manly, strong, knowing one's mind. Psychotherapy knows how difficult knowing mind can be. I can be nasty and say that those who know their minds don't have much mind to know. The dominant culture's emphasis on decisiveness and knowing one's mind is violent. It takes room away from values of reflection, experiencing, feeling and feeling feelings—the time of experience. Now, there are situations requiring speed of thought and action. But this ought not be the dominant ethic. This may be necessary for certain emergencies—but not a criterion of being.

It would have opened new symbolic pathways, built strength and possibility of another sort, had Hamlet borne the tension of failing to enter the revenge chain, which continues fertilizing with bodies the idea of destruction as corrective. But this would have required a new kind of man, psychological man—which, from the warrior viewpoint, might be weak, sissy. Isn't it amazing to be proud of being nonreflective? Ashamed of being self-reflective? I'm rooting for Hamlet to endure more shame, open more pathways. But he did enough. It's now up to us. It's our turn.

ROB: And more shame is what you may have allowed the patient you described in *The Electrified Tightrope* who lived in a shithole that he complained of for so long without doing anything about it until you commented, "It seems you must keep living in your mother's asshole." It was a brilliant interpretation of something we take for granted. When we make comments like "He lives in a shithole," we never ask, "Whose shithole is he living in?" Your interpretation echoed the patient's own state of being and feeling that he no longer could feel! Your comment gave him back the feeling he had about himself as reflected in his place, his apartment, maybe even his place in the world—in this life which his mother first gave him. Is this the turn we must take in psychotherapy, the turn Loewald writes people are looking for? Must we become the vulgarity of the unconscious reinterpreted, to become the "doctors" of the toxic nourishment, to use the title of your later work, that we readminister?

MIKE: I said things like that decades ago. I stand by my early work though. I was way more into body images of that sort then. I guess a lot of my thinking along that line was collected by Adam Phillips in my book *The Electrified Tightrope*, including the patient and remark you mention. I'm not sure I'd do that today. Maybe I take it for granted, and I'm in a somewhat different place now. Hard to say. I'm sure today something else would happen. So I really have a hard time responding to "must's." You bring up my writings on toxic nourishment, where emotional nourishment and toxins are fused, where a person takes in emotional toxins along with nourishment, or even may have to ferret what nourishment he or she can from the emotional toxins that are present. My verbal responses there are less important than a "feel" for things, the attitudinal-emotive atmosphere that arises, the emotional transmissions that occur. Verbal utterances grow from and further feelings, tones, the spirit of the moment. It's the latter that is most important, the felt impact of feeling-to-feeling contact, self-to-self contact.

The earlier quotation you gave from *The Exorcist*—about not listening. That's the opposite of what I feel. We need to listen, listen more and more, with whatever capacities we can muster. We do listen to the devil and keep learning (especially learning to listen). In a way, that's exactly what we do with most people, work with the devil, deconstruct devils, opening demonic clots in the psyche, seeing what's there—devil to devil, self to self, opening psychic arteries or even constructing them for better emotional flow. I think not listening is bad advice. Not listening doesn't make demons go away or save one from them. Except for illusory moments. What devils are doing with us is precisely one thing we learn about. But it may be that one is better off not listening, if one is not ready to. But, I fear, the situation will eventually get bad enough to compel attention, or growth opportunities may be missed. Sometimes survival takes precedence over growth.

You know, it may be that we can only listen a little at a time, that we need to dose it out. Value moments of hearing, seeing, feeling. William Blake speaks of a moment in the day the devil cannot find, and that moment changes everything if rightly placed. I think, given where my patient and I were thirty or more years ago (in some therapy asshole?), my spontaneous remark, which was semihallucinatory, gripped his soul as truth. It was like a fact of life made its way in through the fog. He saw—or in his case, discovered—the value of psychic scent (close to sense). It was just a moment—a moment of coming alive a little more, as Blake describes. A kind of moment in which truth does set one freer, in this instance hallucinated truth (my remark) touching hallucinated/real poison of his emotional morass, therapy asshole meets his mother's asshole, perhaps therapy devils meeting devils he's used to and stuck in but not quite aware of.

I suspect if we do not listen to devils in each other, we will shut each other out, get defensive. Listening opens up whole other dimensions than simply fighting/hiding. Are we ready to let a capacity like listening evolve and become more important (Hamlet was on the verge, almost, almost), or will we do what we do best, fight and run away? It's not just either/or, but each moment does ask us which we will emphasize.

ROB: In thinking about your comments, I can't help but imagine you as a supreme humanist! That you take us from something vulgar as embedded in the early body ego and release it into something spiritual, a word that I often think is misused. People often refer to "spiritual" and "spirituality" as the all-powerful good only, but I've often suspected that it includes the demonic as well, or maybe we'd be better off, less spooked, calling it the daemonic. In thinking of your work *The Psychoanalytic Mystic*, something prompted me to go to Houston Smith's *Forgotten Truth* on my bookshelf. I opened to a bookmark I'd placed there in 1989 when I decided to train as a psychoanalyst shortly after meeting Smith at the University of Pennsylvania. In those marked pages was a paragraph on the word "mystic." On the back of a St. Joseph's Indian School envelope stamped with "1989 Tribal Calendar" I had written with an arrow pointing to the paragraph, "Then this means not that a psychoanalyst is a mystic but that a psychoanalyst must become a mystic." You give us what might be called a theory of mysticism in your work, a feeling of awe and wonder in the work of psychotherapy. I thank you for continuing to open up our minds and the pathways of communication/transmission that can be realized in this labor of love that becomes a love of the labor, from one soul to another.

MIKE: Thank you, too, Rob. You're a great releaser.

CHAPTER 12

Is There Room for Heaven in Psychoanalysis?

Author's note: Jeffrey Eaton interviewed me for a journal that folded before the interview could be published. His questions stimulated the responses below, which are not "answers" so much as musings evoked at the time. Since my responses blend central preoccupations, I've combined them and put the questions that triggered this "reverie" in the first note for the chapter.

When I began practicing in the 1960s, a big distinction was made between psychoanalysis and psychotherapy. It's a distinction I often had trouble with. There were people I saw four or five times per week, but there were also those I saw once a week, and some of the latter had better psychoanalytic experiences. As time went on, I felt frequency, use of a couch, and other "externals" didn't necessarily make for a psychoanalytic experience, and more formal definitions (transference, resistance, understanding, unconscious conflict, etc.) didn't always do the trick either.

Add to that the grim realization that many practitioners who claimed to be proponents of the "pure gold" of psychoanalysis were terribly suffocating—what's a guy whose groping along going to do?

I couldn't believe that what I was told was psychoanalysis by some "classicists" *could* be psychoanalysis. If *this* was supposed to be psychoanalysis, then psychoanalysis either was dead or never existed. Later I found echoes in the work of Bion for the notion that psychoanalysis, if it existed, might be embryonic. We were prematurely codifying something we did not really know much about.

I've never been interested in defining what psychoanalysis is or isn't. I'm not much at definitions. More into living it, whatever it may be. Psychoanalysis has always been a living fact for me, part of my life blood for more than four decades. Part of a search, an ax to crack the frozen sea within (as Kafka said about writing), a probe, a point of entrée into pain, a breaking through crust, a way to open heart. I went into it because I was desperate and it became part of the way I live.

In the early years for me, Harold Searles was a point of light, particularly his paper on phases of therapy. Seeing him perform was fun, but his writings touched me more deeply. I think he opened more doors than he went into. Most fantasies he made use of were oriented around sex-aggression, kind of a fight-fuck mindset. Too boxed in. But I quite enjoyed his wanting to cut patients vertically or horizontally, depending on the sort of split that moved him at the moment. He seemed to want to get close to patients or himself but always was battling tendencies that created distance. He seemed to make the most of the hardship of being him.

Later he repudiated his preambivalent symbiotic love/fusion phase of interaction, feeling that reality always was mixed, ambivalent, never free of hostility or aggression of some sort. Perhaps he's right. It certainly sounds realistic, doesn't it? Yet something claws at the innards, a vision. Radiance. Light. There does seem to be something unambivalent at the core—perhaps what is meant by calling the soul pure. For example, mystical Judaism affirms there is a point of soul ever pure in contact with God. This, even though the empirical self or soul is quite impure. Of course, terms like "pure" and "impure" lead to trouble. But they do try to convey something felt. The garden, the heaven within, is quite a real and central moment. The mix is even more mixed than Searles allows: something truly beatific at the heart's center amidst the agony and vice versa.

The heaven within gets us into all sorts of trouble. A man consulted me because heavens sour. He found heaven with one woman and when that turned hellish, found heaven with another, until hell again made its appearance. He then blamed himself for choosing the wrong women to be in heaven with. He wanted to correct whatever was wrong with him, so he could make better choices, that is, find someone who can sustain his heavenly bent, share heaven with him.

A problem with heaven is that others pay for it. My heaven over yours. Heavens differ and wars are fought over them. How many people spend time supporting another's heaven? Heaven becomes a hot potato one tries to hold onto and others try to get rid of. Everyone's angry at everyone else for not supporting the same heaven.

The trick is to find heaven and ever let it go. Don't force your heaven on others or give yours up too long for someone else's version. There's heavenly etiquette. It's quite a currency we've discovered, negotiating heavens, emotional riches. An amazing thing is heavens keep changing. By going into one, others open. At some point, the I-you business becomes less important. You get tired of having to be in the I vs. you mold too long. It's nice swimming with someone, bobbing up in different places, light glistening in the waves. No one pays much attention to who's where and we don't try to drown each other or want much more than what's happening because it's so good bobbing about.

We bump and bounce, toward-away-in-through-with-against, under and up again: "There you are. Oh, you're the one I was mad at because our heavens were different, the one who wouldn't share the way I imagined things might be? And here we are!"

I had a dream that we transform in each other with a kiss. Not just that we transform each other, but in each other (we = you, me, all people). There is a great battle going on now as to whether it is viable to have "insides." What meaning has the old saying about heaven inside? Insides mean sensitivity, vulnerability, feelings for others, others deep inside us under our skin. A patient tells me that his wife and children touch him and he begins to feel them on the inside of his body, which abruptly makes him grow cold. As soon as he begins to feel warmth inside his body, he turns into a cold void.

I think this man tells me the truth about something happening in our world on a frightening scale. We join those—artists, writers, filmmakers, some scientists and mathematicians (who value feelings, intuitions), historians, and even politicians—who affirm that feelings are important and complex and interesting. The way we touch each other and touch in each other invites reflective wisdom and growth. It may be difficult to make money feeling and dreaming about feelings in a respectful and penetrating way, but not impossible. What does it sound like to an insurance company when you say, well, the patient feels more fetchingly, subtly, intricately than three years ago?

Is there room for heaven in psychoanalysis? Marion Milner

thought so. She was interested in commonalties between the most significant moments of a day and wrote of creativity as symbolizing its own orgasmic joy. She was speaking, partly, of tastes of heaven opening within. Her friend, Anton Ehrenzweig, traced ecstatic-depressive phases in creative work. So much goes on in a moment of feeling: violence, transgression, peace beyond understanding, heightened intensity, loss of feeling, cutting to pieces, putting together, turning things this way and that. How is it possible to feel more than one *can* feel and nothing at the same time (as Bion put it, a simultaneous emotional maximum-minimum)? Everything-nothing and the infinitely infinite sense of all the worlds between.

There are psychoanalytic ecstasies. One follows agonies to the point of reversal, opening to *jouissance*, exquisite self-other perception, staying and staying with the feel of oneself and another. Rubbing the magic lamp of self, following twists and turns of self-other interweavings, discovering a growing love, hunger, devotion to sensing, amplifying mutual impacts.

M. Balint wrote of an early heaven, self-other intermingling, flow in an emotional medium akin to water and air, harmonious inter-penetrating mix-up. Bion tended to emphasize disruption, threat of awakening akin to threat of dreaming, discovery of aliveness. Impact, shock, awe. Birth of ideas, feelings, sensations, self, sense of being. This often is hellish but also heavenly disruption, akin to Rilke's angel piercing the heart with the need for poetry. There is no heaven without inspiration. No inspiration without desperation and imaginative fury.

Winnicott praised intensity and extremes together with a sabbath point of soul that makes turbulence thrilling. He valued moments outside of time, immersion in nothingnowhere, self-restorative vacations from self. Something time cannot saturate makes time richer.

For many years, in my milieu, emphasis tended to be on ego mechanisms, adaptation, ego's conflict with instinctual drives, social conditioning—all valuable up to a point. Also, stultifying. I think of the prophet's voice, "Thou shalt not live by bread alone, but by every word that comes from the mouth of the living God." Bread is wonderful. It's terrific to smell fresh bread as one wakes up in the morning. Good as it is, it is even more wickedly, maddeningly uplifting to find God working in one's life. The "scent" or "feel" of God: a wonder all wonders coalesce in. Why did so much psychoanalytic bread in my country smell so stale? Why did it smell fresher overseas? Because there was more heaven in it?

Also more hell. Melanie Klein related hell to an infant's agony, a stomach pit's burning pain, timeless irritation. She portrayed an array of agonies in infancy, related not only to sensations that lacked a frame of reference, but waves of annihilation dread spreading through emotional fields, magnified and channeled by fantasy related to objects (mother, father, breast, penis, urine, feces, womb, babies). Bion pried loose annihilation from object filters and related it to atmospheric conditions. Let me open some aspects of this thought.

Imagine an emotional atmosphere or field like space or air or water. That is, imagine emotion as a medium like air or water. Objects (mother, father) may mediate it, but, in the moment or dimension I'm pointing toward, the emotional flow is where one lives. Suppose that the emotional medium—our emotional air or water, potential nourishment or arena of movement—is toxic or made of boundless dread. Suppose the medium we are born into *is* annihilation anxiety. We cannot say where it comes from or why it's there. To breathe or move or taste we must breathe it, taste it, move with and through it. There is nowhere else to be, to live. In such a state, the atmosphere of annihilation dread is closer to me than I am. I live on and in it and am made up of it. I cannot live without it—it is my nourishment. It affects my mental-physical organs, my pores, my cells. Any self/other chancing on such a medium will be altered, at least temporarily, by it.

Perhaps there are other worlds, other atmospheres, and beings who live in them. Perhaps some of these atmospheres are joyous, loving, beautiful. A soul growing in such an atmosphere will not feel the same as one feeding on and breathing annihilation dread. Suppose there is a being bred simultaneously in two atmospheres with capacity to grow in both. One lung breathes dread, one love. One eye sees beauty, one horror. One ear hears marvelous music, one hears screams. If both collapse into one world and are inextricably mixed (or never were separated), organs develop to accommodate the atmosphere that must be used.

It is difficult for a being born into an annihilating atmosphere to develop what is needed to use and enjoy a supportive, loving one, and vice versa. Most of us are used to a fusion of both. Atmospheres that nourish have toxic side effects, and toxic atmospheres have nourishing aspects. We use what we can and try to find composites that work. We may jump worlds and be like fish out of water or plunge into mixtures too dense to manage. Disruptions force us to exercise ourselves more fully. If things go decently, we feed on many worlds, breathe varied atmospheres, discover qualities of intensity that fuel a hungry existence.

It may happen that emotional fields are so annihilating that ability to "process" annihilation remains stunted. One way of speaking about this is to say that primary process is warped or damaged or somehow is unable to do its job. Its job is to assist, enable, or begin the processing of affects. It partly does this by nibbling at catastrophic globs of experience, chunks of annihilation dread, overwhelming and paralyzing shocks, traumatic impacts. If primary process works well enough, bits of catastrophe become useable in dreamwork. Impact gives rise to image to symbol to thought. If primary process can not process, if it is too damaged, poisoned-poisonous, annihilated-annihilating, it tends to mirror its own damaged state. It does not process this state so much as flash it over and over, like an SOS, or worse. It may become a meaningless caricature of itself, repeating its disability and going on deteriorating.

The therapist functions as an auxiliary primary processor, in time jump starting the patient's primary process or dreamwork ability. The therapist makes possible an atmosphere where primary process work is valued and counted on. This kind of therapy involves commitment to deep experiencing and learning to process the latter, a kind of primary process love (which is a value, an ethics, a faith). There is support deeper than anything one can hold onto, as life provides support in the face of its own annihilating aspects.

For many years, if I were to give a talk in New York about primary process work as binding or helping to initiate the transformation of affect, I would be told that secondary process binds, primary process discharges. Rycroft, Noy, Milner, Ehrenzweig, and Matte-Blanco were among those who emphasized the profound ordering activity of primary process work, nourished by chaos. It is difficult to convey my joy upon coming across a passage in Ehrenzweig years ago on the rigidity of primary process work in schizophrenia. Rather than emphasize primary process as flooding secondary process, Ehrenzweig believed that in schizophrenia something was wrong with primary processing. Instead of processing, it was spinning. It was too afraid of affect to tolerate and process it. It became rigid and repetitive, cycling more of the same rather than working with news of difference.

The psychoanalytic milieu I lived in (things are changing now!) emphasized building better ego defenses against the flood of a great discharge machine gone mad (largely because of an undeveloped, weak, or malformed ego). To find a group of people across the ocean speaking of spontaneous, affective ordering processes, in which order grows from the ground up rather than from a rationalistic order imposed top down—breath came easier. It was clear to me that no amount of defensive imposition on deep madness would win the day. Something had to happen on the level of the madness itself or we would beat ourselves into the ground in order to make believe we weren't mad or murderers (and then be mad murderers anyway, the worse for it). Doesn't control model murder in subtle ways? Psychoanalysis gives people a chance to open on the deepest levels and keep on opening. If "control" does not grow out of opening, it tends to close off the fullest possibilities of development. Of course, if one can open in the way I'm implying, control tends to become less necessary.

The creative unconscious was informally spoken about by artists and writers and some analysts too, although formal psychoanalytic theory tended to pit secondary against primary process. Now we are more aware of what secondary process owes to primary process work, as the flow between different ways of processing becomes explicitly valued.

We are more concerned with between, transitional areas, links, psychic connective tissue, circulation. In "Analysis Terminable or Interminable" Freud felt stuck points may concern something off in the timing or rhythm of the psyche rather than any particular contents. The timing or rhythm of the psyche may have something to do with movement between states. This is not simply a matter of dissociation or splits but lack of connective tissue or mediating capacity.

Again, we are not speaking of imposition of order from the top down but problems in ordering processes from the ground up. Let us suppose that annihilation waves prevent growth of links between states. One bobs up here (depression, hysteria) or there (paranoia, rage, obsessive panic) without awareness that one is surfacing in different areas of the same water. The therapist is witness that the patient is bobbing in an emotional sea without appreciation of the vast formless support for his momentary state. Little by little, the patient begins to notice that more is happening between emotional seizures than could be seen at first. What happens has less to do with control than with discovery of a new field of experience.

An afterword is another kind of prologue, teasing loose threads, jostling thoughts the way breezes spread dandelion seeds. We are very sensitive beings, and a lot hangs on what we do with our sensitivity. We share sensitivity with other life forms but thread it through symbolic activity that becomes stranger, more delicate, and more dangerous than plant or animal reactivity.

We love to study early signs of sensitivity. Mini–life forms moving toward or away from light. Thermal change, surface impingement triggering irritability, coiling, hardening, softening. We look for signs of responsiveness. If only we could trace life to its beginning, we might be able to hold its secret in our hand. To open and close a hand, all the things hands do from sexuality to precision engineering, signaling peace or war, putting one's palm to one's heart or to the heart of another, signaling a caring core—such sensitive hands. We try to get into each other's sensitivity in good ways, bad ways. We need each other's feelings as much as, sometimes more than, food. Survival needs are embedded in emotional contexts. Exchange of material goods becomes a signifier of emotional nourishment.

Sensitivity is more than twitches in response to physical stimuli. Beings are sensitive, and by the time we get to the use of touch to mediate emotions we must say that *someone* is sensitive. When a mother touches a baby, it is not one blank body touching another. Someone is touching someone. There are physical tasks to be taken care of, but these occur in emotional fields. Any touch has tone and texture, and its own kind of meaning. It takes a particular kind of touch to say, "I am not touching you feelingly but simply to dress a wound or clean a mess." If you ever need a mess cleaned when you are old and helpless, the feel of the clean can be more important than the clean itself. This we know, because old people tell us so. A baby cannot talk but expresses itself all over, and we can feel it tingling or tightening and everything in between. A body is an emotional body, an imaginative body, an expressive body. It is amazing that we have managed to abstract an anatomical body from the person who permeates it, as if it were an uninhabited shell.

We are alive in the under- and over-side of our skin. Its eruptions when emotions erupt testify to our psychosomatic sensitivity. The same might be said of our gut-mind, how sensitive intake-output is to changes of feeling and fortune. Add breathing, heart, nerves—all tied to the felt meaning of things. Indeed, our various organs and their functions contribute images to the language of joy and injury. Freud wrote of the connection between physical sensations and expressive language when he noted that words stab a heart or slap a face. Words cut deep. Looks cut deep. Where are these deep cuts? We point to our heart or gut or neck, but their pain, an emotional pain, signals a living being, a person. *Someone* is injured. And someone is uplifted when the spirit of a word uplifts. In a therapy session, one feels better or worse all over, depending on what one goes through.

This is not to deny the reality of external power—political, economic, military—real power in the real world, where calculated insensitivity too often rules. But human problems will not be solved by machinations of might. Sooner or later, sensitivity to the sensitive core of living beings must evolve if we are to live in caring ways. And, in the end, only a caring life will be effective when it comes to quality of living. Might in the service of sensitivity, sensitivity in the service of might—a false duality, perhaps, but worth reflection.

Meanwhile, subgroups of humanity pay attention to sensitivity, not least among them psychotherapists, in whose work moment-to-moment impact and response is valued. One tastes and talks life into or out of being as two people seek to learn how to be together. The difficulties two people face trying to live better proliferate when you multiply two by thousands, millions, billions. What two people find unbearable brings millions to the precipice.

We are working on many fronts at once. Aesthetic, ethical, political, interpersonal, intrasubjective sensitivity—little by little things open up and we get somewhere. Whether or not economic and military sensitivity follow suit remains to be seen. The coupling of money and ethics leaves much to be desired. Difficulties in bringing ethics and power together have been recorded since antiquity. It is a challenge that exercises psychosocial evolution.

There are individuals who lead good lives, even full lives, who feel the pain the dominant society obscures. There are, too, many broken by the pain tucked under the rug of business as usual, pain through top and bottom, with deformations penetrating all walks of life.

This book is sensitive to basic concerns and structures of sensitivity, rhythms, textures, tones as well as patterns. Sensitivity takes many forms, and one is perplexed as to how they work together. Often they are at odds. Much in practical and intellectual history pits one region or use of sensitivity against another. One lower, one higher, one subject or subjugated to another. Top dog–underdog relationships between areas of sensitivity are enacted by multitudes in the body politic.

It has taken many centuries for the idea to take hold that human capacities feed, balance, offset each other, contribute to creative evolution. It is not that sensation is low, thought high, that one should be victorious. Both belong to a mutually constitutive field, make each other possible, contribute to adaptive plasticity.

Lacan argues that not only are we divided and ambivalent, we are split through and through. Our drives are split, ego is split. We are split off from ourselves in all kinds of ways, mediated as we are through language. And since language has a life of its own, burgeoning with meaning, we can always mean something else. Meanings are always multiple. Our contact with ourselves is split by meaning. Meaning splits our contact with ourselves. We are given to ourselves through the life of meaning, and meaning can never mean one thing. If we want to be only one thing, meaning is frustrating, but if we are willing to open, what a treasure a life of meaning is.

Bion suggests something like this when his supervisee describes a schizophrenic patient waking in terror and turning on a light. "Everyone is entitled to a second opinion," Bion remarks. Dark seeing and feeling and light seeing and feeling are not the same. Each contributes its own perspectives again and again. Terror in the night ties in with subregions of feeling important for the ambience of living. Dispelling or confronting networks of gripping affect accessible in boundless darkness gives to the light of day an important function. Movement between the two offers a kind of division of labor, swinging between emotional access and opportunity for reflection.

Bion's example is an extreme, perhaps a caricature, but it points to complementary contributions different sides of our nature make. Emotional reality, for example, appears now this way, now that way, and waiting on the unfolding of alternative views is some insurance against being swept off by a single, destructive conclusion. Even if one opts to act and throws oneself fully into a particular course, there is a difference between doing so blindly convinced one has reached the end of the matter, and doing so with an underlying sense that no one take is sufficient in the face of compelling situations. Husband and wife need each other's perspectives if they are to correct or amplify each other. This is as true between groups of every sort, within and between individuals and nations, as within a family.

Murder is an attempt to reduce the complexity of meaning, whether literal or symbolic murder. Literal murder attempts to end the flow of possible alternatives, which afflict one as long as there is life. There is always danger of being proved wrong, if meanings keep ticking. To see things in many ways is bewildering, even persecutory, if one is determined to mold shimmering possibilities into a single outcome. One of the great things about works of art—which are singular outcomes—is that many alternatives go into them. The singularity of a great work of art contains a plethora of tensions fed by implicit complexity of meanings.

That murder can succeed in reducing the flow of meaning is delusional. One can dispose of a body but cannot terminate mind. One cannot stop other thoughts from happening, neither one's own nor others'. One cannot stop the ways others think or ways one thinks of oneself. Murder, as an attempt to wipe out sensitivity, can never be more than partly successful, although sometimes it grotesquely approaches totally obliterating moments.

The simplifying delusion of murder is powered by an abiding hallucination of one, a kind of hallucinatory monogamy or monotheism of the mind. There is an abiding and pervasive impulse to simplify, to reduce to one. In science or mathematics such a reduction may approach elegance, but in life it is lethal. An individual tells me he broke off with his girlfriend because he could not stop being alone. It is not simply aloneness he protects, because soon enough he will be off with another girl or back with his old one. "I'm protecting my cave, my cocoon," he says. He cannot take the idea of sharing life with another. He cannot take being at the mercy of changes another will force.

He can relate pulling back to his past, attracted as he was by a beautiful mother and injured by her harshness. He pulled himself up through work, while women became objects of pleasure, playthings. "I remain in the clear, a narcissist, self-centered, looking out for myself. I don't want to deal with who the other is, what the other wants. I want her to fit in with me. X wants to marry. That means sharing. I'm not ready to share, to compromise. She is too messy for me. I'd have to tolerate too much. She says she wants children, a family. I can't go along with her, and she must leave me. A kind of sadness goes deep in my heart, my inner soul, a sense of being lost.

"I picture growing with X, having a meaningful life. Revealing myself as a person, a human being. I understand messy means emotionally messy. But I'm so contained in myself I can't reach for others. I can't program the other person in. What will I be like twenty years from now? I have two pictures. To blossom is one. The other is to crystallize as I am. In my crystallized state I am the god of my world. Nothing can get in and I can't get out. I have to open this god-world if I want to live. I'm trying to get out but am afraid. Sometimes I think I'm opening the cocoon, carving out a space, but I fall into it and it closes more and more."

My patient is sensitive to two states. These states are simultaneous, superimposed and oscillating. He is sensitive to closing off and to how different from closing off opening feels. He lived most of his life unaware of the difference. He took self-centeredness for granted, didn't think twice about it. If difficulties with one woman became insurmountable, he traded her in for another and didn't miss a step. That's what women were there for, to service his narcissism and sexual needs (which were of a piece). Only one person truly existed, the others were replaceable parts. It was not until therapy that his self-focused monotheism became chilling.

Of course, no one is one thing. Some sensitivity to others was part of my patient's life or he wouldn't have listened when friends urged him to seek help. They urged him for several years and finally convinced him he was missing out. He was determined to be number one at work and his drivenness, the way he marshaled his whole being, pushed upward, made others wary and concerned. Even in his high-pressured environment, his me-first, job-first perfectionism became too much.

What is scary is that for years, until this point, he lived his life thinking he was the way you were supposed to be. The achievement-driven world he inserted himself into covered up for him. The fact that he had a problem with attachment never entered his awareness. He early transcended trauma-ridden attachment by the sense of power that compulsive work and getting ahead provided. He was able to go quite some distance up the economic mountain before lack of sensitivity to others in the workplace brought him to an unanticipated ceiling.

My patient brought home to me a kind of contemporary morality play, a quasi-Oedipal morality play. The addiction to being number one, Numero Uno. As if there really is such a thing. It is what I call the hallucination of one. The best, the most, the top. As Mel Brooks says, "It's good to be the king." The ancient Greeks were fond of pointing out difficulties that being on top brings. The suffering that the drive to be first inflicts on individuals can be ghastly. The best fuck, fastest gun, biggest muscles, most money, brightest brains, best looks, top of the heap. And what happens to those on bottom? The losers, the helpless, the ignored, the injured? Or the vulnerable, sensitive corners of oneself that one tramples on in one's rise? No matter how "in" one is, one always is leaving oneself out as well as being left out. One hallucinates unanimity, agreement, unity where inner-outer reality ripples with diversity. The mania of number one is supported by many agonies.

It is fitting that the ending of this book makes its way toward a consideration of ethics—psychoanalytic ethics—in a psychopathic age. Have we circled round from sensitivity to impulse to ethical sensitivity, the importance of our impact on the Other, of the Other on us? An ethics of contact, of sensitivity to self and other, double sensitivity? How out of step an ethics of sensitivity must seem when one's goal—as a nation, group, individual—is to be number one.

To hallucinate oneself—one's group, one's nation—as number one renders one resistant to disconfirmation and inclusiveness. Whether the other is a marriage partner, one's child, other religions or races or classes or nations or perhaps another way of seeing and doing things, other interests—to hallucinate oneself and one's own as number one, grants this *one* inherent "moral" authority, a sense of right (in the double sense of being right and having rights over others).

We once thought that deadness, psychic anesthesia, depersonalization was associated with repression of impulse. I am not sure early psychoanalysis fully appreciated the crucial role of sensitivity to others, the feel of mutual impact and response, in sustaining the sense of aliveness. The fact that sensitivity to others, as well as one's fuller self, is seared on behalf of economic, ideological, and ethnic self-interest, places in jeopardy the evolution of caring that is the ethical basis of living together.

My patients pay the price in a world where sensitivity does not count for much, although it is exploited. Theirs is the battle of the underground, the struggle to work with materials of self, to learn how sensitivity works, what one can do with it, what needs to be done. We study the infrastructure of how things go wrong with no other tools than ourselves.

I've described instances in which sensitivity turns against itself, when aliveness cannot take itself. Similarly, sensitivity turns against the Other, as if there is a psychic immune, allergic response to self or other. Often trauma plays a role, but insufficient evolution also is a factor. What my patients experience marks the social fabric. We cannot take too much of ourselves yet create situations that are too much to take. Perhaps this stimulates growth, but often we (as groups and individuals) undergo deformation or collapse under the strain. Microdetails in therapy bring into view ways we come through ourselves and each other and ways we are stuck.

Sensitivity fans out through many realms, makes use of all capacities. This book touches on sensitivity related to sensation, feeling, thinking and their developed use or misuse as part of ethical, aesthetic, spiritual, vulgar, and, above all, psychological sensitivity. Psychological sensitivity itself spans many realms, although my emphasis tends to be emotional sensitivity.

"Sense," a word that is part of sensitivity, has a range of meanings, from sense related to sensation, to sense related to thinking. Reciprocal interaction of multiple dimensions is hinted at in variable (even opposite) meanings of primary words. Dimensions that sometimes seem far apart betray links embedded in what Freud called "a common source."

Bion speaks of compassion and Truth [his capital] as "senses of man." Be wary when reading the word "sense" or "sensation" in Bion. It can bridge, encompass, pass through many realms. Bion points out, too, that one can be sensitive to a lack of compassion or truth in oneself. Chris, in Chapter 7, is tortured by a felt lack in truthful caring, a capacity he believed in and experienced in selected others, but doubted in himself. He felt compassionate truth's reality and deficiency in extremes. He saw no way out unless incapacity in what he most valued was addressed. Simple reassurance and encouragement were beside the point.

Picture what it is like living in a compassionate, truthful atmosphere. Contrast it with being bombarded with twisted feelings and lies. Imagine two infants, one breathing in a sincere attempt at good care, the other breathing in cruelty, toxins, humiliation. Emotional atmospheres are part of breathing, seep through pores. All kinds of feelings and tendencies are compacted and mixed together, with one or another group of attitudes dominant for shorter or longer times. Still, it does make a difference where one's life tends to land, even if no spot is final.

You can imagine the second baby contracting, tightening, thrashing against the onslaught before giving in. You can picture the first baby opening, rounding out, tasting the fullness of being. Then again, perhaps both taste life's fullness, one more in the key of cruelty, one more in the key of compassion. "Truth" molds itself to either. The feel that truth has in each context makes a world of difference. Each uses truth in its own ways. What our world is like depends, in part, on the results of the interplay of emotive, attitudinal contexts. The quality of sensitivity to sensitivity, our sense of contact with ourselves and each other—emotional tactility—is a ubiquitous, if elusive, factor in the kinds of beings we become, in the kind of world we live in.

Ethics can be superimposed from the outside only up to a point. Its deeper grounding is in maturation of sensitive responsiveness. Like eating or breathing or dying—no one can do it for you. Nevertheless, it needs a lot of help.

NOTES AND REFERENCES

Chapter 1. Introduction

p. 3: S. Freud (1914), "On Narcissism: An Introduction," *Standard Edition*, 14:73–102. Freud wrote that the advent of the ego unified body streaming.

pp. 3–4: Whether sensations somehow give rise to ideas or ideas grow from innate organizational processes was a philosophical issue that informed much thinking in academic psychology. Psychoanalysis plays both ends against the middle, emphasizing radical contributions of "lower" and "higher" processes, especially tensions between them, with passional/ emotional forces taking center stage.

p. 4: M. Klein (1946), "Notes on Some Schizoid Mechanisms," in *Developments in Psycho-Analysis*, ed. M. Klein, P. Heimann, S. Isaacs, and J. Riviere, London: Hogarth Press, 1952. W. R. Bion (1970), *Attention and Interpretation*, London: Tavistock. For a comparison of Klein and Bion, see my *Psychic Deadness* (1996), Northvale, N.J.: Jason Aronson, chaps. 1–7. For overviews of Bion, see M. Eigen, *The Electrified Tightrope* (1993), Northvale, N.J.: Jason Aronson, chaps. 11 and 17; and M. Eigen, *The Psychoanalytic Mystic* (1998), London: Free Association Books, chap. 3.

p. 5: Bion: see note re Bion for p. 4.

p. 7: Samuel Johnson's remark quoted from W. R. Bion, *Cogitations* (1992), London: Karnac Books, p. 114; it comes from a letter by Johnson to Bennet Langton, September 21, 1758, printed in Boswell's *Life of Johnson*, vol. 1.

p. 9: D. W. Winnicott (1992), "The Psychology of Madness: A Contribution to Psycho-analysis," in *Psycho-Analytic Explorations*, ed. C. Winnicott, R. Shepherd, and M. Davis, Cambridge: Harvard University Press, pp. 119–29. For discussions of Winnicott's link of madness, trauma, and psychic beginnings, see my *Toxic Nourishment* (1999), London: Karnac Books, chaps. 9 and 10, and the present book, chaps. 1, 2, 4, and 5.

p. 10: "dramas sensitivity goes through": see my *Coming Through the Whirlwind* (1992), Wilmette, Ill.: Chiron Publications. The title of the present book is taken from the last chapter of *Coming Through the Whirlwind*.

p. 10: J. Breuer and S. Freud (1893–95), "Studies on Hysteria," *Standard Edition*, 2:181.

p. 10–11: S. Freud (1937), "Analysis terminable and interminable," *Standard Edition*, 23:216–53.

p. 11: For damaged dreamwork, see Bion, *Cogitations*, pp. 1–98, and M. Eigen, *Damaged Bonds* (2002), London: Karnac Books, chaps. 1–4. For additional discussion of therapy with damaged primary process, see my *Psychic Deadness*, "Primary Process and Shock" (chap. 12).

p. 11: H. Elkin (1958), "On the Origin of the Self," *Psychoanalytic Review*, 45:57–76; and (1972), "On Selfhood and the Development of Ego Structures in Infancy," *Psychoanalytic Review*, 59:389–416; also, M. Eigen, *The Psychotic Core* (1986), Northvale, N.J.: Jason Aronson, chap. 4.

p. 13: "hallucinatory halo" and "mutilated trauma space": see M. Eigen, *Rage* (2002), Middletown, Conn.: Wesleyan University Press, pp. 164–84, and M. Eigen, *Ecstasy* (2001), Middletown, Conn.: Wesleyan University Press, pp. 4–5, 18, 37–38.

p. 15: "dreaming the patient": Bion, *Cogitations*, p. 43. For connections between dreaming and emotional digestion, see *Cogitations*, pp. 39–72; 143. See this book, chap. 2, p. 31–32, and chap. 9, p. 129–30.

p. 16: "Enough! or Too much": William Blake, *The Marriage of Heaven and Hell*, plate 10:10.

p. 16: My writings on anal imagery: *The Electrified Tightrope*, chaps. 4, 6, 9, 16, and 20; *The Psychotic Core*, chaps. 5 and 8.

p. 17: For connections between E. Levinas's writings on an "ethics of the face" ([1969], *Totality and Infinity*, trans. A. Lingis, Pittsburgh, Penn.: Duquesne University Press, pp. 194–219) and psychoanalytic experience, see my discussion in *The Electrified Tightrope*, chaps. 6–9 and 11. Levinas depicts experience of the human face at the heart of ethical feeling, an expressive dimension requiring sensitive cultivation. Aspects of developmental psychology and psychoanalysis bring out the importance of the face in self-formation (R. Spitz [1965], *The First Year of Life*, New York: International Universities Press; H. Elkin [1972], "On Selfhood and the Development of Ego Structures in Infancy"; B. Beebe and F. Lachman [2002], *Infant Research and Adult Treatment: Co-Constructing Interactions*, Hillsdale, N.J.: The Analytic Press). While my work emphasizes opening areas of experiencing rather than "control," it places a lot of emphasis on the growing ability to wrestle with oneself, a dialectic of struggle and surrender. Gain-ing access to subtly new areas of being requires work, although not exactly what is usually meant by "control." There is an effortless moment in experiencing goodness, but basing more of one's life on it, evolving with it, is another story.

Chapter 2. A Basic Rhythm

p. 18: "When two personalities meet": W. R. Bion (1994), "Making the Best of a Bad Job," in *Clinical Seminars and Other Works*, ed. F. Bion. London: Karnac Books, p. 321.

p. 19: Winnicott, "The Psychology of Madness," p. 129.

p. 19: Bion, *Attention and Interpretation*, pp. 62–71; Eigen, *The Psychoanalytic Mystic*, chaps. 3–6; the present book, chaps. 1–5.

p. 20: H. Elkin, "On the Origin of the Self," and "On Selfhood and the Development of Ego Structures in Infancy."

p. 20: "infinity": Bion, *Cogitations*, p. 372.

p. 20: "background Other": James S. Grotstein speaks of a "background object of primary identification" (*Splitting and Projective Identification*, Northvale, N.J.: Jason Aronson, 1981, pp. 211–13), and "the background presence of primary identification" (*Who Is the Dreamer Who Dreams the Dream: A Study of Psychic Presences*, Hillsdale, N.J.: The Analytic Press, 2001, p. 14).

p. 20: "omnipotent, inscrutable . . .": Elkin, "On Selfhood and the Development of Ego Structures in Infancy," p. 397.

p. 21: "the Other as the eternal, numinous, Source of Being . . .": ibid., p. 398.

p. 21: "For the Self has realized . . .": Elkin, ibid.

p. 21: "Yea, though you slay me . . .": Job 13:15.

pp. 21–22: "in every calm and reasonable person . . .": Phillip Roth (2001), *The Dying Animal*, Boston: Houghton Mifflin, pp. 153–54.

p. 22: Winnicott, "The Psychology of Madness," pp. 119–29.

p. 22: "Some experience of madness . . .": ibid., p. 122.

pp. 22–23: "Psychosis has to do . . .": ibid.

p. 23: "one who does not carry . . .": ibid.

p. 23: For related discussions of beginnings linked to trauma, see my *Toxic Nourishment*, chaps. 6, 9, and 10, and *Damaged Bonds*, chaps. 1–4.

p. 24: "Madness that has to be remembered . . .": Winnicott, "The Psychology of Madness," p. 125.

p. 24: Winnicott's schoolgirl case, ibid., p. 126.

p. 25: "fear of madness . . .": ibid.

p. 25: "Cure only comes if . . .": ibid.

p. 25: "In the simplest possible case . . .": ibid., p. 127.

p. 26: "What is absolutely personal . . .": ibid., 128.

p. 27: "The madness to become": ibid., pp. 128–29.

p. 27: Bion, *Cogitations*, p. 104.

p. 27: "At the point when his blood . . .": ibid.

p. 27: Loss of blood as image of loss of feeling: ibid, p. 12. Splattering of common sense: ibid., pp. 15–19, 23. Double dread associated with gain and loss of aliveness: Eigen, *Psychic Deadness*. See this book, chap. 10, pp. 147–51, and chap. 5.

p. 28: For a discussion of rebirth patterns related to what I call here basic pulse or background rhythm, see my *Coming Through the Whirlwind*, chap. 2.

p. 29. For some primal scene permutations see my early paper (1974), "On Pre-Oedipal Castration Anxiety," *International Review of Psycho-Analysis*, 1:489–98, esp. pp. 489–90.

p. 30: On formless sense of destruction and catastrophic dread, also see Eigen, *Psychic Deadness*, "Disaster Anxiety" (chap. 16), and *The Electrified Tightrope*, "Demonized Aspects of the Self" (chap. 16).

p. 31: For more on coming through each other's destructiveness, see Winnicott, *Psycho-Analytic Explorations*, section 34; Eigen, *The Electrified Tightrope* pp. 112–17, and *Damaged Bonds*, chap. 8.

p. 31: Murderous superego, object that stops dreaming: Bion, *Cogitations*, pp. 33–90; Eigen, *Damaged Bonds*, chaps. 2–4.

p. 32: Dreaming the patient while awake in sessions: Bion, *Cogitations*, pp. 43, 120; W. R. Bion, *Transformations* (1965), London: Heinemann, p. 147; Eigen, *Damaged Bonds*, chaps. 3 and 4.

p. 33: Hamlet betraying his deeper intuition: Eigen, *Rage*, p. 3.

p. 33: Freud, "Analysis Terminable and Interminable," 216–53.

p. 33: "psychical inertia" and following phrases: ibid., pp. 241–42.

Chapter 3. Mysticism and Psychoanalysis

p. 36: "primary ego feeling," "intimate bond . . .": S. Freud (1930), "Civilizations and Its Discontents," *Standard Edition*, 21:59–145.

p. 36: "Mysticism is . . .": S. Freud (1941), "Findings, Ideas, Problems," *Standard Edition*, 23:299–300.

p. 36: P. Federn (1957), Ego *Psychology and the Psychoses*, London: Maresfield

Reprints, esp. chaps. 1 and 2. In addition to his exposition of the natural expansion and contraction of ego boundaries, and an all enveloping I-feeling that draws back with education, Federn succinctly relates loss of self-feeling to shock. Sensitivity to shock jolts the sense of self and cracks the ego's ability to relate boundless and bounded states.

p. 38: Elkin, "On Selfhood and the Development of Ego Structures in Infancy." The material here restates part of chap. 2 above, elaborated to add coloration, to help the reader get a "feel" for relatively unfamiliar work. See also Eigen, *The Psychotic Core*, chap. 4; *Coming Through the Whirlwind*, chap. 1; and *The Psychoanalytic Mystic*, chap. 1.

p. 39: M. Milner (1979), *On Not Being Able to Paint*, New York: International Universities Press; and (1987), *The Suppressed Madness of Sane Men*, London: Tavistock.

p. 40: I. Matte-Blanco (1975), *The Unconscious as Infinite Sets*, London: Duckworth; and (1988), *Thinking, Feeling, and Being*, London: Routledge.

p. 41: "perpetual co-presence and intermingling . . .": Matte-Blanco, *Thinking, Feeling, and Being*, p. 228; "'imprisoning' the ungraspable indivisibility . . .": ibid., p. 316; "I consider . . .": ibid., pp. 316–17.

p. 41: Bion, *Attention and Interpretation*, pp. 64, 74–75, 78, 112; Eigen, *The Psychoanalytic Mystic*, chaps. 3–5.

p. 43: Bion's O diagrams in *Cogitations*, pp. 323, 325.

p. 43: Bion's remarks on a "religious force" that works in love of God or the death pits of Ur: ibid., pp. 369–75. Eigen, *The Psychoanalytic Mystic*, chap. 4.

p. 44: Bion's force that destroys time, space, existence . . . : (1965), *Transformations*, p. 101; Freud's "force against recovery": "Analysis Terminable and Interminable," p. 242; Klein's "destructive force within": "Notes on Some Schizoid Mechanisms," p. 297. For an account of the convergence of these forces, see my *Psychic Deadness*, chaps. 1–7, with clinical explorations in chaps. 8–18. For Winnicott's portrayals of surviving destructiveness, see *Psycho-Analytic Explorations*, pp. 217–46. Eigen, *Psychic Deadness*, chaps. 1, 7; *The Psychoanalytic Mystic*, chap. 2; *The Electrified Tightrope*, chaps. 11 and 12; *Ecstasy*, pp. 80–84. One way of viewing the thrust of *Damaged Bonds* and *Toxic Nourishment* is to see them as depicting crises of faith, intense destructive pressures in sessions (and society), which the therapist must find ways of surviving in order to provide support for psychic development. Learning to live, in part, grows as therapist and patient learn how to survive each other.

p. 46: J. Lacan (1978), *The Four Fundamental Concepts of Psycho-Analysis*, trans.

A. Sheridan, ed. Jacques-Allain Miller, New York: Norton, pp. 33–34, 44–45, 57–60. Eigen, *Ecstasy*, pp. 37–38.

p. 50: For some of Bion's references to "white radiance" and the rosy and messier hues of life that stain it, see his book (1991), *A Memoir of the Future,* London: Karnac Books, pp. 51, 81–82, 85. For "good objects in the womb," see E. Rhode (1994), *Psychotic Metaphysics,* London: Karnac Books.

pp. 50–51: The Omaha Beach landing scene passage is taken directly from *Ecstasy*, pp. 72–73, and I reuse it here because it amplifies a sense of basic goodness surviving destructiveness. The "rightness" that exploits "goodness" is a theme running through *Ecstasy* and, especially, my later book, *Rage* (where I've written that few things have done more harm in human history than a feeling or conviction of being "right"). *Ecstasy* affirms basic goodness surviving destruction. *Rage* brings out how fragile that survival is, especially threatened by hallucinatory "rightness."

p. 52: "Your miracles of every day . . .": from the eighteenth blessing of the *Shemona Esrai* prayer, which is part of every daily and Sabbath Jewish prayer service. "From the stream of your delights . . .": Psalms 36:9–10.

p. 52: For Winnicott, the very sense of otherness depends on the Other surviving my destruction of him or surviving my fantasy of destruction. *Psycho-Analytic Explorations*, pp. 217–39. Eigen, *The Electrified Tightrope*, chap. 11.

p. 54: *Toxic Nourishment*, "Suicide" (chap. 2); also, *Damaged Bonds*, "The Need to Kill Oneself" (chap. 8).

p. 54: "the fundamental reality is 'infinity' . . .": Bion, *Cogitations*, p. 372; "Many mystics have . . .": ibid., p. 371; "the significant thing is . . .": ibid., p. 371.

Chapter 4. Half and Half

p. 62: "Well then, if you want to know . . .": Bion, *Cogitations*, p. 79.

pp. 62–63: mug of beer thrown in patient's face: Bion, *Transformations*, pp. 2–4; ice cream/scream/no-scream: Bion, *Attention and Interpretation*, pp. 13–14; mother "cuts off supplies": Bion, *Cogitations*, p. 29; Eigen, *Damaged Bonds*, "Wounded Nourishment" (chap. 2); and *The Psychoanalytic Mystic*, "Infinite Surfaces, Explosiveness, Faith" (chap. 3).

p. 64: I elaborate on Bion's writings on catastrophic shock in *The Electrified Tightrope* (esp. "The Area of Faith in Winnicott, Lacan and Bion" and "Between Catastrophe and Faith"), *Psychic Deadness* (chaps. 1–6 and 12), *Toxic Nourishment* (chap. 8), and *Damaged Bonds* (chaps. 2–4).

p. 64: patient X: Bion, *Cogitations*, pp. 59, 88–89, 102, but also pp. 29, 33, 40,

81–82, 90, 92, 116, 218–20; madness X: Winnicott, *Psycho-Analytic Explorations*, pp. 119–29; Eigen, *Toxic Nourishment*, chaps. 9, 10.

p. 66: Every dream fails: Bion, *Cogitations*, p. 95.

p. 67: Bion's narcissism-socialism: ibid., pp. 103–6.

p. 71: For my elaboration of psychotic dynamics related to sensitivity to influence, cosmic feeling, dread of invasion, the warp of hate fused with terror, see *The Psychotic Core*.

p. 71: "The schizophrenic relationship . . .": Bion, *Cogitations*, p. 80.

Chapter 5. A Little Psyche-Music

p. 74: S. Freud (1954), *The Origins of Psycho-Analysis: Letters to Wilhelm Fliess, Drafts and Notes, 1887–1902*, ed. M. Bonaparte, A. Freud, and E. Kris, New York: Basic Books; H. Sachs (1942), *The Creative Unconscious*, Cambridge, Mass.: Sci-Art Publishers.

p. 74: For a detailed account of the importance of psychotic dynamics in the formulation of Freud's views, and of the importance of psychosis in the unfolding of psychoanalysis, see my book *The Psychotic Core*.

p. 75: Federn, *Ego Psychology and the Psychoses*; Klein, "Notes on Some Schizoid Mechanisms"; Winnicott, *Psycho-Analytic Explorations*; W. R. Fairbairn (1954), *An Object Relations Theory of the Personality*, New York: Basic Books; Milner, *The Suppressed Madness of Sane Men*; H. S. Sullivan (1992), *Clinical Studies in Psychiatry*, New York: Norton; H. F. Searles (1965), *Collected Papers on Schizophrenia and Related Subjects*, New York: International Universities Press; W. R. Bion (1987), *Second Thoughts: Selected Papers on Psycho-Analysis*, London: Karnac Books. For Freud and sin and madness, see *The Psychotic Core*, chap. 1.

p. 75: Freud's remarks on the stuck psyche and something off in the timing of psychic life: "Analysis Terminable and Interminable," pp. 241–42. My book *Psychic Deadness* focuses on "soul entropy." For the music of the psyche and clinical work, see my *Toxic Nourishment*, pp. 79–83.

p. 75: See chap. 2 of this book for more on the rhythm of trauma and recovery (including Elkin's loss and recovery of primordial consciousness, Winnicott's breakdown and spontaneous recovery in sessions, and Bion's coming alive–being murdered–feeling all right.

p. 75: Blackout and hallucination: Freud (1911), "Psycho-analytic Notes on the Autobiographical Account of a Case of Paranoia (Dementia Paranoides)," *Standard Edition*, 12:3–82. Also *The Psychotic Core*, chaps. 2, 3, and 7.

p. 76: damaged alpha, damaged dreamwork: see this book, chap. 2. Much of what I say about Bion's dreamwork in this and other chapters leans on the first hundred pages or so of his *Cogitations*.

p. 76: P. Noy (1968), "The Development of Musical Ability," in *The Psychoanalytic Study of the Child*, New York: International Universities Press; C. Rycroft (1968), *Imagination and Reality*, New York: International Universities Press; M. Milner, *On Not Being Able to Paint*; A. Ehrenzweig (1971), *The Hidden Order of Art*, Berkeley: University of California Press. Current workers for whom affects are central include A. Green (1999), *The Fabric of Affect in the Psychoanalytic Discourse,* trans. A. Sheridan, London: Routledge; R. Stein (1991), *Psychoanalytic Theories of Affect,* Westport, Conn.: Greenwood; D. Fosha (2000), *The Transforming Power of Affect,* New York: Persea Books; and S. Alhanati (2002), "Current Trends in Genetic Molecular Research of Affective States and Psychiatric Disorders," in *Primitive Mental States,* vol. 2, ed. S. Alhanati, London: Karnac Books. A somewhat earlier emphasis on psychotic states seems to have shifted to one on affect states. In some workers, like Winnicott and Bion, the two converge.

p. 76: S. Freud (1900), *The Interpretation of Dreams*, *Standard Edition*, 4/5, chap. 6, "The Dream-Work," pp. 277–508.

p. 77: alpha function and dreamwork: Bion, *Cogitations*, pp. 1–112; this book, chap. 2; Eigen, *Damaged Bonds*, chaps. 2–4.

p. 77: In 1978, at a seminar in New York, I heard Bion speak of alpha function as a nest where birds of meaning alight. A transcript of the seminar, which was sponsored by the Institute for Psychoanalytic Training and Research, is published as *Bion in New York and São Paulo*, ed. Francesca Bion, London: Karnac Books, 1980.

p. 77: Winnicott's democratic attitude toward carriers of different functions: *Psycho-Analytic Explorations*, p. 155.

p. 77: Bion's emotional storm: "Making the Best of a Bad Job," pp. 321–22.

p. 79: Winnicott's breakdown as personality forms: "The Psychology of Madness," pp. 119–29; this book, chap. 2.

pp. 80–81: Winnicott's list of basic agonies: This and other elements of Winnicott's thought revolving around early breakdown of personality (including moving toward/away from madness X) draws on *Psycho-Analytic Explorations*, pp. 87–95, 103–14, 119–29.

p. 82: Shirah Kober Zeller made remarks like this at my Bion seminar and various meetings, and she has written an unpublished paper relating Winnicott's incommunicado core to Kabbalah's Ain Soph.

p. 82: Grotstein, *Who Is the Dreamer Who Dreams the Dream?: A Study of Psychic Presences*, pp. xxv, 14, 17–22, 164–65.

Chapter 6. Alone with God

p. 92: "Yahrzeit," a Yiddish term, refers to the lighting of a memorial candle on the date of a loved one's death each year. It is customarily lit for the deceased in one's immediate family. It is said that the light, and especially the devotional intention expressed by the light, elevates the loved one's soul. At the same time it elevates the soul of the one who remembers, since it hallows a human link. Sarah turns this custom into a place in one's heart where her mother is honored and where the broken heart of humanity is consecrated, a personal eternal light.

p. 96: Bion's force that continues after it destroys time, space, . . .: *Transformations*, p. 101. See also chap. 3 of this book and the note for p. 44.

Chapter 7. I Could Do It

p. 113: skinning Rabbi Akivah: Eigen, *Ecstasy*, pp. 70–71.

Chapter 9. Dancing

p. 129: "anxiety in the analyst . . .": Bion, *Cogitations*, p. 43. See also the present book, chap. 1, pp. 5–10, and chap. 2, p. 32.

p. 129: A function of therapy; digesting impacts: this book, chaps. 1, 2, and 5; Eigen, *Damaged Bonds*, chaps. 2–4.

p. 131: nourishment from toxic material: Eigen, *Toxic Nourishment*.

Chapter 10. Not Enough

p. 139: Fantasy selves endlessly inform experience. I remember a fat woman who, in her mind, saw herself as thin. She knew she was fat and suffered because of it. Yet she took out a photo of herself when she was young and thin and said, "That's the real me. When I dance I turn into the thin me. I become the real me, the thin me." She danced in my office and became thin as I watched, as we dissolved into her inside image (*The Electrified Tightrope*, p. 28). For Doran, the fantasy woman is the unattainable that haunts and taunts experience. The fantasy self or object can only be met by the un-expected, and for that he hopes therapy will help.

p. 141: Diotima is the wise woman who taught Socrates to ascend the ladder of goodness in Plato's *Symposium*. The method begins with sensuous par-ticulars and rises to an immaterial Vision of Goodness as such.

p. 143: For more on exploding and inner and outer screaming, see my books *Rage*, pp. 151–55; *The Psychoanalytic Mystic*, pp. 68–71; and *Damaged Bonds*, pp. 130–31. The section on screaming in *Rage* relates my personal scream to accounts of screaming in Winnicott and Bion.

p. 147: Blood Restored: This section overlaps with passages from earlier chap-ters, "A Basic Rhythm" (chap. 2), p. 27, and "A Little Psyche-Music" (chap. 5), p. 75. Bion's image of being murdered by restoration of psychic blood (undoing or reversing bloodless murder) is unfamiliar and rich enough to warrant presentation in contexts with different nuances and threads await-ing further development.

p. 147: Loss of blood–loss of feeling: Bion, *Attention and Interpretation*, p. 12; loss of blood–splattering of common sense: *Cogitations*, pp. 15–19, 23; blood being restored–growth of psychic circulation: ibid., pp. 104–5.

pp. 147–48: processing what damages processing: *Damaged Bonds*, chaps. 2–4; Bion, *Cogitations*, pp. 1–112; this book, chaps. 1–5.

p. 148: People often complain that Job lost too much, gained too little. His family and flocks were destroyed, and God shut him up with a show of power. However, I (partly) experience Job as a parable of stripping self to bare points of God-contact—contraction to the God-point, after which expansion and renewal begin again. From this point of view, the Bible can be seen as expressing a rhythm of contraction-expansion, destruction-renewal in many keys, including variations on the death-rebirth structure (see chap. 2 of this book and also, my books *Reshaping the Self*, Madison, Conn.: Psychosocial Press, 1995, pp. 191–92, and *Coming Through the Whirlwind*, pp. 3–11.

p. 148: "At the point when his blood will be fully restored . . .": Bion, *Cogitations*, p. 104. See the section "Bion's Freeing Murder" in chap. 2 of the present book. Bion's formulation of experiencing murder, then being all right, has affective resonance with Job's, "Yea, though you slay me, yet will I trust you" (Job 13:15).

Chapter 11. Sensitivity and Vulgarity

p. 152: This chapter is a slightly revised version of an e-mail interview conducted by Robert Marchesani for the journal *The Psychotherapy Patient* 12 (2003): 99–110. Its original title was "Vulgar Links: Up, Down, All Around: Interview with Michael Eigen." This issue of the journal was also published as a book edited by E. Mark Stern and Robert B. Marchesani (2003), *Inhabitants of the Unconscious: The Grotesque and the Vulgar in Everyday Life*, Binghamton, N.Y.: Haworth Press. The interview is used with the permission of Haworth Press.

p. 153: asshole as a nexus of meaning, holding the body together: see this book, chap. 1, pp. 16–17. Ruth Stein has written on phallic aspects of terrorism ("Evil as Love and as Liberation," at psychematters.com). Important as the phallic register is, I am suggesting that anal tropes bring us to deeper and more pervasive levels of hate and spoiling.

p. 156: On Bion's faith in O, see *The Electrified Tightrope*, chaps. 11 and 17. Bion uses the symbol O for unknowable ultimate reality. He may speak of the O of a session, in which the impact of personalities provokes perturbations that press toward formulation, action, or experiencing. O may remain unknown, but it is, nevertheless, lived, and one grapples with its impact as resources allow. It is a term that grows in meaning through use. Sample references, by no means exhaustive, in two of Bion's works, are *Transformations*, pp. 13, 26, 28–29, 62 141, 147–49, 155, and *Attention and Interpretation*, pp. 26, 27, 30, 53, 118. For more of my amplifications of Bion's O, see *The Psychoanalytic Mystic*, chaps. 3, 4, and 6.

p. 156: "Demonized Aspects of Self": *The Electrified Tightrope*, chap. 16; baby mind: ibid., p. 183.

p. 157: "containerless container . . .": *The Psychotic Core*, pp. 348–57.

p. 157: J. Dewey (1959), *Art as Experience*, New York: Capricorn Books; A. N. Whitehead (1985), *Process and Reality*, New York: Free Press; Lacan, *The Four Fundamental Concepts of Psycho-Analysis*, p. 43; H. Bergson (1994), *The Two Sources of Religion and Morality*, trans. A. Audra, C. Brereton, and W. H. Carter. Notre Dame, Ind.: University of Notre Dame Press; E. Husserl (1984), *Crisis of European Sciences and Transcendental Phenomenology*, trans. David Carr, Evanston, Ill.: Northwestern University Press.

p. 158: The transference arising/unconscious closing . . . : Lacan, *The Four Fundamental Concepts of Psycho-Analysis*. See, for example, "The transference is the means by which the communications of the unconscious is interrupted, by which the unconscious closes up again" (p. 130); comments on the unconscious closing-opening related to temporal pulsation of the subject (p. 125); and chaps. 10–13, which have much to say concerning lack, missed meeting (something always missing), opening-closing of the unconscious and transference.

p. 158: Milner, *On Not Being Able to Paint*, pp. 148–65.

p. 161: hallucinated "rightness" : See my books *Ecstasy* and, especially, *Rage*. The sense of rightness supports rage with hallucinatory/delusional authority, blocking sensitivity to the Other. To be sure, one's being right in ways that are destructive to others often is fueled by restricting sensitivity to a limited, magnified sliver of one's own sensitivity at enormous cost. Too often this comes down to being oversensitive to an aspect of one's oversensitivity, discounting the same sensitive point in others. What is wrong is not sensitivity but the way it is responded to. In a sense, we are raw sensitivity looking for responsive processing, and much depends on what quality of processing is possible. The theme of destructive hallucinatory authority runs through *Rage*, and is stated in general terms (pp. 164–69).

p. 161: Hamlet and the generative aspect of waiting: the introduction to *Rage*, pp. 3–4.

p. 162: "living in mother's asshole": *The Electrified Tightrope*, p. 36.

p. 162: G. I. Fogel, ed. (1991), *The Work of Hans Loewald: An Introduction and Commentary*, Northvale, N.J.: Jason Aronson.

p. 162: Emotional toxins: In *Toxic Nourishment* and *Damaged Bonds* I examine ways we seek nourishment from emotional toxins and draw sustenance from bonds that damage us. Mixtures of rage and ecstasy that adhere to this predicament act, in part, as emotional cement.

p. 163: a moment the devil cannot find: "There is a Moment in each Day that Satan cannot find, / Nor can his Watch Fiends find it; but the Industrious find / This Moment & it multiply, & when it once is found / It renovates every Moment of the Day if rightly placed." William Blake, *Milton*.

Chapter 12. Is There Room for Heaven in Psychoanalysis?

p. 165: Jeffrey Eaton's questions:

1. All of your books could be seen as developing answers to the questions "What is psychoanalysis?" and "What can psychoanalysis be?" What's the current state of your thinking and what directions are you heading in?

2. Your book *The Psychotic Core* was really a gift to all those who struggle to

work in this area. Would you speak about your early work in this area, how it developed, and how you think about working with the psychotic core today?

3. The idea of the embryonic is very evocative. You said recently in another context, "I've lived through this all of my life. Dealing with truncated versions of the human. For me, that's an issue that is perennial. What is a human being? How much of one can one dare to be?" (12/14/98, Bion97 Archive). Is it hatred for the embryonic that leaves so many lives truncated? Is it that we have so few "facilitating environments" for the embryonic to be discovered and grown? Could you speak about how the idea of "embryonic" informs for lived understanding of human encounters? What kind of awareness/experience it takes to tolerate and open to the embryonic?

4. Bion counseled an intense discipline, abstaining from memory and desire. I hope this was in part because he sought to make possible a situation where one might intuit radiance, what Tibetan Dzogchen masters call "the natural great perfection." Direct recognition of heart itself, the nondual center, the ugh! of "just this much" as Stephen Levine says. Bion seemed to make a remarkable life for himself after he died in World War I. The hardship of being Bion must have been immense. But there's so much ordinary hope in the capacities psychoanalysis can help grow. You seem to be living proof. But you go further. You go to the light, to filter systems for God, to the "myriad plus and minus aspects" and to faith in the basic goodness of life. Could you speak about faith? And could you speak about O? I can't imagine psychoanalysis without either. How do you relate to Bion's without memory and desire?

5. In our work with patients sometimes a powerful tangible aesthetic experience opens up. Your openness to this dimension of experience seems to be an important thread running through your work. How do you think about such experiences and, perhaps more to the point, how do you open to them and make use of them?

p. 165: In the 1960s, Bion's great works (*Learning from Experience, Elements of Psycho-Analysis, Transformations, Attention and Interpretation*) amounted to his way of giving expression to the O of psychoanalysis as it impacted him. He did not rest there but sought new means of expression, as seen in *A Memoir of the Future*, a three-book work in which aspects of Bion's being are refracted in an array of characters in search of dreaming experience (i.e., emotional processing). Expression, of course, is always exploration, gestures toward discovery.

p. 166: Searles, *Collected Papers on Schizophrenia and Related Subjects*, pp. 521–59. Searles described moments of love in therapy that were an important part of the healing process. He understood what happened as regression to an early phase of mother-infant connection. Associative overtones link it with divine union and beatific moments that uplift life (see my books *Ecstasy* and *The Electrified Tightrope*). Later Searles emphasized the fact that aggression is never absent in the human psyche and plays a pivotal role in individuation. One might say love is never fully absent either. Not everything is in the foreground at once and many states, including loving plenitude, have their day (qualified by states to come, latent tendencies, background currents). The fact that there is no pure state does not nullify a new X one contacts. It is not simply a matter of love or aggression, but how each is used, the spirit of approach, since mixtures of good and bad faith pervade both.

p. 166: soul is pure: M. M. Schneerson (1986), *The Essence of Chassidus*, Brooklyn, N.Y.: Kehot Publication Society. Schneerson seems to emphasize transformation of lower material reality into higher spiritual aspects, somewhat akin to Freud's sublimation model (energy, like fuel, used for higher purpose). My own emphasis is less on animal to spiritual, than on alternate spirits. The great struggle in humanity's soul is between different attitudes, alternate infinities, expressed in one's feel for things, one's glance, tone, touch (see *The Psychotic Core*). In the midst of struggle there is also, as Schneerson affirms, pure soul contact with God (see *Ecstasy*).

p. 167: The sense of finding heaven and ever letting it go is expressed in Blake's "Eternity": "He who binds to himself a joy / Does the winged life destroy / But he who kisses the joy as it flies / Lives in eternity's sun rise."

pp. 167–68: Milner, *On Not Being Able to Paint*, appendix. Joanna Field (pseudonym for M. Milner, 1934), *A Life of One's Own*, London: Chatto and Windus. Eigen, *The Electrified Tightrope*, chap. 14.

p. 168: Ehrenzweig, *The Hidden Order of Art*.

p. 168: Bion, *Transformations*, pp. 104–5; and *Attention and Interpretation*, pp. 12–15.

p. 168: M. Balint (1968), *The Basic Fault*, London: Tavistock; Bion, *Attention and Interpretation*, chap. 2; Eigen, *The Psychoanalytic Mystic*, chap. 4; R. M. Rilke (1978), *Duino Elegies*, trans. D. Young, New York: W. W. Norton. On Winnicott, see my *Psychic Deadness*, chap. 7; *The Psychoanalytic Mystic*, chap. 2; R. F. Rodman, ed. (1987), *The Spontaneous Gesture: Selected Letters of D. W. Winnicott*, Cambridge, Mass.: Harvard University Press.

p. 168: not by bread alone: Deuteronomy 8:3, Matthew 4:4.

p. 169: M. Klein (1948), *Contributions to Psycho-Analysis, 1921–1945*, London: Hogarth Press.

pp. 169–70: fusions of emotional toxins with nourishment, bonds with damage: see my *Toxic Nourishment* and *Damaged Bonds*.

p. 170: Rycroft, *Imagination and Reality*; Noy, "The Development of Musical Ability"; Matte-Blanco, *The Unconscious as Infinite Sets*.

p. 171: something wrong with primary process in schizophrenia: Ehrenzweig, *The Hidden Order of Art*, pp. 122–27, 194–95.

p. 171: Freud, "Analysis Terminable and Interminable," pp. 241–42. See chaps. 2 and 5 in this book.

Afterword

pp. 173–74: "I am not touching you feelingly but simply to . . .": We have developed a vocabulary of disregard. We signal each other to disregard intentions or subintentions, regions of affective-attitudinal fields. That is, we agree or conspire not to notice what we are doing to each other, perhaps because the deleted or bracketed feelings would be difficult or would interfere with other plans or wants. Our ability to disregard ourselves sometimes functions positively, allowing us to push past danger or weak spots. It can also be calamitous, as tolerance of insensitivity mounts.

p. 174: Freud's writing on words that stab in the heart and slap in the face: Breuer and Freud, "Studies on Hysteria," p. 181. This book, chap. 1, p. 10.

p. 175: The war of higher-lower capacities (e.g., thought/sensation): for a fuller discussion of top-bottom, vertical hierarchies, and the notion of the upright, see Eigen, *The Psychotic Core*, the section "Beyond the Upright," pp. 238–42.

p. 175: Lacan, *The Four Fundamental Concepts of Psycho-Analysis*.

p. 175: I've heard Bion's "second opinion" story a number of times over the years. A. Mason recently wrote of it in "Bion and Binocular Vision," *International Journal of Psychoanalysis* 81 (2000): 983.

p. 178: For casualties of our achievement-dominated milieu, see my *Toxic Nourishment*, which includes discussions of suicide, attention deficit, behavior "disorders" and deformations that "winners" and "losers" in our high-pressured world undergo. In *Damaged Bonds* I focus on damaged affect processing and the pressures affective ties strain to meet and absorb. For depictions of twists and turns of rage in daily life, see my book *Rage*.

p. 179: For the notion of "coming through," see my *Coming Through the Whirlwind*. "Coming through" is also relevant in my use of the story of Job as a model for certain aspects of therapy and living in *Reshaping the Self*.

p. 180: Freud, "a common source": "Studies on Hysteria," p. 181. See, too, "The Antithetical Meaning of Primal Words," *Standard Edition*, 11:155–61.

p. 180: Bion's sense of compassion and truth: *Cogitations*, pp. 125–26.

p. 180: More on Bion's sense and emotional tactility, sense of contact: Ability to make contact with ourselves and others is not only a crucial personal capacity, but also has ethical significance. What kind or quality of contact can we make, with what consequences? If capacity for contact is damaged or deformed or undeveloped, what then? Contact deficit does not ipso facto result in ethical deficit. Things are too complicated for such a simple statement and require more attention than this note can give. Quality of contact, however, *is* important for quality of world. Here is an e-mail I received from Donna Jacobs, after a seminar on Bion, which conveys the urgency, depth, and breadth of a root capacity. I am quoting it as she sent it, with her permission:

> I didn't know if it was as apparent to you as it seemed to me early on in your lecture today that you linked Bion's presentation of truth and compassion as a sense to at least one of the senses—the sense of touch—showing that emotional tactility (contact with truth and compassion) is more powerful (a need, impulse, drive, for survival) than that which is primarily physically tactile. The mind experiences the sensuous perhaps even more profoundly than the eyes, ears, skin, olfactory nerves and taste buds in concert—as discussion around the room gave testimony to. Perhaps Bion was not using the word "sense" loosely, but expanding his use of sense to include truth and compassion as real things-in-themselves, without confounding them in any way with intuition.

p. 180: For related discussions of two worlds, two babies, two atmospheres, see the end of chap. 12 in this book. For Winnicott's two babies, see my *Psychic Deadness*, p. xxii–xxiii.

About the author

MICHAEL EIGEN is a psychologist and psychoanalyst.

He is Associate Clinical Professor of Psychology in the Postdoctoral

Program in Psychotherapy and Psychoanalysis at New York University.

His numerous books include *Rage* (2002), *Ecstasy* (2001), *Damaged Bonds*

(2001), *Toxic Nourishment* (1999), *The Psychoanalytic Mystic* (1998), *Psychic*

Deadness (1996), and *The Psychotic Core* (1986). Eigen is also a Senior

Member at the National Psychological Association for Psychoanalysis.